Understanding the Inte

This book critically analyses the concept of the Intelligence Cycle, highlighting the nature and extent of its limitations and proposing alternative ways of conceptualising the intelligence process.

The concept of the Intelligence Cycle has been central to the study of intelligence. As Intelligence Studies has established itself as a distinctive branch of Political Science, it has generated its own foundational literature, within which the Intelligence Cycle has constituted a vital thread – one running through all social-science approaches to the study of intelligence and constituting a staple of professional training courses. However, there is a growing acceptance that the concept neither accurately reflects the intelligence process nor accommodates important elements of it, such as covert action, counter-intelligence and oversight.

Bringing together key authors in the field, the book considers these questions across a number of contexts: in relation to intelligence as a general concept, military intelligence, corporate/private sector intelligence and policing and criminal intelligence. A number of the contributions also go beyond discussion of the limitations of the cycle concept to propose alternative conceptualisations of the intelligence process. What emerges is a plurality of approaches that seek to advance the debate and, as a consequence, Intelligence Studies itself.

This book will be of great interest to students of Intelligence Studies, Strategic Studies, Criminology and Policing, Security Studies and International Relations in general, as well as to practitioners in the field.

Mark Phythian is Professor of Politics in the Department of Politics and International Relations at the University of Leicester. He is the author or editor/co-editor of twelve books.

Studies in Intelligence

General Editors: Richard J. Aldrich and Christopher Andrew

Understanding the Intelligence Cycle

Edited by Mark Phythian

Routledge
Taylor & Francis Group

LONDON AND NEW YORK

First published 2013
by Routledge
2 Park Square, Milton Park, Abingdon, Oxfordshire OX14 4RN

Simultaneously published in the USA and Canada
by Routledge
711 Third Avenue, New York, NY 10017

First issued in paperback 2014

Routledge is an imprint of the Taylor & Francis Group, an informa business

British Library Cataloguing in Publication Data
A catalogue record for this book is available from the British Library

Library of Congress Cataloging in Publication Data
Understanding the intelligence cycle / edited by Mark Phythian.
    pages ; cm. – (Studies in intelligence)
    Includes bibliographical references and index.
    1. Intelligence service. 2. National security. I. Phythian, Mark.
    UB250.U25 2013
    327.12–dc23

                                                           2012050067

ISBN: 978-0-415-81175-0 (hbk)
ISBN: 978-1-138-85632-5 (pbk)

Typeset in Times
by Wearset Ltd, Boldon, Tyne and Wear

Contents

Illustrations

Figures

Tables

Contributors

Aaron Brantly holds a PhD from the University of Georgia and a Master's of Public Policy from American University. He is a research associate at the Center for the Study of Global Issues at the University of Georgia. He served in the United States Peace Corps in Ukraine from 2005 to 2007 and has worked as a digital democracy training consultant during the Arab Spring and beyond.

Philip H. J. Davies is the Director of the Brunel Centre for Intelligence and Security Studies (BCISS) and originator of Brunel's MA in Intelligence and Security Studies. He is the author of *MI6 and the Machinery of Spying*, and *Intelligence and Government in Britain and the United States: A Comparative Approach*. He has published extensively on the management and organisation of intelligence institutions and on the concept of 'national intelligence cultures'. In 2010–11 he led Brunel's contribution to the latest iteration of the British military's Joint Intelligence Doctrine and a new doctrine for operational commanders on 'understanding'.

Peter Gill is an Honorary Fellow at the University of Liverpool and was previously Research Professor in Intelligence Studies at the University of Salford. He is the author of *Policing Politics* and *Rounding Up the Usual Suspects?* and co-author of *Intelligence in an Insecure World*. He is co-editor of the *PSI Handbook of Global Security and Intelligence: National Approaches* (two volumes) and *Intelligence Theory: Key Questions and Debates*. His current research is into the democratisation of intelligence in former authoritarian regimes, for which he was awarded a Leverhulme Emeritus Fellowship in 2010.

Kristian Gustafson is Deputy Director of BCISS and a Major in the UK's Territorial Army. Formerly a Canadian Army officer, he completed his PhD at the University of Cambridge, and taught at the Royal Military Academy Sandhurst before moving to Brunel. He has written on a range of intelligence topics including horizon scanning and US covert action, especially the case of US intervention in Chile in his book *Hostile Intent*. Along with Dr Davies, he contributed to the latest UK Joint Intelligence Doctrine and new doctrine on 'understanding', and also contributed to the drafting of an additional doctrine on partnering with indigenous force.

Arthur S. Hulnick is Associate Professor of International Relations at Boston University. He is a veteran of 35 years' service in the profession of intelligence, including seven years in US Air Force intelligence and 28 years in the CIA. He is the author of *Fixing the Spy Machine* and *Keeping Us Safe: Secret Intelligence and Homeland Security*, as well as numerous journal articles and book chapters. He is a member of the Board of Editors of the *International Journal of Intelligence and CounterIntelligence*. In 2011 he was awarded the Distinguished Scholar Award from the Intelligence Studies Section of the International Studies Association (ISA).

Sir David Omand GCB is a visiting professor at the Department of War Studies, King's College London. In 2002 he was appointed as the first UK Security and Intelligence Coordinator. He served for seven years on the Joint Intelligence Committee, was Permanent Secretary of the Home Office from 1997 to 2000, and before that Director of GCHQ. Previously, in the Ministry of Defence, he served as Deputy Under-Secretary of State for Policy, Principal Private Secretary to the Defence Secretary during the Falklands conflict, and for three years in NATO as the UK Defence Counsellor. His book, *Securing the State*, was published in 2010.

Mark Phythian is Professor of Politics in the Department of Politics and International Relations at the University of Leicester. His research interests are in the areas of intelligence, national security and foreign policy. He is the author or editor/co-editor of twelve other books on intelligence and security issues, as well as numerous journal articles and book chapters. He is co-editor of the *Journal of Intelligence History*, a member of the editorial board of *Intelligence and National Security*, an Associate Editor of *Crime, Law and Social Change*, and an Academician of the Academy of Social Sciences.

Julian Richards completed his doctorate on political violence in Pakistan at Cambridge University in 1993. He spent nearly 20 years working in intelligence and security for the British government. In 2008, he co-founded the Centre for Security and Intelligence Studies at the University of Buckingham. He is the author of two books: *The Art and Science of Intelligence Analysis* and *A Guide to National Security: Threats, Responses and Strategies* and numerous papers on security and intelligence issues. He is a regular media commentator for BBC television and radio, and has also appeared on Al Jazeera and the Islam Channel.

Ian Rigden is currently Colonel Brigade of Gurkhas, the professional Head of all Gurkhas in British Army Service. He previously served as the Assistant Head of Thematic Doctrine at the UK MOD's Development, Concepts and Doctrine Centre at Shrivenham. He has served on the staff in the MOD, HQ Land Forces, 1st (UK) Armed Division, and as Chief of Campaign Plans HQ MNF-I on General Odierno's CJ5 staff. A graduate of the USAWC Class of 2008 and the Royal College of Defence Studies, Colonel Rigden hold Master's degrees from King's College London and the US Army War College.

James Sheptycki is Professor of Criminology at York University, Toronto, Canada. He has published widely on topics relating to policing and criminology. His most recent book is *Transnational Crime and Policing*. Other recent publications include a co-authored book with Ben Bowling, *Global Policing*, a 2009 co-edited special issue of *Criminology and Criminal Justice* (with Adam Edwards) on 'Guns, Crime and Social Order' and, with Andrew Gold-smith, the co-edited book *Crafting Transnational Policing*.

David Strachan-Morris is a political and security risk consultant with extensive experience in the commercial sector supporting government reconstruction agencies, oil and gas companies, news media organisations and NGOs. He holds a PhD in History from the University of Wolverhampton, and his research interests include intelligence, counterinsurgency and private security companies. He has given numerous papers at academic conferences and has published articles in the *RUSI Journal* and *Intelligence and National Security*, as well as in security industry journals. He also teaches postgraduate courses on intelligence and security at the University of Leicester.

Michael Warner serves as a Command Historian in the US Department of Defense, and has written and lectured widely on intelligence history, theory and reform. He is also adjunct professor at American University's School of International Service in Washington, DC. His most recent book *The Rise and Fall of Intelligence: A Global History*, is published by Georgetown University Press.

Acknowledgements

I would like to thank all of the contributors for agreeing to write for this volume. It has its origins in a panel organised within the Intelligence Studies section of the International Studies Association for the ISA annual conference in San Diego in 2012. Early versions of the chapters by Michael Warner, Peter Gill and Mark Phythian, Julian Richards, and Philip Davies, Kristian Gustafson and Ian Rigden were presented at this conference, and benefited from the acute observations of Loch Johnson as discussant and from the informed discussion that is a characteristic of Intelligence Studies panels at ISA conferences. Thanks to Aaron Brantly, Jim Sheptycki, David Strachan-Morris, David Omand and Art Hulnick for agreeing to join this cast and so help develop the idea behind the panel into a book. The origins of the book also lie more deeply in the succession of panels that have been held at ISA over the last decade or so and which have aimed to develop social science approaches to the study of intelligence. In addition to the contributors to this volume, these have regularly involved Stuart Farson, Loch Johnson, Stephen Marrin and Shlomo Shpiro and have resulted in several previous publications. Thanks also to Andrew Humphrys, Senior Editor at Routledge, for immediately seeing the potential of this book and for his subsequent support, to Ian Howe for his expert copy-editing and to Annabelle Harris for guiding the manuscript through the production process.

Mark Phythian

Introduction

Beyond the Intelligence Cycle?

Mark Phythian

The concept of the Intelligence Cycle presents something of a paradox. On the one hand, it has been central to the study and understanding of intelligence in the post-Second World War era. An intelligence training course, higher education course, or textbook that did not open with a description of the Intelligence Cycle would have seemed unthinkable until quite recently, akin to studying Politics without considering the nature and role of the state. As Robert Clark has noted: "Over the years, the intelligence cycle has become almost a theological concept: No one questions its validity."[1] On the other hand, the Intelligence Cycle has never been a particularly accurate guide to the way in which contemporary intelligence is organised and proceeds. Moreover, a range of developments mean that the gap between representation and reality is widening rather than narrowing. In short, its validity is now being seriously questioned. Hence, as Robert Clark has also noted, "when pressed, many intelligence officers admit that the intelligence process 'really doesn't work like that' ".[2] The core argument of this book is that the time has come to fully recognise this paradox, adopt a more critical approach to the concept of the Intelligence Cycle, and in so doing consider whether it is now time, given developments in both the practice and the study of intelligence (in particular with regard to the latter, the emergence of Intelligence Studies as a distinct subject area[3]), to move beyond the Intelligence Cycle.

The Intelligence Cycle

It is useful to begin with a description of the Intelligence Cycle to ensure a baseline level of understanding among all readers before moving on to engage with the critiques that make up the main body of this book.[4] While there have been some differences in the way in which the Intelligence Cycle has been represented,[5] in its most widely discussed form the Intelligence Cycle can be considered to comprise five distinct stages. The entire cycle begins with the **planning and direction** stage, in which the customers for the intelligence product – policy-makers in the case of national security intelligence – request intelligence on a particular issue or specific target. Once directed by the customer, the second stage of the cycle, **collection**, begins. This involves accessing the raw information that will be required for the finished intelligence product to be produced. Contemporary intelligence collection draws on a wide range of sources, usually categorised in terms of various "INTs". As outlined by the CIA, there are six categories of these, involving a total of nine INTs:

- Signals intelligence (SIGINT) is derived from signals intercepts comprising, however transmitted – either individually or in combination, all communications intelligence (COMINT), electronic intelligence (ELINT), or foreign instrumentation signals intelligence (FISINT).
- Imagery intelligence (IMINT) includes representations of objects reproduced electronically or by optical means on film, electronic display devices, or other media. Imagery can be derived from visual photography, radar sensors, infrared sensors, lasers, and electro-optics.
- Measurement and signature intelligence (MASINT) is technically derived intelligence data other than imagery and SIGINT. The data results in intelligence that locates, identifies, or describes distinctive characteristics of targets. It employs a broad group of disciplines including nuclear, optical, radio frequency, acoustics, seismic, and materials sciences.
- Human intelligence (HUMINT) is derived from human sources. Collection includes clandestine acquisition of photography, documents, and other material; overt collection by personnel in diplomatic and consular posts; debriefing of foreign nationals and US citizens who travel abroad; and official contacts with foreign governments.
- Geospatial intelligence (GEOINT) is the analysis and visual representation of security-related activities on the earth. It is produced through an integration of imagery, imagery intelligence, and geospatial information.
- Open-Source intelligence (OSINT) is publicly available information appearing in print or electronic form.[6]

However, it should be noted that collection methods are constantly evolving in response to technological developments, and these developments can also affect the manner in which collection methods are categorised – for instance, separate categories can emerge from within existing categories as technological change impacts on the volume of material involved and results in increased specialisation of collection methods. For example, in this book two contributors suggest additions or alterations to the list of INTs presented above; in Chapter 5 Aaron Brantly suggests the addition of CYBERINT as a discrete collection category,[7] while in Chapter 8 David Omand suggests the addition of SOCMINT – the collection of information from internet social media – as a separate type of collection, fuelled by the rapid growth of activity in this area.

All but the last of these categories, OSINT, involve covert collection methods. It is worth pausing to consider the wide range of information that is openly available and which can be utilised as OSINT before it is necessary to resort to covert collection methods:

News media: Newspapers, magazines, radio, television, and computer-based information.

Web-based communities and user-generated content: Social networking sites, video-sharing sites, wikis, blogs, and folksonomies.

Public data: Government reports, official data (such as budgets), demographics, hearings, legislative debates, press conferences, speeches, marine and aeronautical safety warnings, environmental impact statements, contract awards.

Observations and reporting: Amateur airplane spotters, radio monitors, and satellite observers.

Professional and academic: Conferences, symposia, professional associations, academic papers, and subject matter experts.

Commercial data: Insurance companies, international aviation organisations, transportation and shipping companies.[8]

As a source, OSINT is particularly important for intelligence customers (whether states, corporations, or other customers) with limited budgets and/or technological capabilities, although, working on the basis that the most important secrets are also the most closely guarded, not all information that a customer might want is likely to be openly available. Some collection will, therefore, inevitably involve more expensive, and ethically questionable, covert methods.

The key point here is that the combined potential of covert and open sources of intelligence is, in the contemporary globalised world, staggering. Anyone who has used a search engine such as Google will have experienced the resulting problem in miniature. For example, the search term "Russian gas industry" can result in 22,200,000 results, returned in a mere 0.275 seconds.[9] Information is not intelligence, and to be transformed into intelligence raw information must pass through the **processing** and **analysis** stages, which together may be thought of as the Rumpelstiltskin stage.[10] **Processing** is the pre-analytical stage in which raw information is filtered and readied for **analysis** via a range of techniques, including decryption (i.e. decoding information that has been encoded in order to protect it), language translation, and data reduction. This, then, is an essentially technical stage. In the **analysis** stage this organised information is transformed into intelligence. In the terms of the 9/11 Commission *Report* (which criticised US intelligence analysts for failing to do this and so provide specific and timely forewarning of the impending 9/11 attacks), this stage is all about "connecting the dots".[11] As described by the CIA, it involves

the conversion of basic information into finished intelligence. It includes integrating, evaluating, and analyzing all available data – which is often fragmentary and even contradictory – and preparing intelligence products. Analysts, who are subject-matter specialists, consider the information's reliability, validity, and relevance. They integrate data into a coherent whole, put the evaluated information in context, and produce finished intelligence that includes assessments of events and judgments about the implications of the information for the United States.[12]

This is a complex process but the essence of it is, as Loch Johnson points out, "straightforward enough: namely, hiring smart people to pore over all the information from open and secret sources, then present the findings to decision-makers in written reports and oral briefings".[13] Hence, in the Intelligence Cycle, **analysis** leads to the final stage, that of **dissemination** – the distribution of the finished intelligence product to the same customers who requested it at the **planning and direction** stage. The logic of the Intelligence Cycle model lies in the assumption that it is at this point that "policymakers, the recipients of finished intelligence, then make decisions based on the information, and these decisions may lead to the levying of more requirements, thus triggering the Intelligence Cycle".[14]

Thinking critically about the Intelligence Cycle

How accurate a depiction of contemporary intelligence practices and processes is this? The chapters that follow present a range of critiques of the Intelligence Cycle model across several intelligence contexts: national security intelligence; military intelligence; police and criminal intelligence; corporate intelligence; and the fast-developing realm of cyber intelligence. They address the following questions. First, how relevant is the Intelligence Cycle model? Second, has the time now arrived to move beyond the Intelligence Cycle? If so, what should replace it? What emerges from these chapters is a plurality of approaches that seek to advance the debate and, as a consequence, Intelligence Studies itself.

In Chapter 1 Michael Warner explores the origins and history of the Intelligence Cycle concept. He locates the origin of the concept in the intersection of military science and psychology, and discusses the way in which it was imported from social science into US military training programmes in the 1940s, around the time that the US Army was solidifying its doctrine for battlefield intelligence support. From there it became a staple of intelligence writings, to the point where academics and practitioners came to accept it as a given, or at least did not give it too much critical attention. However, Warner argues that this wide acceptance of the Intelligence Cycle is, to a significant extent, an artefact of the linear notions of cognition and behaviour that prevailed in the social sciences seventy or more years ago. The nature of the contemporary world means that it is time for the Intelligence Cycle to be re-evaluated in the light of more recent discussions of the social construction of knowledge and risk, as well as the advent of automated decision processes in which cognitive steps occur at machine speeds. In particular, Warner highlights the challenges posed by the growth of threats in the cyber domain and the implications of intelligence activity here for the future relevance of the Intelligence Cycle concept.

Peter Gill and Mark Phythian take an innovative approach to explaining the limitations of the Intelligence Cycle model in the context of what they term the "challenges of complexity". They identify seven specific challenges: the challenge of understanding intelligence via a risk-based approach; the challenge of bureaucratic politics; the challenge of interactivity; the challenge of comparative analysis; the challenge of (covert) action; the challenge of technology; and the challenge of oversight. On the basis of their analysis of these challenges, Gill and Phythian propose an alternative way of conceptualising the intelligence process that involves moving away from the notion of a cycle towards the more complex notion of a web of intelligence.

Julian Richards examines the ways in which the intelligence enterprise has been transformed since the end of the Cold War. He anchors his critique of the cycle model in his argument that a process that was embedded during the Cold War, when "the monolithic and slow-moving target of the Soviet threat had allowed an industrialisation of the intelligence business", is not appropriate to meeting the challenges of post-modernity. He shares with Warner and with Gill and Phythian a concern with the impact of technological change, but offers a different approach to thinking about this, reflected in his alternative to the cycle model, the "synthesised actor-oriented model".

From 2009 to 2011, Philip Davies, Kristian Gustafson and Ian Rigden were involved in the development of the British military's new Joint Intelligence Doctrine. As they point out in Chapter 4, rethinking the classic Intelligence Cycle model became one of the review's central tasks. They give a detailed reflective account of the review process, analysing the alternative approaches that were considered and highlighting the considerations that arise from the conceptualisation and representation of the intelligence process in a military context. In doing this, they make the useful distinction between what they term "proceduralist" and "conceptualist" approaches to the Intelligence Cycle. As they explain, one outcome of the review was the formulation of a new "core functions of intelligence" paradigm that supplanted the Intelligence Cycle model and was incorporated into the new intelligence doctrine.

As noted above, a number of chapters in this volume address the way in which technological advances have impacted on the continued relevance of the cycle model. Aaron Brantly focuses on a key domain in this respect: cyber. He provides a framework for understanding the role of intelligence in this poorly understood domain; for example, exploring the implications for understandings of intelligence collection. He explains that the role of intelligence in cyber is not dissimilar to elsewhere, that there are "new areas in which collection and analysis need to occur, yet its overall objective remains the same". At the same time, he emphasises the importance of anticipating future threats rather than simply countering known ones. This means that intelligence in the cyber domain needs to be action-oriented, highlighting the question of reflexivity raised by Gill and Phythian in Chapter 2. His chapter also highlights a related question raised elsewhere in this volume, of whether the Intelligence Cycle model is too limited in the range of activities it encompasses. Key here is the question of covert action, which is fundamental to the conduct of intelligence in the cyber domain.

The chapters thus far have been largely concerned with national security intelligence. Another key issue is whether and how far the Intelligence Cycle model applies to intelligence in contexts other than national security intelligence – for example, in relation to the policing sector. Here, intelligence-led policing has been advanced as the best way to organise and operationalise the allocation of scarce policing resources. In Chapter 6, James Sheptycki critically engages with the literature concerning policing, crime, and the Intelligence Cycle in order to highlight shortcomings in Intelligence Cycle thinking and practice. In doing this he provides a full spectrum critique via identification of a chain of pathologies that operate within the cycle of intelligence-led policing. He argues that the net effect of these pathologies has been to generate ineffectiveness, albeit an ineffectiveness that has had the ability to masquerade as agency success, pointing to a clear need to move beyond the police Intelligence Cycle.

David Strachan-Morris analyses the continued relevance of the Intelligence Cycle model in a further context: that of the corporate sector. In the contemporary world, most large organisations have their own intelligence departments. However, he argues that in this area corporations are far less bound by doctrine and methodology than governments. This makes notions of an Intelligence Cycle distinctive in a number of respects. The relationships between the customer and intelligence provider can differ: it may be a very close relationship with an "in-house" provider or the company may contract this work out to an external organisation on a regular or ad hoc basis, keeping the provider at arm's length. The type of decision is also very different. Rather than making political or diplomatic decisions, corporations are seeking to maximise profits and/or reduce risk. This can often lead to very different questions being asked of an intelligence provider. Expectations of the intelligence provider are also different. In discussing these and related issues, Strachan-Morris provides a clear guide to understanding how the intelligence process works in the corporate sector and the implications of this for the cycle concept.

In Chapter 8 David Omand argues that the classic Intelligence Cycle model should be seen as incorporating three distinct concepts: that of an intelligence narrative; that of a professional intelligence identity; and the meta-concept of the model of intelligence. His chapter provides a critique of the assumptions embedded in each of these. In doing so he reflects on a range of issues, including the implications of the introduction of a National Security Strategy in the UK, the impact of technology, and the importance of risk awareness – of the capacity of intelligence to alert governments to potential risks before they fully emerge – a requirement that the Intelligence Cycle model is unable to accommodate.

The final chapter of the book is by Arthur Hulnick. His 2006 article in *Intelligence and National Security*, "What's Wrong with the Intelligence Cycle"[15] represents an important milestone in the development of this debate – indeed, he can be said to have kick-started it. At the time of writing it remains the most-read article published in that journal.[16] In Chapter 9 he discusses his own experience with the Intelligence Cycle and its shortcomings. At the same time, he cautions that alternatives to the cycle risk exhibiting a common weakness that, in turn, point to the principal advantage to be gained from the cycle model; namely that as "more and more modifications are made to the traditional model, the diagrams become almost incomprehensible, and perhaps misleading". Nevertheless, Hulnick sees two key problems with the cycle model: its omission of the key intelligence functions of counter-intelligence and covert action. In response, he proposes what he terms the "matrix model" of the intelligence process. He concludes with a call for those involved in teaching intelligence, whether in academic or training contexts, to move beyond the Intelligence Cycle model and incorporate consideration of the kind of alternatives presented throughout this volume. Hence, Hulnick has the final word (for now) on a debate he has done much to promote and in which he has been an influential voice. To facilitate further critical thinking about the cycle concept and alternatives to it, a select bibliography of key works relevant to the Intelligence Cycle debate is provided at the end of the book.

Notes

1 Robert M. Clark, *Intelligence Analysis: A Target-Centric Approach* (Washington, DC: CQ Press, 2003), p. 11.
2 Ibid.
3 See Peter Gill and Mark Phythian, *Intelligence in an Insecure World* (2nd edn, Cambridge: Polity Press, 2012), pp. 1–9.
4 A number of subsequent chapters provide a brief outline of the Intelligence Cycle in contextualising their own critiques or alternatives. As editor I have retained these outlines, even though this can result in some duplication of information, as doing so makes each individual chapter more comprehensible if read in isolation from the remainder of the volume than would otherwise be the case. The following paragraphs are intended in particular for those readers who have not encountered the concept of the Intelligence Cycle previously. More experienced readers may prefer to move on to the next section (p. 4).
5 Most strikingly, while US versions (the basis of the discussion below) have involved five stages, the UK version has included just four stages. Whereas the US version regarded "processing" and "analysis" as distinct stages, in the UK model both of these stages were combined. This difference is considered in more detail in Chapter 4.
6 https://www.cia.gov/library/publications/additional-publications/the-work-of-a-nation/work-of-the-cia.html, last accessed 20 November 2012.
7 See Table 5.1 and the related discussion, pp. 77–82.
8 This categorisation is taken from Joint Staff, Joint Publication 2–01, *Joint and National Intelligence Support to Military Operations*, revised 5 January 2012, Appendix D, available at www.dtic.mil/doctrine/new_pubs/jp2_01.pdf. Last accessed 20 November 2012.
9 Search conducted 20 November 2012.
10 After the Brothers Grimm fairy tale about the "little man" with the ability to spin straw into gold, www.cs.cmu.edu/~spok/grimmtmp/044.txt, last accessed 20 November 2012.
11 See Thomas Keen and Lee H. Hamilton, *The 9/11 Commission Report* (New York: W. W. Norton, 2004), pp. 400, 408, 416–17; Mark M. Lowenthal, "Towards a Reasonable Standard for Analysis: How Right, How Often on Which Issues?" *Intelligence*

   and National Security, Vol. 23 No. 3, 2008, pp. 303–15; Mark Phythian, "Intelligence Analysis Today and Tomorrow", *Security Challenges*, Vol. 5 No. 1, 2009, pp. 69–85.
12 www.fas.org/irp/cia/product/facttell/intcycle.htm, last accessed 20 November 2012.
13 Loch K. Johnson, *National Security Intelligence* (Cambridge: Polity Press, 2012), p. 54.
14 www.fas.org/irp/cia/product/facttell/intcycle.htm, last accessed 20 November 2012.
15 Arthur S. Hulnick, "What's Wrong with the Intelligence Cycle", *Intelligence and National Security*, Vol. 21 No. 6, 2006, pp. 959–79.
16 According to the journal's own website, www.tandfonline.com/toc/fint20/current, last accessed 20 November 2012.

1   The past and future of the Intelligence Cycle

Michael Warner[1]

Introduction

The Intelligence Cycle needs no introduction to intelligence professionals or scholars. Its circle of links representing a set of sequential and repeated operations – educing decisionmakers' *requirements* for information; *collecting* relevant data; *evaluating* the data for reliability; *analyzing* their significance; *disseminating* the resulting intelligence product to decisionmakers; and then starting the process all over again by passing the decisionmakers' updated requirements to the collectors – sounds familiar to anyone who has sat through a college or staff-school course on intelligence. The Cycle per se now seems less interesting than its significance. To wit, we have grounds to suspect that the Cycle, even as a teaching device, has passed its point of maximum utility. Indeed, the usefulness of any classroom tool, analogy, or thought experiment must lie in increasing the mental agility and acuity of the student, analyst, or decisionmaker employing it. A good teaching device should not require more explanation to clarify it than it returns in increased understanding, and it should not predispose analysts toward inaccurate judgments (or decisionmakers toward courses of action that are likely to fail). Based on that criterion, growing evidence suggests that the Intelligence Cycle – even as a heuristic device, not to mention as a doctrine for real-world intelligence operations – could be doing more harm than good.

This examination of the Intelligence Cycle comprises discussions centered around three questions. First, where did we get the Cycle in the first place? Second, how is it working now, and how do we understand it? Finally, where is it going; i.e. how are intelligence scholars and practitioners of the future likely to view it? Considering the possible answers to these three questions might induce greater caution among teachers who employ the Intelligence Cycle as a learning tool.

Whence came the Intelligence Cycle?

Around the time of the French Revolution the world witnessed an astounding technological upheaval, and a military revolution to accompany it. During the

Napoleonic wars, military staff work developed in scale and sophistication to assist generals in commanding the huge patriotic armies of France and the masses that France's opponents mobilized in response. Such forces required specialized staffs to plan and prepare commanders to make decisions – and then to ensure the decisions were properly implemented. These staffs consumed information voraciously, and they initiated a rationalization of warfare that continues today.

A Prussian general named Carl von Clausewitz spent much of his life fighting the armies of the French Revolution and of Napoleon, and in reflecting upon his experience he became a ready guide to legions of staff officers to come. In his age he pondered what made for victory and defeat for all generals, leaving a manuscript that his widow soon published as *On War* (1832). Clausewitz regarded information as vital for commanders, but he also viewed it as inherently suspect and thus counted it as only one factor for a general to consider. In the heat of the fight a general should be a wise and imperturbable rock against the shifting emotions and alarms of all engagements:

> Many intelligence reports in war are contradictory; even more are false, and most are uncertain. What one can reasonably ask of an officer is that he should possess a standard of judgment, which he can gain only from knowledge of men and affairs and from common sense. He should be guided by the laws of probability.[2]

On War nonetheless implicitly raised the expectation for military intelligence by defining it as "every sort of information about the enemy and his country – the basis, in short, of our own plans and operations."[3] If steady generals were rare in any army, however, Clausewitz thus hinted that another answer to the problem of generalship was to improve the information that reached them, thus reducing the uncertainties of command.

The Prussian army subsequently applied the new rationality to war first and most thoroughly, and as a result beat the Austrians in 1866 and the French in 1870 with stunning efficiency and dispatch. The Prussians became famous for their diligent preparation and meticulous attention to the details of modern war, all of which came under the all-knowing General Staff. Someone had to take notes on the methods and means of real and potential enemies, moreover, and this chore fell to the new army intelligence bureaus created for the purpose from the 1860s on. Indeed, armies planning to fight on foreign soil also needed maps of where they might have to march, and those maps had to be kept up to date as new roads, rail lines, and industries re-shaped the landscape. It was no accident that the first military information bureaus were usually in charge of map-making offices as well, or at least were quartered near the cartographers.

While Clausewitz and contemporary military theorists covered lightly the types of information needed by commanders and the ways of attaining it, later authors would fill in these details. The provision and quality of that information, as opposed to its use, became a primary topic of consideration. In 1895 a British colonel named George Furse contributed to a growing literature in his book *Information in War*. From the outset he used information and intelligence as synonyms and explained, in Clausewitzian terms, why his topic was so important:

> No military operations can be carried out without having first acquired such intelligence as will assist in making the most suitable dispositions. A commander must not only see that he gets information, but also that what he obtains is the best and most reliable. The greatest talent will be of little avail to him if he cannot devise means for acquiring a knowledge of his adversary's strength, positions, and movements. All great captains have attached very considerable importance to this matter.[4]

Within a generation of Furse's *Information in War*, the First World War added signals intelligence and imagery intelligence to the sources of information for commanders. A generation after that, the Second World War refined these disciplines and arguably added another (scientific intelligence) as well. These new technological means amply served commanders, but they were themselves hard taskmasters, demanding of their armies thousands of men (and women as well) who could be trained in the analytical and technical tasks necessary for their functioning.

So who first conceived of this provision of information for commanders as an Intelligence Cycle? Kristan Wheaton of Mercyhurst College has helpfully researched what must be some of the earliest uses of the phrase "intelligence cycle."[5] He employed Google's Ngrams program to date it to a 1948 book, *Intelligence is for Commanders*, authored by a pair of lieutenant colonels, Robert R. Glass and Philip B. Davidson, then teaching at the US Army Command and General Staff College at Fort Leavenworth. Their Intelligence Cycle comprised four phases: direction of the collection effort, collection of information, processing of information, and use of intelligence.[6] Wheaton inferred from their explanation of the Intelligence Cycle (which even includes a diagram) that the phrase was not original with these authors, who thus presumably drew from some earlier source. His conclusion seems eminently sensible. Indeed, one speculates with him that the Cycle was a teaching device used in training officers at Fort Leavenworth during the Second World War.

Wheaton also suggests that the Intelligence Cycle might have been used synonymously with other phrases to describe the intelligence process. Following this suggestion one finds (as Wheaton seemed to do as well) that that very phrase, "intelligence process," was used to mean roughly the same thing as the Intelligence Cycle in the 1940s and 1950s. One also finds something interesting from another angle.

The notion of an Intelligence Cycle seems related to concepts emerging in the academic discipline of psychology (i.e. scientific descriptions of the workings of the human mind) before the Second World War. Indeed, the original occurrences of the phrase "intelligence process" in Google Ngrams appear in medical writings early in the twentieth century. Harvard psychologist Hugo Münster-berg's *Psychology, General and Applied* (1914) makes a good example. The textbook discussed education and "the problem of grading the general intelli-gence" possessed by students. Münsterberg defined that intelligence as the "ability to adjust one's mind to a task." For each student, the "intelligence process" involved in such adjustment included "his ability to perceive, to learn, to retain, to discriminate, and so on." That was "the one mental factor which is most significant for the later practical life."[7]

Münsterberg's definition of the intelligence process resembles the later Intel-ligence Cycle in incorporating a set – if not yet a sequence – of discrete opera-tions for gathering and processing inputs. Just a few years later another discussion of mental acuity showed that psychologists were moving even closer to something recognizable as the Intelligence Cycle. Dr. J. Victor Haberman's article in the weekly *Medical Record* on measuring intelligence explained how the mind understands the world: first it notices things and events; then it registers or remembers how present impressions associate with those that the mind already recalls; then it analyzes and comprehends similarities and differences; and finally it combines the resulting knowledge elements to complete a train of thought or to span gaps in available evidence. Dr. Haberman called that latter step "combination" and classed it as "the highest of all mental functions." This whole sequence of these four elements constituted the "intelligence process." "When we speak of intelligence," Haberman insisted, "we should imply all func-tions mentioned: attention, memory, comprehension, and combination."[8]

One suspects that some intelligence officer in Britain or the United States, sometime around the Second World War, remembered a college course in psy-chology and lifted the "intelligence process" from his notes or his textbook in crafting a lesson on military intelligence practice. Indeed, the US Army's 1940 Basic Field Manual for military intelligence (FM 30–5) already had chapters [III through VII] titled "Collection of information"; "Collation of information"; "Evaluation and interpretation of information"; "G-2 estimate of the enemy situ-ation"; and "Dissemination of intelligence." All an instructor had to do was to note that this "intelligence process" is iterative, and hence cyclical, and the term "Intelligence Cycle" was born. Scholars may never know just who made this mental leap, but by 1948 it was an accomplished fact well understood and ready for diagramming by the authors of *Intelligence is for Commanders*.

The historical link between the origins of the Intelligence Cycle and the early literature on measuring human intelligence should give the reader pause. Not necessarily because "intelligence" seems shadowed by a cloud of disagreement wherever it travels, as it perhaps inevitably became associated with ideologies of group or even racial differences. Discussions of human intelligence often allude to a vague but nonetheless important mental capacity that makes a person more readily able than her peers to draw and apply useful lessons from patterns, cases, and life events. What is that capacity, which has proven time and again to be both experimentally present and yet profoundly elusive? Around the time of the First World War researchers sought to avoid subjective associations by giving the relative acuity of mental processes the tactfully neutral label of "intelligence quotient," or IQ. Since that time, the acronym "IQ" itself has become controversial, and psychologists by the 1970s referred to that not-quite-definable but still roughly quantifiable something in an actor's mental processes as the "general intelligence factor" or "*g*." It appears to be something unique but intangible about each person – a private capacity that helps one to know and respond to one's environment.[9]

This is not to suggest there has been no progress in our understanding of how the mind works; indeed, it is just that progress that makes the Intelligence Cycle problematic. The inventors of the phrase implicitly drew an analogy between the behavior of organizations and nations and an early twentieth century notion of a linear, step-by-step sequence of mental operations. By doing so, they tied themselves to hypotheses that decades of findings by psychologists would challenge. Indeed, the last 15 years have seen major books by psychologists trying to explain why intuitive or "snap" judgments can frequently be more correct or reliable than decisions made after long reflection.[10] Insight can be as important as information. Historian Walter Laqueur hinted at this in *A World of Secrets: The Uses and Limits of Intelligence* (1985), noting a similarity between the demands on doctors and intelligence analysts. Both disciplines rely on sustained data gathering and dispassionate calculation, but success in both also stems from intuition. Indeed, "it is precisely in critical situations in which there are elements of ambiguity that the dramatic insight comes back into its own, and this applies to both clinical medicine and intelligence."[11] Perhaps that was what Napoleon famously meant with his "*coup d'œil militaire*," that indefinable eye of command, and why he allegedly preferred his generals to be lucky rather than brilliant. One is tempted to say we have come full Cycle, as it seems we have arrived back with Clausewitz and his model general as an imperturbable rock:

> When all is said and done, it really is the commander's *coup d'œil*, his ability to see things simply, to identify the whole business of war completely with himself, that is the essence of good generalship. Only if the mind works in this comprehensive fashion can it achieve the freedom it needs to dominate events and not be dominated by them.[12]

Where has the Intelligence Cycle been?

This chapter makes no pretense of judging the merits of competing lines of inquiry in a field (psychology) well removed from this author's expertise. It does suggest, however, that intelligence scholars should recognize at least two ways in which conceiving of intelligence as a process of linear and iterative operations – i.e. as the Intelligence Cycle – has caused and is causing problems for students and practitioners. This irony might best be illustrated with a look at one of the clearest applications of the Intelligence Cycle to intelligence practice: the issue of warning.

Recall that the Intelligence Cycle is like an endless chain of a few processes. Any number of authors have studied the links in that chain, particularly as they show signs of stress in warning situations. Indeed, the literature on warning is voluminous, from intelligence community post-mortems to blue-ribbon commission reports to academic tomes. The writings in that veritable library tend to concentrate on improving the functioning of the collection component of the Cycle, or its analysis phase, or its dissemination to decisionmakers. Two famous examples help to illustrate this point. Roberta Wohlstetter's *Pearl Harbor: Warning and Decision* (1962) concluded that warning failures rarely stem from too little information; more commonly, analysts find themselves unable to distinguish "signals" from "noise" in the torrent of events and data rushing past.[13] By contrast, Richard Betts's seminal article, "Analysis, War and Decision: Why Intelligence Failures Are Inevitable" (1978), explained that most surprises emerged not from intelligence mistakes but rather from decisionmakers misreading or dismissing the intelligence provided to them.[14] In short, better collection and even analysis does not always mean better warning if the decision link of the chain is flawed. One can cite any number of other studies of warning that focus on other phases of the Intelligence Cycle.

Wohlstetter and Betts would surely agree that perfect warning is impossible – but that improvement is both feasible and imperative. Successful warning, they hint, requires an entire process and all its elements to function properly: intelligence collection must feed into insightful analysis that shares timely counsel with decisionmakers, who then respond effectively. The chain can break at any point, and thus has to be strengthened in every link. Studies of warning failures have thus tended to examine the "links" in the warning chain and what makes them stronger or weaker. Nonetheless, a different approach is possible.

Instead of discussing the discrete elements in the warning process, one can study why and when the entire chain is likely to be stressed to breaking – and the warning that decisionmakers expect is not provided. This author's own examination of the history suggests that warning failures for the United States, at least since 1940, seem to fall in a recognizable pattern. Three "generic types" of warning failures, moreover, share a common feature. All involve situations where there are active information-denial efforts (and occasionally deception as well). The motivations behind such denial efforts seem quite logical to the actors and adversaries seeking to shield their plans from outside observation:

1   We see surprise attacks against US forces when an adversary is stressed by American military or diplomatic moves, and wishes to shock the United States and alter the trend of events.[15]
2   We also see warning failures when we are monitoring dictatorships. The intentions and plans of dictators are notoriously difficult to fathom, as they are typically "hard targets" for intelligence collection. Some dictators, moreover, craft their plans on the fly, as it were, and do not always decide what their next moves will be until the last moment.

3 Finally, weapons of mass destruction programs are notoriously difficult to
monitor. States developing such weapons have almost always sought to
prepare for crucial but politically, diplomatically, and technologically risky
advances in the greatest possible secrecy. In such instances, even a democracy like India can briefly make its weapons program into a very tough
intelligence target.

What of this pattern? While agreeing with Wohlstetter and Betts that surprise
can never be eliminated, we can still work to ensure that warning failures are
reduced and mitigated. Warning experts agree that "intelligence" is rarely if ever
the sole or even the principal source of vital information available to decision-
makers. Nevertheless, both intelligence professionals and leaders will continue
to expect that intelligence – given the resources and talent allotted to it – should
provide clearer and earlier clues to events than those coming from other information sources. The trick is in the calibration – in tuning the metaphorical dials to
make both the intelligence "sensors" and the policy interface sensitive enough to
recognize all signs of serious danger (no false negatives) while leaving sufficient
slack to avoid crying wolf (minimal false positives). Understanding the three
types of situations in which we have historically been vulnerable to warning failures might help us in tuning our collective alert level to help everyone involved
recognize when we are entering such situations in the future – as a driver
watches for ice when the road is damp and her car's thermometer slips below
freezing.

Returning to the "endless chain" metaphor for the Intelligence Cycle, this
analysis also suggests that studying the links in that chain (requirements, collection, evaluation, analysis, dissemination) will only take us so far, whether toward
improving our knowledge of intelligence per se or toward improving the work of
intelligence agencies. It can be just as important to include factors that are
wholly exogenous to intelligence – such as the relative openness of a target
regime or its interest in acquiring weapons of mass destruction – if one wants to
understand intelligence outcomes.

Where is the Intelligence Cycle going?

Despite such issues, the Intelligence Cycle lives on for a great many intelligence
practitioners. Lately, however, we can see signs that its reign as the supposed
essence of intelligence could be nearing its end. For example, in the US military,
the Joint Staff's recent revision of its most relevant doctrinal statement on the
matter, Joint Publication 2–01, *Joint and National Intelligence Support to
Military Operations*, leaves the Cycle to Appendix D. Instead of focusing on the
Cycle, the main text of Joint Pub. 2–01 discusses the "intelligence process" that
brings a commander timely and accurate information on the adversary. That
process comprises the familiar elements of the Intelligence Cycle, but the Joint
Pub. takes pains to keep readers from viewing the process as a linear sequence
of discrete steps:

There are no firm boundaries delineating where each operation within the intelligence process begins or ends. Intelligence operations are not sequential; rather, they are nearly simultaneous. Additionally, not all operations necessarily continue throughout the entire intelligence process. The increased tempo of military operations requires an unimpeded flow of automatically processed and exploited data that is both timely and relevant to the commander's needs. This unanalyzed combat information must be simultaneously available to both the commander (for time-critical decision making) and the intelligence analyst (for the production of current intelligence assessments). Likewise, the analysis, production, and dissemination of intelligence products must be accomplished in time to support the commander's decision-making needs.[16]

Appendix D of the Joint Pub. finally gets around to a more traditional presentation of the Cycle, only now it is called – rather more accurately – the "Intelligence Analytical Cycle." No pretense is made that the Intelligence Cycle defines intelligence per se, or that activities outside the Cycle, such as covert action or counter-intelligence, are somehow "not intelligence" but rather some species of operations.

Why has the Cycle been relegated to an appendix? Joint Pub. 2–01 does not elaborate, but if it did, one suspects the answer might relate to the fact that intelligence and the military art are in the midst of profound changes that this author has elsewhere dubbed "the digital revolution."[17] With regard to this tectonic shift in the ways people amass, use, store, and transmit knowledge, one can observe certain problems in the ways in which intelligence organizations are trying to adjust to it. Chief among them is speed, and hence the Joint Pub.'s note above that intelligence operations are "nearly simultaneous," and that the tempo of modern military operations "requires an unimpeded flow of *automatically processed* and exploited data" (emphasis added). The US Air Force has recently reflected on this as well in its own doctrine. According to Air Force Doctrine Document (AFDD) 3–12, *Cyberspace Operations*, among the challenges of cyberspace operations is the compressed decision cycle; there is little if any time to gather, process, and share information for decisions: "The fact that operations can take place nearly instantaneously requires the formulation of appropriate responses to potential cyberspace attacks within legal and policy constraints. The compressed decision cycle may require predetermined rules for intelligence, surveillance, and reconnaissance (ISR) actions."[18]

In addition:

In cyberspace, the time between execution and effect can be milliseconds. Nonetheless, the observe-orient-decide-act (OODA) loop remains a valid construct for examining the decision cycle in cyberspace. Ongoing operations can be considered those operations that span past the phases of warfare. Even for ongoing operations, planning at the strategic level is imperative because cyberspace operations can create effects simultaneously at the strategic, operational, and tactical levels across multiple domains. Planners should provide inputs to and receive feedback from appropriate intelligence and targeting organizations across the full range of government organizations and partner nations. Cyberspace's unique attributes and potential for speed require the ability to react to rapidly changing situations.[19]

Of course, cyber operations can take days, months, or years to plan and execute, as Jason Healey of the Atlantic Council notes,[20] and in that sense the traditional Cycle can be quite relevant. But cyber attacks themselves can occur literally in nanoseconds. A victim has no time to consider a response until after the damage is done. It is as if the intelligence problem had become not the deployment and tactics of battleships but the trajectories of the shells they just fired. There is no room for a human commander in this segment of the decision loop. Indeed, as Healey suggests, the corporal on the cyber firing line might be making a decision of national significance – and thus has more need of intelligence support than his or her commanding general, for whom the Cycle was ostensibly designed. As noted above, Joint Pub. 2–01 seems to be moving toward some way of making sense of that development, for instance in its note that raw data must sometimes pass simultaneously to commanders and analysts.

Nonetheless, various organizations still invoke the Intelligence Cycle, perhaps to demonstrate that they are firmly grounded in traditional ways of understanding the issues in looking at new material and thus are not just making up their procedures for intelligence handling. Two examples suffice to make this point. First, the non-governmental Intelligence and National Security Alliance (INSA) in 2011 released a white paper intended to help private and national security decisionmakers "define an emerging cyber intelligence discipline." That discipline, of course, requires "an effective connection between intelligence provider and the customer." Such a connection, as "good intelligence professionals" know, in turn requires that data be

> collected, analyzed, and conveyed; the intelligence serves customers' purposes; and some action is being taken (or deliberately not taken). This cycle can be referred to as a constant process of story-finding, story-telling, story-updating, story listening, and story-heeding. A concept to institutionalize this ad hoc community is currently missing.[21]

What looked so promising is the old Cycle with new names for its links.

Another take comes from Verisign, Inc. which manages two of the Internet's 13 root servers. The company's website advertises a white paper that looks timely and relevant for explaining how the Intelligence Cycle functions in the compressed confines of cyberspace. The paper notes that organizations the world over are recognizing the need for a "formal cyber intelligence capability." It promises to help meet that need with an intelligence model "based on methodical, proven processes" that the company itself has "tested and refined." The paper goes on to describe "a proven, repeatable process with clearly established steps."[22]

What is that process? Of course, it is the classic Intelligence Cycle, comprising direction, collection, analysis, and dissemination. Indeed, this Cycle's presentation could almost have been lifted from *Intelligence is for Commanders* – it has hardly changed a wit. The promised "formal cyber intelligence capability" turns out to be a way of giving a corporation a battalion S-2 shop; a good idea for fighting the *Wehrmacht* in Normandy, but not exactly a detailed prescription for taming that compressed cyber decision loop noted above.

One must not unfairly single out any particular organization or group. These examples were picked almost at random. They illustrate not a lack of seriousness or effort on the part of those who created them, but rather a collective lack of insight. The assumption seems to be that if people need intelligence, they must invoke the Intelligence Cycle. Such is a use of the Cycle not as a tool of analysis but as a talisman.

The right metaphor?

Microsoft Corporation in early 2012 posted an opening for a "Principal Analyst – Threat Intelligence" at its Redmond, Washington headquarters. The posting noted under job responsibilities that candidate applicants would be "expected to understand the intelligence cycle and how to apply this cycle to the cyber environment." One sincerely hopes they can.

The roots of the Cycle in a century-old conception of how the mind works should instill caution in intelligence scholars and practitioners alike. If one insists on defining and viewing intelligence according to psychological analogies, one should at least use modern notions of psychology – and read Clausewitz to boot. If we still need a biological metaphor for the intelligence process, however, perhaps we might find one in a different place. We could search not in the mind, but in the cells. After all, an intelligence system or "community" can be conceived of as animated organism, doing its business while reacting to stimuli and developing within the constraints of the available resources and the parameters in which it dwells. A plant or animal develops in accordance with the resources and threats prevalent in its environment. An intelligence system does likewise. Both biological entities and institutions have internal ordered relations tying together their various related parts in vital structures that serve the whole: the nervous or skeletal systems in animals, or the missions of internal security, combat support, assistance to foreign policy, and so on in a state's intelligence community. Those missions or relations in turn break down into functions: an animal's functional systems work by means of organs like the stomach or liver, while the intelligence missions are all served by the disciplines of signals intelligence, human intelligence, and the like. And finally, each organ or discipline has its own internal components – at the cellular level in animals and plants, and at the level of specialties sorted by teams in intelligence organizations. The processes employed in those fundamental units are constant, reiterative, and cyclical. In an intelligence community – and indeed in any knowledge-based organization – something like the Intelligence Cycle works at that cellular level of analyses and processes.

If we want healthy pets, or people, we should study medicine, which means closer attention to organisms as such as well as to the processes inside of their cells. We learn what makes dogs or cats healthy, or what does likewise for men or women or old people or infants. For the study and good practice of intelligence, we should do likewise in understanding intelligence institutions as such, and not take processes common to all knowledge-based organizations and systems as unique to intelligence systems. We might start by updating our assumptions or conceptual model; doing so might help us in two ways. First, it might nudge forward the eternal debate over warning. It could do so by studying the situations that stress all the links of the chain that produce warning rather than by continuing to focus on those individual links themselves. In other words, analysts and policymakers might improve the efficacy of warning if they could be made more fully aware that they are entering international situations that are prone to warning failures – and thus could double their caution about their evidence, analyses, and conclusions. Second, as intelligence grows ever more digitized and "cyber-ized" (in its subject matter, its methods, and its forms), a clearer understanding that the Intelligence Cycle is actually quite a dated heuristic device – rather than a constitutive dimension of intelligence as such – can liberate analysts, operations officers, commanders, policymakers, and the providers of oversight to think about intelligence and the reform of practices and organizations in more innovative ways better suited to contemporary needs than the Industrial Age methods that served when the Intelligence Cycle was first charted.

Notes

1 This article extends and amends comments made at the International Studies Association annual conference in San Diego, April 2012. The views expressed herein are mine alone and do not necessarily reflect those of the Department of Defense or any other US government entity.
2 Carl von Clausewitz, *On War*, edited and translated by Michael Howard and Peter Paret (Princeton, NJ: Princeton University Press, 1989 [1976]), see Book I, Chapter 6 on "Intelligence War," p. 117.
3 Ibid.
4 George Armand Furse, *Information in War: Its Acquisition and Transmission* (London: William Clowes & Sons, 1895), p. 3.
5 See Kristan J. Wheaton, "Let's Kill the Intelligence Cycle," available at http://sourcesandmethods.blogspot.co.uk/2011/05/lets-kill-intelligence-cycle-original.html, last accessed November 20, 2012.
6 Robert R. Glass and Philip B. Davidson, *Intelligence is for Commanders* (Harrisburg, PA: Military Service Publishing, 1948), p. 5.
7 Hugo Münsterberg, *Psychology, General and Applied* (New York: Appleton, 1914), p. 391.
8 J. Victor Haberman, "The Measures of Intelligence Diagnostically Remeasured," *Medical Record* 97 (March 20, 1920), pp. 467–8.
9 For more on *g*, see Linda S. Gottfredson, "The General Intelligence Factor," *Scientific American*, Winter 1998, available at www.sciam.com. See also Charles Murray, "Intelligence in the Classroom," *Wall Street Journal*, January 16, 2007, p. A21.
10 See, for instance, Daniel Kahneman, *Thinking, Fast and Slow* (New York: Farrar, Strauss and Giroux, 2011), and Gary Klein, *Sources of Power: How People Make*

Decisions (Boston, MA: MIT Press, 1999). I thank psychiatrist Dr. David Charney for this observation.

11 Walter Laqueur, *A World of Secrets: The Uses and Limits of Intelligence* (New York: Basic Books, 1985), p. 305.

12 Clausewitz, *On War*, see Book VIII, Chapter 1, p. 578.

13 Roberta Wohlstetter, *Pearl Harbor: Warning and Decision* (Stanford, CA: Stanford University Press, 1962), p. 3.

14 Richard K. Betts, "Analysis, War and Decision: Why Intelligence Failures Are Inevitable," *World Politics*, Vol. 31 No. 1, 1978, pp. 61–89.

15 One can argue that Pearl Harbor and 9/11 fit in this category, as both Imperial Japan and Osama bin Laden viewed America as an encircling and stifling force that had to be pushed back.

16 Joint Staff, Joint Publication 2–01, *Joint and National Intelligence Support to Military Operations*, revised 5 January 2012, pp. xvi–xxvi, available at www.dtic.mil/doctrine/new_pubs/jp2_01.pdf, last accessed March 21, 2012.

17 Michael Warner, "Reflections on Technology and Intelligence Systems," *Intelligence and National Security* Vol. 27 No. 1, 2012, pp. 133–53.

18 US Air Force, Air Force Doctrine Document (AFDD) 3–12, *Cyberspace Operations*, 15 July 2010, with Interim change 1 published November 30, 2012, pp. 9, 29; available at www.au.af.mil/au/cadre/aspj/digital/Doctrine/du_afdd3-12.pdf, last accessed November 20, 2012.

19 Ibid.

20 See, for example, Jason Healey, "Claiming the Lost Cyber Heritage," *Strategic Studies Quarterly*, Vol. 6 No. 3, Fall 2012, pp. 11–19.

21 Intelligence and National Security Alliance, *Cyber Intelligence: Setting the Landscape for an Existing Discipline*, pp. 3, 13–14; September 13, 2011, available at https://images.magnetmail.net/images/clients/INSA/attach/INSA_CYBER_INTELLIGENCE_2011.pdf, last accessed March 20, 2012.

22 Verisign [no author or date], "Establishing a Formal Cyber Intelligence Capability," p. 3; available at https://www.verisigninc.com/assets/whitepaper-idefense-cyber-intel.pdf, last accessed March 20, 2012.

2 From Intelligence Cycle to web of intelligence

Complexity and the conceptualisation of intelligence[1]

Peter Gill and Mark Phythian

Introduction

Over the last twenty years Intelligence Studies (IS) has developed significantly to represent a distinctive branch of Political Science/Political Studies. As all distinct areas of enquiry must, it has developed its own foundational literature within which the specific concepts that underpin its study have been articulated, debated and refined. The model at the core of IS is the intelligence 'cycle' – a common thread running through all social science approaches to the study of intelligence as well as post-1945 intelligence training manuals. However, there is a growing acceptance that it neither accurately reflects the intelligence process nor accommodates important elements of or related to it, for example covert action, counterintelligence and oversight. There is a strong argument for conceptual parsimony so long as this can clearly and fairly accurately describe the core process on which it focuses. However, it is increasingly clear that the cycle concept looks dated in respect of technological and other developments in intelligence. For example, while the idea was originally conceived with respect to foreign intelligence, variations have been developed in other areas, such as the UK national intelligence model for law enforcement, and business models for the assessment of 'risk'. Changing threats and targets and the information revolution have all contributed to a sense that the classic model requires at least a major re-fit, if not actually discarding. This chapter analyses these developments and concludes by suggesting an alternative way of presenting the intelligence process that addresses the shortcomings of the cycle model.

Beyond the Intelligence Cycle?

Academic studies of intelligence tend to open by outlining the Intelligence Cycle, a linear model which presents the intelligence process as occurring in four or five sequential stages involving planning and direction, collection, processing,[2] analysis and production and ending in dissemination. The dissemination stage generates fresh intelligence requirements, and so the process is repeated. At the same time, however, a number of these studies also express varying degrees of reservation as to the accuracy and hence utility of the concept.[3]

All social sciences make use of models to simplify the study of complex social and political processes. The key question is the extent to which they are useful for the purposes of education, research and training. These purposes are somewhat different, though connected, and we also need to be aware of whether our questions about the intelligence process are empirical (how does it work?) or normative (how should it work?) (see Table 2.1). There is no questioning the importance of a model that can describe the intelligence process in easily under-standable terms, but how useful is the current Intelligence Cycle model in seeking answers to the questions set out in Table 2.1? If the answer is 'not very', can an alternative model be developed to describe the intelligence process better?

As noted elsewhere in this volume, the origins of the Intelligence Cycle are difficult to identify,[4] but it seems that the antecedents can be found in wartime requirements to explain quickly and clearly the process by which intelligence is acquired and individual roles within this process. After 1945, this experience began to appear in US training manuals, such as *Intelligence is for Commanders* by LTC Phillip Davidson and LTC Robert Glass.[5] In this, the cycle ended in 'use'. The concept of the cycle was not explicitly referred to in UK deliberations at this time; for example, there is no mention of the 'cycle' in the comprehensive report by the Joint Intelligence Committee (JIC) Chairman for the Chiefs of Staff in January 1945 on the future machinery for intelligence. Similar principles to those enshrined in the cycle were being discussed, but the cycle terminology was absent.[6] The cycle concept was popularised in the United States through the work of Sherman Kent, notably in his seminal 1948 work *Strategic Intelligence for American World Policy*.[7] This was a key text used in the training of intelli-gence professionals, and represented an important advance in the process of pro-fessionalisation. While not a training manual, it did seek to explain to intelligence analysts their relationship to collectors and their responsibilities towards policy-makers. In the United States this came to be understood as ulti-mately meaning elected officials. The cycle began with direction: policy-makers

Table 2.1 Understanding the intelligence process: empirical and normative questions

	Education/research	*Training*
Empirical	How does intelligence, as an example of a knowledge-power process, actually work? How can we best model the process in order to understand the broader role of intelligence in security governance?	How does the intelligence process actually work within specific agencies? Does it work in the same way in foreign, domestic, police or other intelligence units?
Normative	Given the dysfunctionalities to which intelligence is prone, as shown by research, how should it be organised in order to achieve more effective outcomes?	Given the specific mandate in an agency, what changes might be made to the process of producing intelligence that would improve organisational performance?

determined what was targeted and so, within a broad framework, what was collected. Hence, implicitly, if not by design, the process was firmly linked to the democratic notion of control and direction of security intelligence by elected representatives who were accountable for their actions.[8] However, while targeted collection responds to international developments, this response – the determination of the information to be targeted – is usually the business of intelligence managers, because it is they who are aware of the gaps in existing knowledge. As Arthur Hulnick has argued: 'Filling the gaps is what drives the intelligence collection process, not guidance from policy makers.'[9] Yet, as Agrell observes, this is the equivalent of 'the mopping-up operations of normal science' and is unable to answer the normative question of how the process *should* be organised in order to cope with increased uncertainty.[10]

This increased uncertainty arises from the fact that the world that intelligence inhabits today is more complex than it was in 1948 – the process of identifying and tracking potential threats is more complex, the technologies on hand to assist in these processes are more sophisticated, and so too is our understanding of intelligence – in part, an outcome of the application of social science theories. It is not clear that the logic of these developments necessarily provides the reassurance for democrats implicit in the model as presented by Sherman Kent. Hence, we suggest that the challenges confronting the Intelligence Cycle model are a consequence of two developments: first, technological innovations that have impacted on intelligence; and second, changes in how 'intelligence' is understood and studied. We argue that this increased complexity has generated seven principal challenges which, for normative as well as professional reasons, we need to interrogate. Collectively, these mean that the extreme parsimony of the traditional cycle model is no longer an asset and that the failure to accommodate complexity within the model has rendered it misleading – a distortion rather than a simplification of reality.

Accommodating complexity: challenges to the Intelligence Cycle

The questions posed in Table 2.1 provide an important clue as to the reason why the Intelligence Cycle faces these challenges. Intelligence is a process that occurs at multiple levels – individual, small group, organisation, state and transnational organisation.[11] Yet, at the same time, most academic discussion of the Intelligence Cycle is focused at the level of the state. Within this state-focused discussion, much is concerned – implicitly or explicitly – with the US experience. Hence, criticisms of the Intelligence Cycle can be made on the basis that 'it doesn't work like this' in a specific national system. At the same time, the concept of the cycle cannot be held to apply equally well across all of the lower levels noted above. The smaller the group setting, the more likely it is that collection and analysis, or analysis and decision-making, will be the business of the same person. Perhaps even more significantly, higher levels of intelligence organisation exhibit greater degrees of complexity as a consequence of understandings of the optimal way to organise the intelligence process – that is, as a consequence of the bureaucratisation of intelligence. The larger (and wealthier) the intelligence group, the greater the specialisation it can be expected to develop. Competition between different national agencies may well include distinct variations of the cycle.[12] Since the cycle is a poor reflection of organisational processes at both the lower and higher ends of the intelligence spectrum, it is a poor starting point to begin answering the questions set out in Table 2.1.

Having identified the principal challenges to the cycle as being a consequence of complexity, let us now consider each of them in turn.

The challenge of understanding intelligence via a risk-based approach

The notion of a cycle fails to fully capture the fact that the end product of intelligence is an assessment designed for the customer that may be used in formulating policy or operations. As such intelligence analysis feeds into, and has the capacity to alter, the future environment in which the information that fed into the analysis was collected and the analysis undertaken, intelligence interventions clearly have the capacity to impact on the risk/threat environment; that is, there is a reflexive dimension to intelligence that the concept of a cycle cannot adequately capture. The 'cycle' may include a 'feedback' loop to a new set of requirements but this can be highly self-referential, resembling a 'closed' system. What is needed is something more akin to an 'open' system in which interaction with the environment is a significant variable; policy-maker direction is not the only factor driving the process. There are models drawn from Foreign Policy Analysis which seek to do this – for example, via application of the concept of the funnel of causality (see Figure 2.1).[13] This funnel concept has the advantage over the traditional cycle model of illustrating the reality that not all information is necessarily translated via analysis into policy, and that much is filtered out. However, while capturing the reflexive nature of intelligence, the funnel model is still limited and repeats the error of the cycle concept in assuming that the process is sequential and linear. For example, information collection may be 'covert' but its occurrence, or the suspicion thereof, may have an impact on targeted individuals and groups or, in the terms of Figure 2.1, an 'outcome' results directly from 'collection'.

These outcomes of intelligence operations may be impossible to calibrate and 'boomerang' or 'blow back' in a way that undermines the intentions of their initiator.[14] Furthermore, the application of the 'precautionary principle' to counterterrorism since 9/11 has meant that action may be based on little evidence at all. In the most extreme case, under the so-called 'Cheney Doctrine', action may be taken on the basis of 1 per cent of 'knowledge'; that is, almost perfect ignorance. Thus the notion of an Intelligence Cycle informing action is completely subverted.[15] Hence, while providing an alternative way of thinking about intelligence to that provided by the cycle concept, the 'funnel' is similarly flawed.

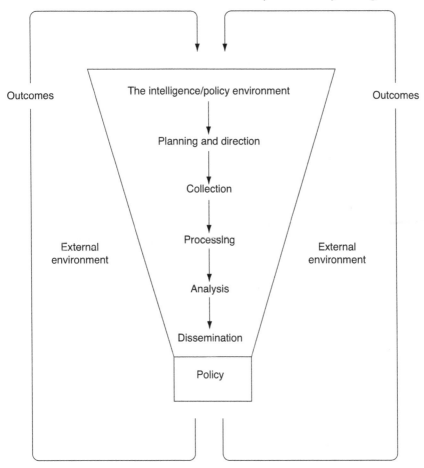

Figure 2.1 The intelligence process as a funnel of causality.

The challenge of bureaucratic politics

As noted above, the cycle model begins with direction from policy-makers. However, in practice, states do not invest in vast and expensive intelligence collection capabilities and then wait for policy-makers to determine the targets of collection. The fact that the Bush Administration had failed to appreciate the imminence of the threat posed by al-Qaeda in the months prior to 9/11, let alone insist on prioritising it as an intelligence target, offered no protection from widespread charges of intelligence failure after 9/11, notably from policy-makers.[16]

It is also worth bearing in mind that in writing about intelligence and deploying the cycle concept, Sherman Kent was writing about foreign intelligence. In the US literature, *strategic* intelligence was always understood to mean *foreign* intelligence. However, the precise arrangements by which priorities are established for agencies vary depending on whether their focus is primarily internal or external. For example, in the UK the JIC establishes the 'requirements' for MI6 and GCHQ but MI5 retains autonomy in determining its own priorities. This is held to be important given its internal focus. As its former Director-General Eliza Manningham-Buller has explained, it is

> an important constitutional principle, enshrined in law ... that the operations of the Security Service are the responsibility of the Director-General who reports to the Home Secretary. The government cannot direct whom the Service investigates. This is an important safeguard against the politicisation of the Service's work.[17]

After 9/11, MI5 formally allocated some institutional resources to looking ahead for 'emerging threats', but this does not seem to have survived renewed emphasis on counterterrorism after the London bombings of 7 July 2005.[18] Hence, the determination of risks and threats needs to be understood as a more complex, varied process involving intelligence managers and their judgement of uncertainties.

There is a further danger that organisational cultures and bureaucratic interests ignore or are slow to react to evidence that a threat has receded sufficiently to require information collection no longer. The Intelligence Cycle tells us how targeting supposedly starts – the process of threat recognition – but is less clear as to how threats end.[19] Who determines that a threat exists, and who determines that a threat has ceased to exist? There is a bureaucratic politics dimension to contemporary intelligence processes that the cycle model, as an abstract and idealised representation of a process, cannot capture. As Morton Halperin observed some 40 years ago, organisations with missions 'strive to maintain or to improve their (1) autonomy, (2) organizational morale, (3) organizational "essence", and (4) roles and missions. Organizations with high-cost capabilities are also concerned with maintaining or increasing their (5) budgets.'[20] Moreover, the cycle model cannot capture the reality of complex organisations in which varying interests compete as to how issues should be channelled; for example, the competition in the UK in the 1990s over which law enforcement or security intelligence agency should lead on the question of Irish Republican terrorism in Britain.[21] Again, the notion of a simple linear process cannot accommodate the complexity of the bureaucratic politics 'game' at this stage. This is itself a consequence of organisational environments in which:

> Typically, issues are recognized and determined within an established channel for producing policies or decisions. Where a deadline or event initiates the game, that trigger influences the selection of the action channel. In most cases, however, there are several possible channels through which an issue could be resolved. Because action channels structure the game by preselecting the major players, determining the usual points of entrance into the game, and by distributing particular advantages for each game, players maneuver to get the issue into the channel they believe is most likely to yield the desired result.[22]

The challenge of interactivity

The concept of the Intelligence Cycle suggests that the collection and analytical functions are sequential, that the latter can only begin once the former is complete. This is clearly not the case, and in practice collection and analysis are interactive processes which occur broadly concurrently. In this key respect, the cycle model distorts rather than simplifies. It does not adequately deal with the reality that much intelligence comes from open sources available to the analyst in advance of the collection of secret intelligence, and that the role of secret intelligence will not usually have a transformative impact on analysis, but more usually an incremental one.[23] Here, it is useful to consider the implications of David Omand's use of the term 'access' rather than 'collection' to draw attention to the quantities of open source information available via the internet and personal protected data before it is necessary to consider (much more expensive) covert collection. As Omand notes, a 'whole branch of intelligence work is having to be created to access (not a straightforward matter), monitor and exploit such internet-based material'.[24] This faces the complication that quality control needs to be applied to a vast range of material and that reliable performance of this quality control is problematic. Nevertheless, it is essential given that, 'once incorporated into a government product the limitations of the original source can easily be lost sight of'.[25] We would also add that, in the interests of efficiency, agencies should consult their own 'store of memory' – full of previous 'products' – so that at least they 'know what they know' before embarking on a fresh operation.

With regard to the sequential logic of the cycle model, there are also contexts in which analysis might be said to lead collection – as, for example, in the case of Echelon, a system for targeting the interception of global communications operating as part of the UKUSA agreement.[26] Here, the monitoring of electronic traffic by a 'dictionary' of key words (presumably selected on the basis of past experience) will produce a number of 'risky' communications that will lead to further investigation of senders, recipients etc. Analysis can identify patterns of behaviour – such as in travel or financial transactions – that are 'suspicious' and, once spotted, through pattern analysis, will give rise to further collection. In many operational settings, interaction between analysts and collectors can be continuous.

The cycle concept also rests on the implicit assumption that policy-makers await objective analysis before deciding on a course of action. This assumption has been criticised by several commentators in the wake of the Iraqi Weapons of Mass Destruction (WMD) case. For example, Stephen Marrin has argued for an alternative understanding of the relationship between intelligence analysis and decision-making where, 'rather than start with the intelligence analyst, it starts with the concepts and values being pursued by the decision-maker which determine the meaning and the relevance of the intelligence analysis that is provided to them'.[27] Certainly, policy-maker memoirs that cover the Iraq WMD debacle offer no indication that they awaited intelligence analysis before forming judgements, although this did not stop them, in the same memoirs, blaming the intelligence picture for misleading them on this issue.[28]

Hence, it is wrong to think, as the Intelligence Cycle seems to imply, that policy-makers wait for the analytical product before embarking on an action. They may well seek intelligence analysis that matches and supports an existing policy or policy preference. If they do not get it they may ask for further analysis – or even question analysts personally, as Vice President Dick Cheney did in relation to US intelligence on Iraqi WMD in the lead-up to the 2003 Iraq war.[29] It is also wrong to assume, as the cycle model seems to, that they are the only customers for the intelligence product. The more complex the structure, the more numerous and varied the customers are likely to be. Overall, Arthur Hulnick argued long ago, it 'is much more useful to consider the intelligence process as a matrix of interconnected, mostly autonomous functions'.[30] More recently, David Omand has suggested an 'interactive network'.[31]

The challenge of comparative analysis

This leads to the next challenge: the idea that intelligence agencies await and then respond to policy-maker direction is one that is most relevant to liberal democratic contexts, and is an extension of the principles governing civil–military relations in established democracies. Is the concept of the cycle limited to liberal democratic contexts? It would be absurd to propose some 'one size fits all' model of or for intelligence regardless of political culture and type of regime but what we can do is develop a model of the process that facilitates comparative analysis by identifying key similarities and differences.

Outside of democratic contexts, intelligence agencies may enjoy greater autonomy in determining targets and direction. For example, in the former GDR, the Stasi clearly enjoyed a considerable degree of autonomy in determining targets, to the extent that it has been discussed in terms of its representing a 'state within a state'.[32] In its early years a foreign intelligence agency – the KGB – played a key role in setting its agenda. Further complicating this picture is the question of the relationship between intelligence structures, the party and the state in communist regimes, where the party constitutes (or constituted) the vanguard precisely because it is best able to apply Marxism–Leninism to the specific national context, and the extent that the party defines risks and threats through the prism of the official state ideology – i.e. that targeting is partly determined by ideology and that analysis is (mis)shaped by the application of ideology.[33] Even in formal democracies, intelligence agencies can operate with a significant degree of autonomy – for example, the ISI in contemporary Pakistan, and the Servicio de Inteligencia Nacional (SIN) in Peru under spy chief Vladimiro Montesinos.[34]

A related question is whether and how far it applies to intelligence in contexts other than security intelligence – for example, in relation to criminal intelligence.[35] As with security intelligence, one can find examples of the traditional 'cycle' at work in law enforcement but, equally, there are many cases where it does not model the process actually at work. Some years ago, one of us wrote that any cyclical representation of the police intelligence process would over-simplify something that is 'highly complex and frequently messy'.[36] Similarly, Jerry Ratcliffe has acknowledged his intelligence 'heresy' in recommending to time-pressured law enforcement analysts that they 'think back' from what their client wants to the type of analysis that would produce it and then back to the information they would need to collate in order to complete the task. Policing has developed a number of models for knowledge management and operational planning that depart to a greater or lesser extent from the basic 'cycle'.[37] However, in other respects 'national security' and 'policing' intelligence increasingly converge, which leads to the next challenge.

The challenge of (covert) action

The Intelligence Cycle concept also omits a core intelligence function: covert action. Intelligence is not simply passive. Some intelligence agencies, for example the CSIS in Canada, are charged just with advising government, but many are called upon to implement the policy responses arising from their own collection and analysis. At times these will be overt – for example, through a diplomatic response or the application of sanctions. At other times these will be covert; and at others policy will be a mixture of both. While during the Cold War such actions were covert so as to provide deniability and avoid destabilising the prevailing 'balance of terror', the situation is somewhat different in the post-Cold War, post-9/11 world. Here, intelligence 'actions' can be overt as well as covert, or can even fall somewhere in between. Armed US Predator drone strikes on al-Qaeda suspects inside Pakistan, Yemen and Somalia provide a good example. These are not avowed by the CIA, which carries them out. But neither can their occurrence be denied (see further below). Hence, in the contemporary international environment it is now perhaps more accurate to speak of 'actions' rather than simply 'covert actions'. In matters of internal security and intelligence regarding organised crime, police or other intelligence operations will feature 'disruption' as an activity designed to prevent bad things happening and in which the targets may well be aware of who is responsible; so, again, the idea of covert action is too limiting.

While one feature of IS has been a debate as to whether covert actions should be considered a part of the intelligence process, or are actually a separate realm of activity,[38] in part this has rested on their absence from the Intelligence Cycle: a dated model may well serve to reinforce a dated understanding of 'intelligence'. However, the extent and regularity of recourse to covert actions, and the nature of these, help to define the wider security and intelligence culture and, to an extent, reflect the form of government that intelligence agencies serve. In this respect, separation of covert action from intelligence is artificial; and, as we noted earlier, some forms of covert collection, such as the use of informers, can themselves constitute (intentional or unintentional) action. More broadly, if police or security agencies do not act in some way on the basis of intelligence, or at least consider its implications for their policies and practices, then, one might ask, what is the point of intelligence? Thus it seems artificial to exclude the possibility of covert actions as a policy response from models of intelligence activity when these are carried out or funded by intelligence organisations and use secret intelligence methods in pursuit of policy objectives. One option would be to simply extend the cycle to accommodate an optional further stage of covert action, although this should also be able to convey the reflexive nature of this form of intelligence activity.

The challenge of technology

All of this suggests the need to consider the impact of technological advance. A common rule of thumb with regard to intelligence collection has always been that it is important to cast the net wider than is considered strictly necessary. As Ray Cline, a former head of the CIA's Directorate of Intelligence, reflected in 1976:

> There is no way to be on top of intelligence problems unless you collect much more extensively than any cost-accounting approach would justify ... You might think you could do without most of what is collected; but in intelligence, in fact, as in ore-mining, there is no way to get at the nuggets without taking the whole ore-bearing compound.[39]

Hence, with sophisticated but still limited technologies, the wealthiest agencies could aim to collect much more broadly than deemed strictly necessary to minimise the risk of missing anything. However, contemporary technological advances mean that the wealthiest collectors – principally the US government – can aim to collect *everything* that they consider might be of importance (aided and abetted by a highly active security industry and the bureaucratic politics of national security) in the vain hope of eliminating the risk of missing *anything* of potential importance. This has implications for what we understand 'targeting' to mean. There is a form of technological determinism at work here, in that technological innovation is determining intelligence practice, and in that there is an inevitability around intelligence adopting new technologies, as it is these technologies, rather than human agency, that are held to be the key to progress in solving security problems and so to hold out the prospect of realising the chimera of *total* security.

To give two brief examples: James Bamford has recently written of the US National Security Agency's construction of a one-million-square-foot data storehouse in Utah in which it proposes to store the product of its targeted interception of both the public internet and deepnet.[40] Its potential is much enhanced by the simultaneous development of supercomputers capable of cracking public encryption. By 2008, proposals existed for a similar data-mining approach in the UK, via the anodyne-sounding Intercept Modernisation Programme, described by Richard Aldrich as comprising a 'surveillance concept so vast that it was beyond the bounds of the imagination'.[41] Then Home Secretary Jacqui Smith explained:

Our ability to intercept communications and obtain communications data is vital to fighting terrorism and combating serious crime, including child sex abuse, murder and drugs trafficking. Communications data – that is, data about calls, such as the location and identity of the caller, not the content of the calls themselves – is used as important evidence in 95% of serious crime cases and in almost all security service operations since 2004.[42]

Although in the run-up to the 2010 General Election the Conservative Party criticised the Labour government for the rise of the 'surveillance state',[43] in office the principle underpinning the Intercept Modernisation Programme was retained as an element of the new government's 2010 Strategic Defence and Security Review.

The key point to make with reference to the impact of such developments on the Intelligence Cycle is that they subvert the original model. The liberal notion implicit in the concept of the Intelligence Cycle – that intelligence collection is only undertaken discriminately following a legitimating targeting request from an elected official – is rendered obsolete. Therefore it is not just individuals, groups or buildings that are targeted for initial collection but whole groups who fit some profile of 'risky' behaviour or pattern of behaviour that is classified as 'suspicious'. The 'targeting' that takes place prior to accessing or collecting is less discriminating than previously because, first, this reduces the risk of missing anything and, second, the technologies to facilitate it are emerging. This clearly has implications for the relationship between intelligence and democracy (the subject of the final challenge we discuss below), nowhere more so than in contexts where intelligence collection has traditionally been understood to refer to foreign collection, but where, for the reasons discussed above, it must now involve significant domestic surveillance. As described by Bamford, the systems being constructed are awesome in scale and expense, but whether they can solve the problem of 'information overload' remains uncertain.

The use of drones as an intelligence tool gives rise to another technology-based challenge and provides another reason why 'action', whether overt or covert, now needs to be incorporated within models of intelligence. The traditional cycle models a process that has a clear temporal dimension. While intelligence must be timely, it also requires time for the cycle process to be engaged – to go through the process by which *information* is transformed into *intelligence*. Implicit within the analysis stage are two processes – which could arguably be thought of as distinct sub-stages – of evaluation (i.e. credibility, reliability etc. of source) and reflection (what does it mean?). Absent these (and this is an assumption that can be read into the cycle model) it might be concluded that, following analysis, conclusions are obvious and/or easily agreed upon. In reality, the process is not so straightforward, and can require going back to collectors for further raw information, asking constituent parts to deliberate or reflect on their own micro-analysis which has contributed to contested macro-analysis, possibly while engaging in a process of *resistance* to political pressure. Moreover, absent these sub-stages it is difficult to gauge from consideration of the model just what function intelligence management performs outside of carrying the finished product to the policy-maker. These will inevitably be time-constrained, but they are nevertheless important to the generation of considered and agreed analytical product. Arguably, any product that has bypassed these stages, or where they have been excessively compressed, cannot be fully regarded as *intelligence* and as such carries potentially significant risk.[44]

However, within armed drone operations intelligence officers can take decisions on action arising out of intelligence within a highly compressed time-frame due to 'window of opportunity' pressures. In the case of the armed Predator drone, individuals are *targeted* and information is *collected* by the officers remotely piloting the drone and watching the real-time footage it relays, the *analysis* is undertaken immediately by the same people involved in collection, and the *response* (action) can follow immediately from the analysis (to launch a Hellfire missile with the intention to kill/not to launch a missile). There is no need for any wider *dissemination*. Analysis and action are so closely linked in this case as to be inseparable.[45] This compression can lead to erroneous targeting and puts considerable pressure on the ethical judgements that drone operators are required to make rapidly about possible and permissible levels of incidental civilian casualties. In the US case, these are judgements they are required to make for the drone programme to meet the standards publicly outlined by Harold Koh, Legal Advisor to the Obama Administration State Department, rooted in observance of the Just War principles of distinction and proportionality.[46] There is now a greater body of law relating to intelligence collection than there was throughout the Cold War, though its symbolism has been greater than its actual impact on operations. But as the technology spreads, the potential implications of widespread deployment of drones will provide a sharp test of law's impact on intelligence in an arena where might is so often 'right' and victor's justice prevails.

A technological challenge of a different order can be seen in the efforts of the intelligence community to make use of Web 2.0 tools such as blogs and wikis.[47] One of the more successful innovations has been Intellipedia, developed by CIA analysts and deploying the same software as Wikipedia, which by 2009 contained 900,000 pages, had 100,000 user accounts, and received 5,000 page edits a day.[48] Working on the principle of putting information out to the broadest audience possible while respecting three levels of classification – unclassified, secret (hosted on SIPRNet) and top secret (on JWICS) – wikis clearly increase the possibility of the bottom-up collaboration and sharing that were missing prior to 9/11, and provide an audit trail of who added what. More recently still comes A-Space, which enables analysts to create workspaces on specific topics on which they can share information and collaborate on projects. This has been described as 'essentially a mashup of Facebook, LinkedIn and GoogleDocs'[49] and has expanded significantly the information available to analysts and their awareness thereof. It started in September 2008; a year later it was reported that 150 new people were signing up to A-Space each day.[50] As well as its potential as a social networking tool, it incorporates access for all analysts to the Library of National Intelligence, which is intended to create a repository of summaries of all the intelligence community's disseminated intelligence, regardless of the original classification of the document.[51]

The challenge of oversight: towards a holistic approach to understanding intelligence?

Implicit in all of the above challenges is the question of how intelligence should be defined and understood. However, in this final challenge it is quite explicit. The Intelligence Cycle was designed to describe the intelligence production process. In a contemporary liberal democratic context, should oversight and accountability be factored into it? At the time when the cycle concept was first used in relation to non-military intelligence, oversight was conducted (to the extent that it was at all) by policy-makers, who sat at the end point of the cycle. This was the day of the gifted amateur, and gave rise to the excesses that led to the introduction of formal legislative oversight.[52] Today, however, few would accept a situation where oversight of intelligence in a liberal democratic context resided solely in the hands of the executive. Given this, and bearing in mind David Omand's suggestion that the intelligence process today might 'best be thought of as an interactive network rather than a cycle', should that interactive model not reflect (not to say, require) the input of and interaction with overseers? If so, what is the optimal form, and how do overseers avoid the risk of being co-opted by the agencies – that is, becoming in effect a part of the management process, serving as advocates for the agencies in the legislature and at a national level? Overseers should not confuse their role with that of management and seek to direct operations. If they have responsibility for budgets, their decisions will have inevitable implications for the efficiency and effectiveness of agencies, but they must retain sufficient distance from day-to-day operations that their ability to provide effective and rigorous monitoring is not compromised.

From a cycle to a web

Having identified so many inadequacies of the cycle model, rooted in its inability to meet the challenges of complexity, it seems incumbent on us to suggest an alternative that addresses them. One problem with alternatives that seek to provide greater accuracy is that they invariably do so at the expense of simplicity. In the more extreme cases this can call into question who the alternative models are aimed at, given the complexity that they can achieve,[53] and hence the question of the purpose of a model in the first place. How far is it possible, taking on board the issues we have discussed, to move beyond the Intelligence Cycle to provide a better representation of the intelligence process while retaining the degree of simplicity that is the purpose of a model?

Inevitably, any alternative model will need to reflect a greater degree of complexity than the traditional cycle model. It should be applicable to the variety of organisational environments within which intelligence is developed. At the root of this requirement is the fact that intelligence *is* a process that operates at all social levels: individual,[54] small group, organisation, state and transnational organisation. It also operates within particular social, political and economic contexts that constitute its *environment* which, for the reasons discussed above, must also be factored in.

Given all of this, our alternative is to move away from the notion of a 'cycle' and replace this with the more accurate notion of a 'web', as in Figure 2.2. This has an immediate linguistic advantage. We suggest that the intelligence process is not a 'cycle' in the literal sense (defined in the *Oxford English Dictionary* as 'a recurrent round or course (of successive events, phenomena, etc.); a regular order or succession in which things recur; a round or series which returns upon itself'), and in its complexity approximates more to a web (OED: 'something of complicated structure or workmanship'). However, we are not proposing to confuse things by replacing a 'process' with a 'structure': one of the weaknesses of the cycle as commonly used is that it appears to exist in a vacuum. While the central purpose of any model is to simplify, if it removes a process from its context then it can be plain misleading. Therefore, we suggest two main innovations: first, a model of the intelligence process itself that reflects better the complex and multiple interactions that occur between the main points of targeting, collection, analysis and so on; and second, a clearer exposition of the main environmental or contextual factors that influence the process and which may, in turn, be altered by the outcomes of the process. What we are proposing is still clearly a model, but it is more complex and, as such, more appropriate to the task at hand. In Figure 2.2 the five main contextual factors that impact on the way in which the process works – culture, external liaison, secrecy, political control and oversight – are shown in the outer boxes.

Culture is used as a shorthand term to describe the amalgam of values, attitudes and beliefs that influence the way in which the process is conducted. We are familiar with discussions of national intelligence cultures or, more broadly, of cultures of national security;[55] similarly, organisational culture is a useful term for understanding the basis for bureaucratic politics in more complex governmental systems – i.e. culture here covers both the ideas that contribute to the prevailing individual and institutional world view and the organisational processes and principles that govern the bureaucratic operation of intelligence organisations. *External liaison* indicates that intelligence processes necessarily are part of larger environments in which other agencies at home and abroad are also working and may well provide short cuts to information or enhanced leverage when it comes to implementing policy. What distinguishes intelligence from most other governmental information processes is *secrecy*. This reflects the fact that the object of intelligence is security and that it will be subject to resistance from other countries and/or agencies working in competition if not actual hostility.[56] In Figure 2.2 this is represented in the form of a 'ring of *secrecy*', enclosing the intelligence process and representing the subjects of counterintelligence and protective security. *Political control* in authoritarian regimes will be aimed principally at the maintenance of the ruling party or elite. In democratic regimes it reflects the belief that intelligence must be subject to direction by elected officials – for example, with regard to policy management as to targets, intelligence methods and compliance with the law. Equally, *oversight* reflects the Lockean principle of democratic accountability and the related recognition that public confidence will only be achieved and maintained if intelligence agencies are subject to scrutiny by external bodies – for example, legislative committees, inspectors general, ombudsmen etc. This last factor will normally be absent in authoritarian regimes. The thick outer arrows indicate the ways in which these contextual or environmental factors interact with the intelligence process itself.

Recalling Table 2.1, examining these contextual variables contributes to both empirical and normative analysis of an intelligence process. Factoring in 'the environmental' gives the intelligence web a normative dimension absent from the cycle model. We cannot understand how the process works, and reforms cannot be developed, without an understanding of the prevailing security culture. This culture is reflected in specific secrecy and liaison practices; for example, under what circumstances does an agency in country A cooperate with one in country B? Is it purely a pragmatic decision or is it influenced by beliefs that cooperation would be inappropriate whatever the potential information gain? Similarly, we need to compare how political control and oversight actually work (or not) in different countries in order to be able to develop better ideas on how they might work if we are to secure more effective and accountable intelligence processes.

The lettered arrows are explained below; note that most of them are double-headed, indicating the multiple relationships within the intelligence process.

A   In the cycle model everything starts with a political or managerial decision to identify some target which is passed to collectors. However, as a result of environmental scanning for risks or applying a profile of 'suspiciousness' to a data warehouse, some potential new target is identified and suggested to managers as appropriate for more specific attention.

B   Those responsible for collection will establish what the agency already knows, as contained in the store of 'organisational memory'. Here we encounter the problem of 'overload': much that is accessed or otherwise collected will remain unanalysed since there simply are not the resources to do so. But the information will remain in the store and may be of potential future use or, one day, will be 'weeded' and discarded.

C   In the context of an ongoing crisis some item of information is obtained which is perceived as so significant as to require direct transmission to those responsible for the response. (Of course, this can be very dangerous if the information subsequently turns out to be wrong, as in the case of the last-minute MI6 information in 2002 that Iraq could mobilise WMD within 45 minutes that was withdrawn within a year.) Similarly, those responsible for developing a specific action or policy bypass the usual planning process in order to ask for immediate collection relevant to their considerations. Information collection of itself may constitute a form of action, for example the deployment of an undercover officer.

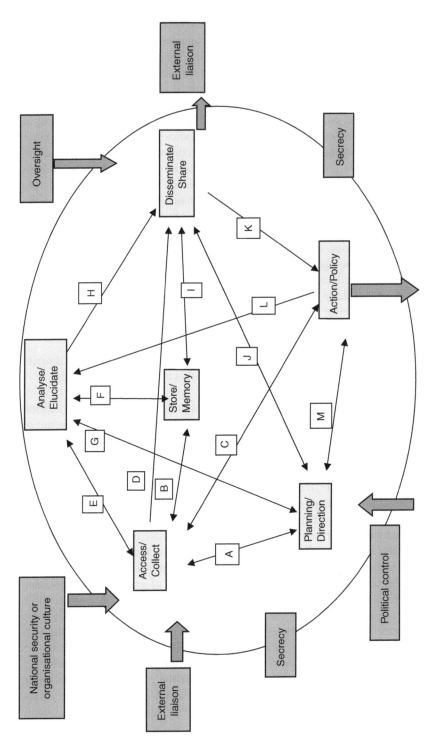

Figure 2.2 The intelligence web.

D   Similarly to C above, some new item of raw information is considered to be so important as to justify direct dissemination to other domestic or foreign agencies. Equally, intelligence may be received from a liaison partner.

E   Once collected or accessed, information is passed to analysts for evaluation, as in the cycle model. But, in carrying this out, analysts will often require immediate further collection to try to clarify a problem on which they are working. In another technique, analysts develop a profile or pattern of behaviour that is then used to 'mine' a data warehouse in the search for risks or threats that require further investigation (and see A above).

F   In order to evaluate new information, the organisational memory is drawn on by analysts in the production of all-source analysis. After analysis the intelligence produced may be seen as insufficiently relevant to the stated requirement or the known needs of customers to justify dissemination but it will be stored.

G   Aware that intelligence has already been developed with respect to some threat or opportunity, managers go directly to analysts, asking 'what is known?' If, on some issue, managers and/or policy-makers are known to have clear preferences then analysts may be tempted (or feel pressured) to provide analysis that confirms those preferences, or analysts may provide judgements that are in line with what they believe policy-makers wish to hear (cf. 'politicisation') or which conform with the official ideology.

H   In line with the traditional cycle, intelligence is disseminated within and between agencies. In some cases it will also go to trusted foreign partners.

I   A partner agency may ask 'what is known' about a target and previously developed intelligence located in the 'store' may be passed to them through liaison arrangements. Other intelligence will be disseminated within and between agencies but will not lead immediately to some action or policy; whether it does or not, it enters the organisational memory.

J   Managers, aware that intelligence has already been developed, direct that it be disseminated to executives who are developing a policy/action or to partner agencies. Intelligence may be developed but there is no immediate policy-maker interest, so it is transmitted to managers who can take its existence into account in planning future requirements.

K   In line with the traditional cycle, intelligence is disseminated to those who can use it as the basis for action – these officials may be in the same agency (if it is empowered to act) or an executive agency – to liaison partners (appropriately caveated) or, more generally, to government policy-makers.

L   Those responsible for some operation or policy go directly to analysts for their latest judgement on the current situation and future prospects.

M   As a consequence of some action taken, policy-makers see that fresh intelligence is required. Also, policy-makers may be informed by managers that some new law or policy is required in order to enable future information-gathering, as, for example, in response to new technologies.

Conclusion

Crucially, this better reflects the complexity that characterises intelligence, its non-linear form, the centrality of environmental factors in its production, and its impact on its own environment. Among the advantages to be gained from replacing a misleading model, this also has the potential to better educate users about the complexities of intelligence and inform thinking about the nature of intelligence failure. In terms of the questions posed in Table 2.1 it can stimulate thinking about normative questions and provide an empirical basis for education, research and training. This is beyond the capacity of the one-dimensional Intelligence Cycle model.

Notes

1 An early version of this chapter was delivered as a paper to the panel on 'Beyond the Intelligence Cycle?' at the International Studies Association annual conference in San Diego, April 2012. Thanks to those present for their helpful comments.
2 US versions of the model have tended to represent processing and analysis as separate stages, while UK versions have tended to consider them as constituting a single stage.
3 Recent examples include Peter Gill and Mark Phythian, *Intelligence in an Insecure World* (2nd edn, Cambridge: Polity, 2012); Loch K. Johnson, *National Security Intelligence* (Cambridge: Polity, 2012); and Julian Richards, *The Art and Science of Intelligence Analysis* (Oxford: Oxford University Press, 2010).
4 See the work done by Kris Wheaton on this, presented on his blog: 'Who Invented the Intelligence Cycle?' posted 4 January 2011: http://sourcesandmethods.blogspot. com/2011/01/rfi-who-invented-intelligence-cycle.html, last accessed 15 October 2012. Wilhelm Agrell has suggested that it developed out of the traditional military chain of command: 'Intelligence Analysis after the Cold War – New Paradigm or Old Anomalies?', in Gregory F. Treverton and Wilhelm Agrell (eds), *National Intelligence Systems: Current Research and Future Prospects*, (Cambridge: Cambridge University Press, 2009), pp. 93–114. See pp. 107–8.
5 Wheaton, 'Who Invented the Intelligence Cycle?'
6 We are grateful to Sir David Omand for drawing this to our attention.
7 Sherman Kent, *Strategic Intelligence for American World Policy* (Princeton, NJ: Princeton University Press, 1966).
8 Certainly this 'direction' may only have been in the general terms of 'national security', and more specific targeting decisions would be made by the agencies or some coordinating body such as the UK Joint Intelligence Committee. In authoritarian regimes, of course, 'intelligence' was driven primarily by the search for dissenters and would be determined by the ruling party or military elite, or, in some cases, by agencies acting as 'states within the state'. See further the discussion of 'The challenges of comparative analysis' later in the chapter.
9 Arthur S. Hulnick, 'What's Wrong with the Intelligence Cycle', *International Journal of Intelligence and Counterintelligence*, Vol. 21 No. 6, 2006, p. 960.
10 Agrell, 'Intelligence Analysis After the Cold War', p. 106. See further, for example, Mark Phythian, 'Policing Uncertainty: Intelligence, Security and Risk', *Intelligence and National Security* Vol. 27 No. 2, 2012, pp. 187–205; Peter Gill, 'Intelligence, Threat, Risk and the Challenge of Oversight', *Intelligence and National Security* Vol. 27 No. 2, 2012, pp. 206–22; and David Strachan-Morris, 'Threat and Risk: What's the Difference and Why Does It Matter?', *Intelligence and National Security* Vol. 27 No. 2, 2012, pp. 172–86.

11 See the discussion in Gill and Phythian, *Intelligence in an Insecure World*, esp. Ch. 2.
12 Kris Wheaton, 'Critiques of the Cycle: Which intelligence cycle?' 26 May 2011, http://sourcesandmethods.blogspot.com/2011/05/part-5-critiques-of-cycle-which. html, last accessed 15 October 2012.
13 For a full discussion of the role it can play in Foreign Policy Analysis, see Charles Kegley and Eugene Wittkopf, *American Foreign Policy: Pattern and Process* (5th edn, New York: St. Martin's Press, 1996), Ch. 2. See also James Rosenau, *The Scientific Study of Foreign Policy* (New York: Nicholas, 1980). This discussion of the funnel of causality draws on Gill and Phythian, *Intelligence in an Insecure World*, pp. 13–14.
14 See Phythian, 'Policing Uncertainty', pp. 191–2.
15 Gill, 'Intelligence, Threat, Risk and the Challenge of Oversight,' pp. 215–16. See also Jessica Stern and Jonathan Wiener, 'Precaution against Terrorism,' in Paul Bracken, Ian Bremmer and David Gordon (eds), *Managing Strategic Surprise: Lessons from Risk Management and Risk Assessment* (Cambridge: Cambridge University Press), pp. 110–84.
16 The memoirs of Bush, Cheney, Rice and Rumsfeld are clear on this: George W. Bush, *Decision Points* (New York: Crown, 2010); Dick Cheney, *In My Life: A Personal and Political Memoir* (New York, Threshold Editions, 2011); Condoleezza Rice, *No Higher Honor: A Memoir of my Years in Washington* (New York: Crown, 2011); Donald Rumsfeld, *Known and Unknown: A Memoir* (New York: Sentinel, 2011). However, compare these with the accounts of George Tenet and Richard Clarke: George Tenet, *At the Center of the Storm: My Years at the CIA* (New York, Harper-Collins, 2007); Richard A. Clarke, *Against All Enemies: Inside America's War on Terror* (New York, Free Press, 2004).
17 Eliza Manningham-Buller, 'Security', Reith Lectures 2011, first broadcast on 13 September 2011, www.bbc.co.uk/programmes/p00k0jy2, last accessed 15 October 2012.
18 Ibid.
19 See the example of the reluctance to concede the end of the domestic subversive threat in the immediate post-Cold War years on the part of some within MI5 management described in former MI5 officer Annie Machon's memoir, *Spies, Lies and Whistleblowers: MI5, MI6 and the Shayler Affair* (Lewes: The Book Guild, 2005), Ch. 2. The proportion of MI5's work devoted to counter subversion reduced from 12.5 per cent in 1990–91 to 3.0 per cent in 1995–96 and shortly thereafter to nothing. However, UK police intelligence arguably 'resurrected' the work some years later via the concept of 'domestic extremism'. Gill and Phythian, *Intelligence in an Insecure World*, pp. 58–9.
20 Morton H. Halperin, 'Why Bureaucrats Play Games', *Foreign Policy*, Vol. 1 No. 2 Spring 1971, pp. 70–90. Quote at p. 76.
21 Christopher Andrew, *The Defence of the Realm: The Authorized History of MI5* (London: Allen Lane, 2009), pp. 771–6.
22 Graham T. Allison and Morton H. Halperin, 'Bureaucratic Politics: A Paradigm and Some Policy Implications', *World Politics*, Vol. 24, Spring 1972, Supplement, 'Theory and Policy in International Relations', pp. 40–79. Quote at p. 50.
23 Hulnick, 'What's Wrong with the Intelligence Cycle', p. 961.
24 David Omand, *Securing the State* (London: Hurst & Co. 2010), p. 31. See also Chapter 5 of this volume.
25 Ibid., p. 32.
26 See, for example, Patrick Radden Keefe, *Chatter: Uncovering the Echelon Surveillance Network and the Secret World of Global Eavesdropping* (New York: Random House, 2006), esp. pp. 115–29.
27 Stephen Marrin, 'Intelligence Analysis and Decision-Making: Methodological challenges', in Peter Gill, Stephen Marrin and Mark Phythian (eds), *Intelligence Theory: Key Questions and Debates* (London: Routledge, 2009), p. 144.

28 See, for example, George W. Bush, *Decision Points*, Ch. 8, esp. p. 262; Tony Blair, *A Journey* (London: Hutchinson, 2010), Ch. 13, esp. pp. 400, 406–7.
29 Walter Pincus and Dana Priest, 'Some Iraq analysts felt pressure from Cheney visits', *Washington Post*, 5 June 2003.
30 Arthur S. Hulnick, 'Controlling Intelligence Estimates', in Glenn P. Hastedt (ed.), *Controlling Intelligence* (London: Frank Cass, 1991), p. 84.
31 Omand, *Securing the State*, p. 119. See also the diagram on the same page.
32 See, for example, the discussion in Mike Dennis, *The Stasi: Myth and Reality* (Harlow: Longman, 2003), pp. 44–9.
33 For a case study, see Beatrice de Graaf, 'How the MfS' Worldview Affected the Intelligence Cycle: A study based on operations against the Netherlands', in Thomas Wegener Friis, Kristie Macrakis and Helmut Müller-Enbergs (eds), *East German Foreign Intelligence: Myth, Reality and Controversy* (London: Routledge, 2010), pp. 162–81.
34 See Sally Bowen and Jane Holligan, *The Imperfect Spy: The Many Lives of Vladimiro Montesinos* (Lima: Ediciones PEISA, 2003).
35 See James Sheptycki, Chapter 6 in this volume, and Stuart Farson, 'Security Intelligence Versus Criminal Intelligence: Lines of demarcation, areas of obfuscation, and the need to re-evaluate organizational roles in responding to terrorism', *Policing and Society*, Vol. 2 No. 2, 1991, pp. 65–87.
36 Peter Gill, *Rounding Up the Usual Suspects? Developments in Contemporary Law Enforcement Intelligence* (Aldershot: Ashgate, 2000), p. 23.
37 Jerry Ratcliffe, *Intelligence-Led Policing* (Cullompton: Willan, 2008), pp. 104–14.
38 For a thoughtful argument as to why it should not be regarded as part of 'intelligence', see Jennifer Sims, 'Defending Adaptive Realism: Intelligence theory comes of age', in Gill, Marrin and Phythian (eds) *Intelligence Theory*, pp. 151–65. See also Michael Herman, *Intelligence Power in Peace and War* (Cambridge: Cambridge University Press, 1996), esp. pp. 54–6.
39 Ray S. Cline, *Secrets, Spies and Scholars* (1976), cited in Charles E. Lathrop, *The Literary Spy* (New Haven, CT: Yale University Press, 2004), p. 41.
40 James Bamford, 'The NSA is Building the Country's Biggest Spy Center (Watch What You Say)', *Wired.Com*, www.wired.com/threatlevel/2012/03/ff_nsadatacenter, 15 March 2012, last accessed 22 November 2012. Bamford reports that:

> Flowing through its servers and routers and stored in near-bottomless databases will be all forms of communication, including the complete contents of private emails, cell phone calls, and Google searches, as well as all sorts of personal data trails – parking receipts, travel itineraries, bookshop purchases, and other digital 'pocket litter'.

41 Richard J. Aldrich, *GCHQ* (London: HarperPress, 2010), p. 543.
42 BBC News, 'Giant Database Plan "Orwellian"', 15 October 2008, http://news.bbc.co.uk/1/hi/uk_politics/7671046.stm, last accessed 12 February 2013.
43 Dominic Grieve and Eleanor Laing, *Reversing the Rise of the Surveillance State* (September 2009), www.conservatives.com/News/News_stories/2009/09/~/media/Files/Policy%20Documents/Surveillance%20State.ashx, last accessed 12 February 2013.
44 One clear example is provided by the 'intelligence' indicating that Saddam Hussein's Iraq could launch a chemical weapon within 45 minutes. See Brian Jones, *Failing Intelligence: The True Story of How we were Fooled into Going to War in Iraq* (London: Biteback, 2010), and BBC News, 'Iraq inquiry: 45 minute claim "asking for trouble"', 20 January 2010, http://news.bbc.co.uk/1/hi/8471091.stm, last accessed 15 October 2012.
45 By 2012 the Obama administration had developed a bureaucratised approach to the process of adding names to a targeting list. Nevertheless, it is unclear, because of the

high degree of secrecy that attaches to the drone programme, how far this is routinely applied and the extent to which strikes occur which bypass some or all of this process. The existence of 'signature strikes' – where the target is determined on the basis of patterns of behaviour rather than identification of a named target – provide proof that the process is bypassed at times. See Greg Miller, 'Plan for hunting terrorists signals US intends to keep adding names to kill lists', *Washington Post*, 24 October 2012; Karen DeYoung, 'A CIA veteran transforms US counterterrorism policy', *Washington Post*, 25 October 2012.

46 Harold Hongju Koh, 'The Obama Administration and International Law', speech to the Annual Meeting of the American Society of International Law, Washington, DC, 25 March 2010, www.state.gov/s/l/releases/remarks/139119.htm, last accessed 20 October 2012.

47 Matthew S. Burton, 'Connecting the Virtual Dots: How the web can relieve our information glut and get us talking to each other', *Studies in Intelligence*, Vol. 49 No. 3, 2005, https://www.cia.gov/library/center-for-the-study-of-intelligence/csi-publications/csi-studies/studies/vol49no3/html_files/Intelligence_Networking_6.htm, last accessed 20 October 2012. This paragraph is drawn from Gill and Phythian, *Intelligence in an Insecure World*, Ch. 5.

48 Massimo Calabresi, 'Wikipedia for Spies: The CIA discovers Web 2.0', *Time*, 8 April 2009; see also http://en.wikipedia.org/wiki/Intellipedia, last accessed 12 February 2013.

49 Mark Drapeau, 'Government 2.0: Intelligence renaissance networks', http://mashable.com/2008/09/22/government-intelligence-renaissance-networks, last accessed 20 October 2012.

50 Rutrell Yasin, 'National security and social networking are compatible', *Government Computer News*, 23 July 2009, http://gcn.com/articles/2009/07/23/social-networking-media-national-security.aspx, last accessed 22 November 2012.

51 Robert Cardillo, 'Intelligence Community Reform: A Cultural Evolution', *Studies in Intelligence*, Vol. 54 No. 3, 2010, https://www.cia.gov/library/center-for-the-study-of-intelligence/csi-publications/csi-studies/studies/vol.-54-no.-3/a-cultural-evolution.html, last accessed 13 February 2013; http://en.wikipedia.org/wiki/A-Space, last accessed 13 February 2013.

52 For a discussion of the US context, see, for example, Evan Thomas, *The Very Best Men – Four Who Dared: The Early Years of the CIA* (New York: Simon & Schuster, 1996); Burton Hersh, *The Old Boys: The American Elite and the Origins of the CIA* (New York: Scribner, 1992); David Fromkin, 'Daring Amateurism: The CIA's Social History', *Foreign Affairs*, Vol. 75 No. 1, Jan–Feb 1996, pp. 65–72. The history of British intelligence can, similarly, be read as an (uneven) journey towards professionalism.

53 For example, see the model suggested by Rob Johnston in his 'Analytic Culture in the US Intelligence Community', https://www.cia.gov/library/center-for-the-study-of-intelligence/csi-publications/books-and-monographs/analytic-culture-in-the-u-s-intelligence-community/index.html, last accessed 20 October 2012. Logically, there must come a point where a model is so complex as to lose the benefits sought by the process of simplification through modelling. Equally, it can be suggested that a model will provide only diminishing returns as that point is approached.

54 The study of information-gathering, problem-solving and decision-making in individuals in cognitive psychology parallels the intelligence process in many respects. The quality or otherwise of people's cognitive processes is centrally important to intelligence analysis and policy but cannot simply be modelled identically with intelligence as a collective social and political phenomenon. For discussion of the individual level 'nesting' within more complex environments, see Gill and Phythian, *Intelligence in an Insecure World*, pp. 47–52.

55 On national intelligence cultures see, for example, Stuart Farson, Peter Gill, Mark Phythian and Shlomo Shpiro (eds), *PSI Handbook of Global Security and Intelligence: National Approaches: Volume 1 – The Americas and Asia* and *Volume 2 – Europe and the Middle East* (Westport, CT: Praeger Security International, 2008); Philip H. J. Davies, 'Intelligence and the Machinery of Government: Conceptualizing the Intelligence Community', *Public Policy and Administration*, Vol. 25 No. 1, 2010, pp. 29–46. On cultures of national security, see, for example, Peter Katzenstein, *Cultural Norms and National Security: Police and Military in Postwar Japan* (Ithaca, NY: Cornell University Press, 1996).

56 See the discussion in Gill and Phythian, *Intelligence in an Insecure World*, Ch. 1.

3 Pedalling hard

Further questions about the Intelligence Cycle in the contemporary era

Julian Richards

Introduction

Both during and after the Cold War, the Intelligence Cycle became ingrained as the standard framework for explaining the workings of a standard intelligence establishment. More recently, various commentators have started to question the sanctity of the Intelligence Cycle, noting that "it doesn't really work like that" in the contemporary era. The cycle seems to be resilient to these challenges and still persists. This chapter examines the transformations within the intelligence business since the end of the Cold War and considers how far they challenge the traditional view of the Intelligence Cycle. Since the beginning of the twenty-first century, a number of major strategic shocks have suggested that the intelligence business needs to work smarter, in ways which run very much counter to the industrialised principles of the Intelligence Cycle. Experiences such as the Al Qaeda threat have provided a taste of how the landscape may have changed very fundamentally. Do these changes spell the end of the Cycle as a useful concept, or does it just need a refresh? The chapter concludes with some thoughts on how the Cycle might appropriately be recast and re-presented to better meet the needs and realities of contemporary intelligence practice.

The origins and purpose of the Intelligence Cycle

Anyone who has worked in a state, defence or law enforcement intelligence analysis role, certainly in the Anglo-Saxon world and most probably in any number of other contexts around the globe, almost without exception will have experienced a moment fairly early in their career where they found themselves looking up at a screen onto which the standard Intelligence Cycle was projected. Whether this had the four components (as has been usual in the UK), or five (as is more common in the United States), or indeed any number of extra boxes around the swirling arrow of process flow, the basic principles would have been the same. The Cycle, they would have been told, describes the transactional process from a requirement being levied by a policy-maker or intelligence "customer", through the processes of collection, processing and analysis of resultant intelligence data, and back around to the dissemination of the finished intelligence product to the original requestor.

The standard Intelligence Cycle first appeared in the early 1970s in the United States.[1] It is not insignificant that this was a time when Western economies were at the zenith of the Fordist mode of production. In many ways, intelligence production was no different. The monolithic and slow-moving target of the Soviet threat had allowed an industrialisation of the intelligence business, encompassing increasingly technological approaches such as satellite imagery, and Sigint and encryption attacks using massive computing power. It had also delivered a production-line process of intelligence reporting which could be established and stratified over many years. With little change to the essential dynamics over three decades, intelligence producers in the West positioned themselves to supply industrial-scale amounts of intelligence reports on Soviet military dispositions around Europe to their policy-makers. This was a process which lent itself very well to a linear and codified process-map.

As Castells notes, however, from the 1970s onwards, an increasing flexibility and dynamism of markets, coupled with technological changes that made single-use equipment too lacking in utility, was leading to what Coriat described as an emerging "post-Fordist" period of economic development.[2] Such a transformation ensured that more dynamic and flexible companies, with flatter management hierarchies and greater capabilities in unleashing innovation, would be the winners in the new economy. In essence, industrialism was becoming "informationalism".[3]

While these changes were happening to society at large, intelligence customers found themselves faced with a growing complexity of requirements. The process of securitisation described by the Copenhagen School of security analysts,[4] whereby the referent object in security threats was perceived to be changing and diversifying away from purely military concerns, was well under way by the early 1990s, when the Soviet Union finally collapsed. The new picture of security threat, at least as articulated in the West, and increasingly so since the emergence of Al Qaeda and contemporary international terrorism, is now an extremely complex web of interwoven risks, actors and response strategies.[5] Military threats are still there, but they are now supplemented with complex transnational threats such as terrorism and organised crime, and human security factors such as threats to populations from pandemics, natural disasters and climate change.

Such transformations in society and the economy, and parallel changes in what constitutes intelligence requirements, together may have contributed to a growing awareness that the old Intelligence Cycle was perhaps no longer fit for purpose. A number of issues and problems have started to be raised by various analysts both inside and outside the intelligence business, and various new models have been proposed which may be better suited to contemporary intelligence production. I will analyse these in more detail below, but it is worth taking a closer look at the original Cycle and the purpose it was intended to serve.

As Quarmby and Young very presciently observe, the traditional Intelligence Cycle "is not designed to be taken literally or provide an exact process map" for how a modern intelligence organisation should be structured and should operate.[6] In essence, the Cycle is a very basic theoretical model which is to be used as a training tool. My own experience of the Cycle was at a very early stage of becoming an intelligence analyst, and I later taught it to a number of successor analysts who were newly joining the organisation, or transferring into analysis from non-analytical roles. One of the first and most important points in considering the Cycle, therefore, is to remember that it should not be taken as a template for structuring an organisation, but merely as a loose conceptual model for new recruits. There is a tendency within large bureaucracies, which need to organise, train and manage large numbers of people, to seek formatted process models which can be easily conveyed and administered. This may be more the case within the military, which has a valid need for "doctrine" to be established around its various activities, than within largely civilian organisations. Within the policing sphere, the National Intelligence Model (NIM), published by the National Criminal Intelligence Service (NCIS) in 2000 and subsequently adopted as the process model for all British police forces, is perhaps a good example of a system which is entirely about management and administration of transactional processes rather than the finer elements of doing intelligence analysis per se.[7]

As a basic instructional tool, the Cycle conveys a number of important concepts to new analysts. First, it establishes that there are different actors in the intelligence process, and that the differentiation between them is very important. Policy-makers raise requirements, and intelligence analysts serve them. Intelligence collectors, in turn, serve the analysts with the data that they need to meet the requirements. If ever these differentiations become blurred or perverted, such that the intelligence producers are setting their own requirements, or that the policy-makers are doing their own analysis, or indeed that the collectors are providing raw and unanalysed data directly to the policy-makers, then a traditional understanding of the Intelligence Cycle suggests there is a severe risk that the whole system will start to fray at the seams. This, essentially, was a large part of the problem with the development of the intelligence case for invading Iraq in 2003, in which "politicisation" of intelligence was a constant accusation, and intelligence chiefs started to warn that intelligence was being "fixed around the policy".[8] It is also an argument, from a British perspective, for the Joint Intelligence Committee (JIC), one of whose functions is to ensure that intelligence – at least at the strategic level – is coordinated and properly analysed for its policy significance, over and above any separate and direct back-channels between collectors and policy-makers.

The Intelligence Cycle also conveys the fact that collection priorities should be driven by real intelligence requirements, and not by the whims or preferences of the intelligence collectors themselves, and that collected data needs to be analysed for its intelligence significance before it is disseminated to the policy-makers, lest they jump to the wrong conclusions. There is a question of relative expertise here: policy-makers are the experts in forming policy; analysts are the experts in analysing data for its significance; and collectors are the experts in translating intelligence requirements into collection strategies. Each group should not presume to be experts in each other's disciplines and to stray into unfamiliar territory, since they will probably get things wrong.

Finally, the cyclical nature of the Cycle aims to emphasise the point that the process is, in some ways, not truly linear in the sense of a production line,[9] but that each piece of disseminated intelligence will shape subsequent requirements that flow back into the system, as understanding among the policy-makers is shaped. The cycle never finishes, as such, but is constantly reiterated. In this way, intelligence *can* shape and drive policy-makers' requirements in a very specific way, but not necessarily in the sense of setting strategic agendas.

All of these factors are critical ones for new analysts to learn, and are not necessarily completely intuitive for those who have arrived cold into the business from outside. I would argue that they are still just as critical today – perhaps even more so given the experience of Iraq, 9/11 and other recent intelligence failures – so any adapted process model for the twenty-first century will still need to find ways of embedding these basic principles in the minds of new analysts.

Problems with the Cycle

So what, as Arthur Hulnick recently asked, is wrong with the Intelligence Cycle?[10] A number of observers have noted that, in the post-Cold War and indeed post-9/11 world, the "linear neatness" implied by the Intelligence Cycle is rarely seen in practice.[11] Hulnick describes the Cycle as "not a very good description of the ways in which the intelligence process works",[12] and Clark suggests that most analysts, when asked, will say of the Cycle that the intelligence process "really doesn't work like that".[13]

Hulnick broke down the issues into a number of factors. First is the question of how requirements are articulated, and the fact that policy-makers are notoriously poor at articulating clear and specific intelligence requirements. This is due to a range of factors, including a sometimes weak understanding of what intelligence can do for the policy-maker and thus not knowing what to ask for. The result is that intelligence analysts will actually help to define requirements collaboratively with the policy-maker, or more frequently will have to divine what the specific requirements are, based on a developed understanding of the policy-makers' objectives and needs. In this way, intelligence analysts do need to sit within policy-makers' space to a certain extent, even if only intellectually.[14]

In the intelligence production sphere, the processes of collection and analysis do not usually happen in a sequential, transactional way, but more often in parallel. This is partly for the same reasons, namely that collectors sometimes receive vague or unrealistic requirements from the analysts, again based frequently on a lack of technical understanding about what is possible. Collectors often feel that they cannot wait for the analysts to articulate specific requirements, or that they should not be expected to use their own initiative in thinking about the best ways to gather data to meet specific requirements. Being, in a sense, in third place along a transactional relationship involving policy-maker, analyst and collector, the collectors often feel somewhat neglected and dislocated, and like to show what they can do.

It has traditionally been the case in the intelligence business that placing barriers between these three sets of actors has been seen as necessary and appropriate. Analysts and collectors should not get too close to policy-makers, lest they fall under the spell of politicisation, or end up in a situation where they feel compelled to give the policy-makers what they want to hear rather than what the data is saying. There have been numerous examples in history of where the system has fallen into such traps, including the Iraq situation. Similarly, it has not always been seen as desirable for analysts to get too close to the collectors, partly because collection can be a very technical and arcane business and the analysts would not necessarily have the right skills to understand it, but also because many collection capabilities are often particularly sensitive and it makes sense to restrict access to them as far as possible. There is sometimes an argument that, as long as the analysts receive the data they need, they do not necessarily need to know exactly how it is obtained.

Such thinking makes sense in many ways but it can lead to unintended consequences. Aside from the problems of a lack of understanding between the three sets of actors which can undermine and distort the articulation of clear requirements, the situation can become one in which sensitive or valuable information can be withheld selectively for political purposes. Scoring intelligence successes can sometimes be a competitive business, and an unhealthy situation can arise where a particular actor wishes to be the one who fires the golden bullet and wins the heart of the president or prime minister. Similarly, over-protection of certain types of information can ascribe to it a certain cachet, which can be politically useful when the auditors are trying to get to the bottom of the real value of a particular operation or capability. Not being able to tell all can sometimes be useful in these situations.

Finally, Hulnick noted that the linear and transactional nature of the Intelligence Cycle process can mean that analysis can sometimes take too long for the policy-maker's needs, and this can lead to a situation in which certain lines of intelligence make their way much more quickly and directly to the policy-maker in order to ensure the value of the information.[15] Tactical military situations are an obvious example of this: the appetite for "sensor-to-shooter" capabilities such as RTIC (Real-Time Information into the Cockpit) in live conflict situations means that "raw" intelligence can and often does make its way straight from collector to policy-maker without any processing or analysis.[16] Such tactical intelligence has a very short shelf-life before it becomes useless for directing an operation, so this makes sense, although it also introduces the risk that mistakes can be made if the intelligence is misinterpreted or is wrong. At any rate, this process demonstrates that some activities jump across the Cycle rather than follow it round. At the same time, there are certain activities such as counter-intelligence or covert action which do not really conform to the Intelligence Cycle at all in the way they operate, in terms of the relationship between requirements, intelligence and action.

Not postmodern enough

These are, therefore, some of the specific mechanical problems with the Intelligence Cycle which mean that intelligence production often does not work as simplistically as the process model implies. Relating the Cycle more broadly to the strategic-level changes in intelligence requirements and security threats, the essence of the problem would appear to be that the Cycle is essentially just not postmodern enough. Leaving aside, for one moment, the recognition that post-modernity is a contested concept,[17] it is clear that the radical transformation that society has been experiencing since the end of the twentieth century, whereby "all cultural codes can be mixed without sequencing or ordering"[18] and space and time are being increasingly compressed,[19] is transforming the nature of organisations very considerably. The Intelligence Cycle is perhaps an avowedly Fordist, Taylorian model which is not suited to notions of postmodernity.

As argued, the intelligence agencies are not immune to such changes outside the fence, partly because their own staff are changing their expectations and pre-ferred modes of working, but also because the threat picture is becoming more dynamic and interlinked. Castells notes that the changes in organisations in society at large were noticeable from the 1970s onwards, and were connected with two developments. First, change became economically necessary to cope with "uncertainty caused by the fast pace of change in the economic, institutional and technical environment". Second, rapid technological developments in information technology and multimedia were starting to make themselves felt, and to suggest new ways of working which promised much greater interconnec-tivity and immediacy of transactions.[20]

Such technological changes started to pervade all levels of society properly from the mid-1990s onwards, when the first commercial web browser came on the market and the personal computer started to become a standard household item, at least in the Western world. Ten years later, the advent of smart-phones, and the convergence they have allowed between personal, mobile communica-tions and the networked world, has meant that technologies such as social media have started to have wide-reaching significance across society. Again, there is much debate as to how far the influence of social media can go, particularly in the context of such developments as the Arab Spring of 2011,[21] and early research is showing a complex picture of cause–effect relationships.[22]

For the intelligence process, there are three potential impacts. First, the manner in which targets are undertaking social networking themselves means that analysis of it is becoming a central element of intelligence production. At the same time, new recruits to the intelligence business, who are increasingly living in a socially networked world in their private lives, will find the Fordist bureaucracy of the intelligence business increasingly dissonant with the outside world, and will inevitably press for change. In designing and effecting this change, the new technologies offer a tremendous new set of possibilities that affect every stage of the Intelligence Cycle, whether it is the articulation of requirements, the collection of data and the analysis of it, or the dissemination of the results to the policy-makers. At the core of the change is the fact that, as Treverton outlines, policy-makers will increasingly favour models which "pull" intelligence and information rather than having it "pushed on them".[23] The new revolution in information technology is all about choice and selection: if the old world was typified by the newspaper, in which readers of the news had available to them that which the editors had decided to make available, then the new world is typified by filtered query engines such as Google in which readers can select and access the information they want from the morass of the open internet.

This model has the potential to completely break down the old transactional process between the actors in the Intelligence Cycle. Now, if a policy-maker wishes to fill an information gap, the first thing they will be likely to do is not to levy a formal requirement on the intelligence agencies, but to run a Google query or switch on a rolling news service. This may result in an intelligence requirement to fill in the gaps, but just as frequently it will provide the policy-maker with the level and depth of information they need at that particular time. It may be the case that intelligence providers need to see their secret product not as a separate and different thing from open-source intelligence (OSINT), but as a supplement to that which can be accessed at the same time and in broadly the same ways. As Wark suggests, the intelligence producers need to recognise that they are in the information business rather than the secrecy business, and that they no longer have a monopoly on the production of, or access to, key knowledge.[24]

Concepts such as Intellipedia recognise and reflect this way of thinking. A vibrant literature has grown up recently about OSINT and the ways in which it can and should be incorporated into the intelligence business. Whether everyone would put it quite as strongly as Steele, who claims that any government that persists in spending most of its budget on secret intelligence-gathering and virtually nothing on OSINT is "clinically insane (or insanely corrupt) at the highest levels"[25] is a moot point. But the fact remains that the intelligence services are almost certainly lagging far behind where they should be in properly deriving benefit from the information revolution. This may be as much about organisational process as about technical capabilities. To be sure, the specific issues that entail barriers to change and flexibility within the intelligence business are not trivial. Intellipedia, for example, may be a great idea, but questions of how to properly handle sensitive material; how to ensure audit trails concerning the dissemination of specific pieces of information are clear; and how to protect source sensitivities and equities, to name but a few problems, are all very real issues in considering how to adopt such a system in the intelligence realm in ways that do not always apply in other parts of the information economy.

At the same time, the technologies inherent in the information revolution offer numerous opportunities to deal with these issues. These technologies are all about selecting, sharing and fusing different types of information with maximum speed and efficiency. This is essentially what intelligence organisations need to do, both within their own organisations and in terms of connecting with partner organisations nationally or internationally, even if they are needing to do so in complex ways. The new technologies also revolutionise information dissemination, compressing time and space. For intelligence organisations to not make use of such technologies to maximum effect in revolutionising their processes and capabilities perhaps is somewhat negligent, if not exactly an issue of mental health.

Such imperatives are recognised in senior circles within the intelligence business, and there has been a growing tendency to look at organisations for whom information and innovation are central, to see if there are any pointers for how to transform the business. Such comparisons can be very telling. A sense of the principles of modern information-economy organisations can be seen in some of the "nine principles of innovation" put forward by Marissa Mayer at Google, for example.[26] These include "ideas come from everywhere" (any member of staff from the top to the bottom of the organisation could have an innovative idea, and mechanisms need to be in place to capture them) and "data is apolitical" (successful products are those that work in the market best, rather than those preferred by particular members of the organisation). The first of these principles stresses the fiercely non-hierarchical ethos of such companies, whereby flat management structures and multi-dimensional networking allows for maximum information-sharing and innovation. Government bureaucracies still generally find such concepts to be anathema. In the case of the second principle, while intelligence is also very much supposed to be apolitical, intelligence organisations are avowedly not so and this will prove to be a very difficult situation to change. Despite the mantra from senior managers in the intelligence business that intelligence-sharing between agencies is the future, the picture is still a very tribal and competitive one where very little real progress has been made in this area.

How to modernise?

Can intelligence agencies be like Google, therefore? Clearly there are dangers in assuming all types of organisation can be compared, and the business of Google is, at one level, very different from the business of an intelligence agency. For a start, Google's primary driver is making money, while intelligence organisations must positively not give policy-makers what they like and most want to hear. At another level, however, both sets of organisations are in the information business (albeit in different parts of the forest), and there is much that can and should be learnt from the leading lights in that business. To put it another way, can modern intelligence organisations afford not to learn from these organisations?

The question, therefore, is whether and how the Intelligence Cycle can change and adapt to capture the environmental changes in society in the information age. To consider how this might happen, it is useful to focus on the core elements of the Cycle. I would suggest that the Cycle can be seen in terms of three dimensions: the actors involved in the process; the process flows and transactions between those actors; and the intelligence outcomes that the process aims to deliver.

The traditional Intelligence Cycle is essentially a process-oriented model, whose four or five (or sometimes more) boxes describe the set of processes that are undertaken between actors in the intelligence business. The actors themselves are implied rather than specified in the model, and this is one of its strengths as a conceptual process model, since it allows it to be applied to any number of organisations and situations. Indeed, other sectors have developed similar process models, such as Microsoft's four-box Business Intelligence cycle (which comprises Analysis, Insight, Action and Measurement).[27] That the commercial world has adopted a very similar notional model attests to its simplicity and validity.

Within the intelligence domain, some analysts have sought to build on the essential essence of the original Intelligence Cycle and update it for the modern intelligence picture. Quarmby and Young's "Intelligence System of Systems" is an interesting example of this approach. Taking processes within the intelligence business as the starting point again, this model attempts to incorporate a wider and more complex set of processes, including both tactical and strategic intelligence production, but also activities such as data mining, risk reviews, liaison and audit reporting, depicted within a complex butterfly-shaped model moving outwards in two wings from a central spine structured around the interplay between monitoring and analysis, and evaluation.[28]

While this model has much to commend it and is again easily translated across a number of different intelligence scenarios, from state and defence intelligence to law enforcement, regulatory environments and commercial organisations, it runs the risk of becoming overly complex and difficult to conceptualise. What the model achieves in the completeness of the processes covered and the appropriately conveyed notion that modern intelligence is a complex and multi-faceted business, it loses in the essential simplicity of the original Intelligence Cycle. As a training tool therefore, it may be less useful for immediate new starters in the intelligence business than for more advanced analysts and their managers.

One of the problems with process-oriented models is that they run the risk of looking through the wrong end of the telescope, in that they describe the set of activities within the intelligence organisation but not the essential *raison d'être* of the organisation, namely to produce intelligence. As noted, this was a criticism of NCIS's National Intelligence Model (NIM) adopted by the UK police, in the sense that it was actually a management model that said little or nothing about the intelligence itself. In this way, the NIM could have been applied to any organisational process, from intelligence production to producing widgets on a production line. The organisational risk here is that the actors in the process become too bound-up in administrative and bureaucratic issues, and forget what it is that they are supposed to be producing. It can also be an inflexible approach when faced with a much more dynamic set of challenges such as those described as being at the centre of the contemporary threat picture.

Robert Clark noted these weaknesses within the traditional process-oriented model and proposed another model which places the intelligence challenge at the centre, and builds the actors and their transactions around it.[29] He called this a "target-centric" approach, and correctly claimed that it has gained an increasing degree of currency within modern intelligence agencies.[30]

In designing his model, Clark drew the analogy with Fordist modes of production and the way in which they have changed through the end of the twentieth century:

> Fifty years ago, the automobile production "cycle" looked a lot like the traditional intelligence cycle ... Today automobile production is a team effort – with marketing, sales, design and production staff sitting in the same room with consumer representatives, working together on a common target: the new automobile. This complex, interactive, collaborative and social process results in faster production of higher-quality, more market-oriented products.[31]

In this way, the principles of the target-centric model stress the importance of collaborative working, and many of the organisational best-practice imperatives of information-age businesses, which cut across hierarchies and stove-pipes both within organisations and between them. As Clark observes, the aim of the target-centric model is "to make all stakeholders (including customers) part of the intelligence process" in order that "the process can take full advantage of evolving information technology and handle complex problems".[32]

The target-centric approach has indeed generated much interest within Western intelligence organisations in particular, as it offers a model for tackling many of the institutional problems which have been considered to be at the centre of numerous intelligence failures in history, and particularly the problems of faulty or non-existent sharing of intelligence. With modern information exchange and social networking technologies, such problems can and should be confronted more robustly now than ever before. Such organisational transformations move the intelligence business towards the network-centric model that defence has increasingly recognised as being an essential capability in the modern threat arena, and also echo problem-centric and customer-centric approaches that commercial business are increasingly developing in the contemporary information age.[33]

This notion of networking brings us back, I would argue, to the central importance of the actors in the intelligence business. As noted, the sorts of working across boundaries and moving of information that many commercial enterprises are recognising as being essential for survival in the modern age are not always easy propositions for the intelligence sector, for a host of complex and specific reasons of information source sensitivity and equity. Despite recognition of the imperatives of network-centric warfare and intelligence, it is arguably the case that contemporary intelligence agencies have made very poor progress towards implementing the changes that are needed in this area, for all their bold words and new process models.

I would therefore propose my own new Intelligence Cycle model for the contemporary world, which attempts to encapsulate the key drivers and issues discussed in this analysis. This is shown in Figure 3.1, which I call a "synthesised actor-oriented model".

In the best traditions of such modelling, this proposal encompasses many of the key elements of the other models described above. First, it recognises that the two key constituencies in the overall intelligence process are the policy-makers and the intelligence producers (who comprise both analysts and collectors). The heart of the intelligence process, I would argue, is the interaction between these two sets of actors. The two communities are separate but do

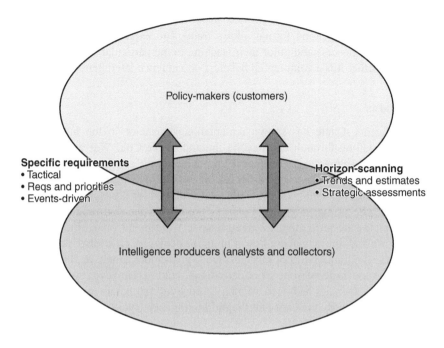

Figure 3.1 Synthesised actor-oriented model.

overlap to a certain extent, in that the intelligence producers will need to sometimes sit very close to the policy-makers in order to understand their objectives and drivers, and to translate these into intelligence collection strategies. At the centre of the model, therefore, these two constituencies network together. The difference between analysts and collectors is not drawn out, since there are many reasons why they should be working very collaboratively, notwithstanding the need to protect sensitive sources and capabilities. The policy-makers, furthermore, do not really need to be troubled by the internal organisation of the intelligence agency, but merely to receive good intelligence from it. The two key sets of processes linking these two constituencies together can broadly be delineated as tactical and strategic intelligence production, described here as "specific requirements" and "horizon-scanning". Both entail a large subset of potential activities, and both are generic concepts which apply across a number of public and private organisations to whom some form of intelligence is essential to the business. Note that the interactions between the actors in these two processes are two-way interactions, capturing the dynamic, interlinked and non-sequential nature of the relationship.

The model is very simple and generic, involving a minimal degree of detail. The purpose of this is to capture the best principles of the original Intelligence Cycle, whose durability probably owes much to its simplicity. As mentioned right at the beginning of this chapter, the Intelligence Cycle is, I believe, primarily intended as a teaching aid for new members of the intelligence organisation. Its clean and generic format allows trainers to expand upon the central elements of the process and tailor their teaching to the particular organisation in question, whether it is a commercial business or a defence intelligence agency.

Conclusions

The Intelligence Cycle has shown remarkable persistence in the intelligence business, pedalling through and beyond the end of the Cold War and into the modern information age of asymmetric and complex threats. It does, however, contain many throwbacks to an earlier age of monolithic and industrial production-line intelligence, and, as such, is not well equipped for the modern world. In this way it reflects many of the organisational challenges that modern intelligence agencies are struggling to meet, despite widespread recognition of the need to do so and thinking about how it might be achieved. Of course, producing new process diagrams will not change such organisations alone, as the change required is a much deeper one of organisational culture. However, as new personnel join the agencies and need training on how best to operate in the information age, it is certainly the case that the old Intelligence Cycle is overdue for an overhaul.

Notes

1 N. Quarmby and L. J. Young, *Managing Intelligence: The Art of Influence* (Sydney: The Federation Press, 2010), p. 13.
2 Manuel Castells, *The Rise of the Network Society – The Information Age: Economy, Society, and Culture, Volume 1* (Oxford: Blackwell, 2010), p. 166.
3 Ibid., p. 164.
4 See Barry Buzan, Ole Waever and Jaap de Wilde, *Security: A New Framework for Analysis* (Boulder, CO: Lynne Rienner, 1998).
5 Julian Richards, *A Guide to National Security: Threats, Responses and Strategies* (Oxford: Oxford University Press, 2012), p. 14.
6 Quarmby and Young, *Managing Intelligence*, p. 12.
7 Jerry Ratcliffe, *Intelligence-Led Policing* (Cullompton: Willan, 2008), p. 113.
8 Michael Fitzgerald and Richard Ned Lebow, "Iraq: the Mother of all Intelligence Failures", *Intelligence and National Security*, Vol. 21 No. 5, 2006, pp. 884–909. See pp. 884, 895. See also, James P. Pfiffner and Mark Phythian (eds.), *Intelligence and National Security Policymaking on Iraq: British and American Perspectives* (Manchester: Manchester University Press, 2008).
9 Clark notes that, despite being circular, the Intelligence Cycle reflects a "sequential, orderly and linear process". The problem with this is that thinking and relationships in real life are often not linear in nature. Robert M. Clark, *Intelligence Analysis: A Target-Centric Approach* (Washington, DC: CQ Press, 2007), p. 12.
10 Arthur S. Hulnick, "What's Wrong with the Intelligence Cycle", *Intelligence and National Security*, Vol. 21 No. 6, 2006, pp. 959–79.
11 Peter Gill and Mark Phythian, *Intelligence in an Insecure World* (Cambridge: Polity, 2006), p. 32.
12 Hulnick, "What's Wrong with the Intelligence Cycle", p. 959.

13 Clark, *Intelligence Analysis*, p. 11.
14 Across the intelligence community internationally, and to a growing extent within the UK system through the 1990s, there was a recognition that the intelligence agencies had to work harder physically at building a relationship and an understanding with the policy-makers. Aside from frequent visits between the two, this also led to the permanent installation of intelligence secondees and liaison offices in a number of policy departments, breaking down the walls between the two to a certain extent.
15 Hulnick, "What's Wrong with the Intelligence Cycle", pp. 964–5.
16 William G. Chapman, *Organizational Concepts for the "Sensor-to-Shooter" World: The Impact of Real-Time Information on Air-Power Targeting*. School of Advanced Airpower Studies, Alabama (June 1996), p. 2, at www.dtic.mil/cgi-bin/GetTRDoc?Location=U2&doc=GetTRDoc.pdf&AD=ADA349387, last accessed 15 October 2012.
17 Andrew Rathmell, "Towards Postmodern Intelligence", *Intelligence and National Security*, Vol. 17 No. 3, 2002, p. 92.
18 Castells, *Network Society*, p. 492.
19 David Harvey, *The Condition of Postmodernity: An Enquiry into the Origins of Cultural Change* (Oxford: Blackwell, 1991), p. 284.
20 Castells, *Network Society*, p. 165.
21 Gladwell, for example, argues that social media merely makes "the existing social order more efficient": Malcolm Gladwell, "Small Change: Why the Revolution will not be Tweeted", *The New Yorker*, 4 October 2010, at www.newyorker.com/reporting/2010/10/04/101004fa_fact_gladwell, last accessed 15 October 2012. DeLong-Bas, meanwhile, argues that, if social media did not actually cause the revolutions in the Middle East, it "clearly played a role in accelerating the events": Natana J. DeLong-Bas, "The New Social Media and the Arab Spring", *Oxford Islamic Studies Online*, at www.oxfordislamicstudies.com/Public/focus/essay0611_social_media.html, last accessed 15 October 2012.
22 For example, Zhang, Johnson, Seltzer and Bichard's empirical study suggests that social networking increases the degree of interpersonal discussion about politics and, in turn, the level of civic and political participation, but not necessarily the level of confidence in government. This could suggest, as the title of the paper proposes, that "the revolution will be networked". Weiwu Zhang, Thomas J. Johnson, Trent Seltzer and Shannon L. Bichard, "The Revolution will be Networked: The Influence of Social Networking Sites on Political Attitudes and Behavior", *Social Science Computer Review*, Vol. 28 No. 1, 2010, p. 87.
23 Gregory F. Treverton, *Reshaping National Intelligence for an Age of Information* (Cambridge: Cambridge University Press, 2003), pp. 103–4.
24 Wesley K. Wark, "Introduction: Learning to Live with Intelligence", *Intelligence and National Security* Vol. 18 No. 4, 2003, pp. 3–4.
25 Robert David Steele, "Open Source Intelligence", in Loch K. Johnson (ed.), *Handbook of Intelligence Studies* (London: Routledge, 2009), pp. 129–47. See p. 134.
26 Chuck Salter, "Marissa Mayer's 9 Principles of Innovation", *Fast Company*, 19 February 2008, at www.fastcompany.com/article/marissa-mayer039s-9-principles-innovation, last accessed 15 October 2012.
27 Elizabeth Vitt, Michael Luckevich and Stacia Misner, *Business Intelligence: Making Better Decisions Faster* (Washington, DC: Microsoft Press, 2002), pp. 17–22.
28 Quarmby and Young, *Managing Intelligence*, pp. 215–18.
29 Clark, *Intelligence Analysis*.
30 Ibid., p. 13.
31 Ibid.
32 Ibid.
33 Ibid., pp. 21–2.

4 The Intelligence Cycle is dead, long live the Intelligence Cycle

Rethinking intelligence fundamentals for a new intelligence doctrine

Philip H. J. Davies, Kristian Gustafson and Ian Rigden

Introduction

In the spring of 2009 the UK Ministry of Defence elected to undertake a review of the existing military Joint Intelligence Doctrine. Its doctrine, Joint Warfare Doctrine 2-00 (JWP 2-00) *Intelligence Support to Joint Operations*, had been promulgated in 2003 largely on the basis of coalition-oriented expeditionary and peace support operations in the Balkans, West Africa, Middle East and Afghanistan. This had replaced an earlier, first edition of JWP 2-00 issued in 1999. By 2009, the UK's intelligence doctrine had escaped scrutiny for six years, two years longer than its predecessor and under conditions which had witnessed wide-ranging and accelerating changes in the intelligence, surveillance and reconnaissance (ISR) environment and the longest interval of sustained, high-tempo operations by UK forces since the Second World War. Regardless of how sound a piece of work the 2003 doctrine might have been, by 2009 too many goalposts had moved too far and there was a widespread and growing dissatisfaction with it.

Given the often radical transformations to ISR and the conduct of operational and tactical intelligence in the decade since the first edition of JWP 2-00, the view was also taken that an equally radical approach needed to be used in producing the new doctrine. First, the new doctrine would be compiled on the basis of widespread, cross-government consultation on key issues and concepts rather than worked up narrowly in-house. Second, that breadth of engagement was to be extended to include the comparatively recently established realm of scholarly intelligence and security studies. Within the UK, the principal team working on conceptual and policy issues in intelligence in the university sector (as opposed to historical work which dominates the so-called 'British school of Intelligence Studies') was the Brunel Centre for Intelligence and Security Studies (BCISS) based at Brunel University in London. After an initial approach by the Development, Concepts and Doctrine Centre (DCDC) followed by a preliminary, advisory memorandum on military intelligence doctrine produced by the BCISS team,[1] a three-way partnership was established between DCDC, Defence Intelligence[2] and BCISS to develop the new doctrine which would go forward under the NATO- and US-compatible designation Joint *Doctrine* Publication 2-00.

There was a range of running debates that the new doctrine would need to address. These included: how to incorporate human terrain analysis (HTA) and its embedded academic subject-matter experts effectively into a doctrine for the armed services (and discomfort with the term 'terrain' which seemed too 'land-oriented' to two of the three armed services); adjudicating a running and sometimes vituperative dispute over whether the prevalent term for operational and tactical intelligence should be the US- and NATO-standard ISR or the prevalent term in British practice of intelligence, surveillance, *target-acquisition* and reconnaissance (ISTAR);[3] articulating the increasing vertical overlap between national intelligence and ISR/ISTAR activities and products; and trying to locate military and defence intelligence in the fast-changing national intelligence governance structures under the administrations of Gordon Brown and David Cameron.[4]

No single matter of discussion was more earnestly disputed, or more completely divided supposedly 'progressive' critics of current practice from 'old guard' conservatives, than the status and prospects of the Intelligence Cycle. Rethinking and revising the Intelligence Cycle rapidly became one of the central tasks for the JDP 2-00 team. What emerged, and eventually won comparatively widespread support, was an approach designated the 'core functions of intelligence paradigm'. The core functions approach was intended to reckon with the substantive and often well-considered concerns on both sides of the debate. Ideally the new formula would be an emergent property of dealing with those concerns rather than taking one side or another or simply postulating a third alternative that neither side would want or accept. In the event, the 'core functions of intelligence' paradigm was adopted for the new intelligence doctrine. As a result, the formula described herein is not a hypothetical proposal but in fact constitutes the accepted doctrinal standard for today's British armed services and the wider UK defence community and is currently being incorporated into the new NATO intelligence doctrine being produced as Allied Joint Publication 2-00.

Variations on a theme

At the outset it is important to keep in mind that there is some variation in the constituent components of what makes up the Intelligence Cycle. One of the earliest public references to the concept appears in the final report of the Church Inquiry, subsequently used by numerous authors, in which, in Walter Laqueur's words:

> the first stage in the intelligence cycle is an indication by [intelligence] consumers of the kind of information needed. These needs are conveyed to senior intelligence officials, who in turn inform the collectors. The collectors then obtain information, then 'raw' intelligence is turned into finished intelligence which is eventually supplied to consumers.[5]

In US practice, however, at least since the 1990s, the Cycle's intermediate process between collection and dissemination has been broken out into two steps, 'processing' and 'analysis', the former referring chiefly to the interpretation of data generated by collection activities and systems, the latter identifying its implications for wider judgements and contextual issues that the collected 'raw' intelligence is supposed to clarify.[6] By much the same token, the relatively narrow notion of 'tasking' has been generally supplanted by the broader concept of 'direction' within which the laying of requirements and priorities is but one component part. The resulting formula is often referred to as the 'DCPAD' (dee-cee-pad) model.

The NATO practice, and consequently that of the UK (which frequently takes NATO conventions as the point of departure for sovereign practice), has employed a somewhat simpler four-step cycle of 'direction–collection–processing–dissemination' at least since the 1970s. In this formulation, 'processing' subsumes both 'processing' and 'analysis' (see Figure 4.1). Slightly confusingly, the DCPD sequence also appears in British operational and tactical intelligence discourse as the 'ISTAR chain'.[7] What is consistent is the degree to which the UK's defence intelligence community is committed to the DCPD convention. Consequently all of the deliberation, and the subsequent formulation of the 'core functions' paradigm, was in terms of the NATO DCPD formulation.

There are reasons to suggest, however, that the five-step DCPAD model is a somewhat clearer expression of the process on the grounds that 'analysis' is a fundamentally different task from 'processing'. There are, for example, indications that the four-step NATO formulation has been found somewhat limiting by some UK commentators. For example, John Hughes-Wilson, a twenty-year veteran of the Intelligence Corps, prefers to employ a five-step scheme in which 'collation' and 'interpretation' are distinct.[8] Alternatively, when drafting the first

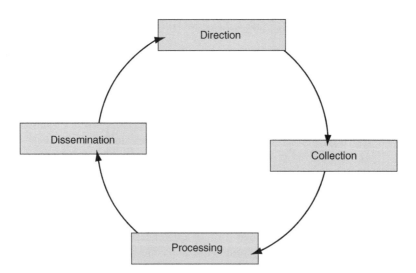

Figure 4.1 Traditional NATO DCPD intelligence cycle (Canadian B-GJ-005-200/FP-000, 2003).

chapter of Lord Butler's *Review of Intelligence on Weapons of Mass Destruction*, the late Peter Freeman drew a painstaking distinction between 'analysis' and 'assessment'. In this formulation, analysis is examining 'the factual material inside the [raw] intelligence report ... in its own right', partly by placing the raw intelligence in a wider context but also as 'the process required to convert complex technical evidence into descriptions of real-world objects or events'.[9] By contrast, assessment seeks to identify 'patterns' and 'extend a picture' by taking the available analysed information and forming net judgements about the conclusions it supports *in toto*, marshalling alternative interpretations against accumulations of reporting that may be mutually consistent or inconsistent.[10] In Freeman's sense, analysis identifies what intelligence reporting *means* and assessment seeks to establish what that reporting *implies*. Such a distinction leans strongly in the direction of a DCPAD approach.

Consequently, considerable thought was put to moving from DCPD to DCPAD by the JDP 2-00 team. However, it was eventually concluded that trying to sell both DCPAD *and* the core functions paradigm in a single revision to the UK Joint Intelligence Doctrine would prove, in one participant's words, 'a bridge too far'. Consequently it was decided to shelve the case for DCPAD, at least until the next revision to JDP 2-00 in the second half of the decade. As should become apparent, however, the basic idea of the core functions paradigm is as applicable to DCPAD as to DCPD.

Institutional background: intelligence doctrine

It is important, especially for a civilian readership, to understand what 'doctrine' is about and its role in military thought and practice. Common operating standards, common concepts and a common professional dialect are essential to a community that depends for its effectiveness on quick, clear and effective communication of information and instructions, and which has a high level of regular staff turnover even in key staff positions. Ambiguity and consequent confusion can have hazardous and potentially lethal ramifications that a conceptual difference in the civilian sector is unlikely to imply. This is the practical context for the internal military discussion of whether doctrine is 'what is taught' or 'what is believed', or as Lt Gen. John Kiszely has put it, 'what to think' as opposed to 'how to think'.[11] As a common cognitive and communicative framework, doctrine will likely end up as the latter even if intended to be the former. An intelligence doctrine is, therefore, liable to hold a greater intellectual authority (literally and figuratively) with its subscribers than any 'intelligence theory' that might be debated in the corridors of the Cabinet Office or Langley. Its users will also look to doctrine to mitigate and minimise uncertainty and nuance rather than resting upon them and then articulating them as 'issues' or intellectual 'problems'.

This can also lead to another level of uncertainty about what doctrine ought to provide. If doctrine is expected to articulate common operating standards as well as common concepts then it is not a leap to expect it to articulate common operating *procedures*. Indeed, the British Army's own *Doctrine Primer* is explicit about this, stating that 'higher levels of doctrine establish the *philosophy* and *principles* underpinning the approach to military activity' while 'lower levels ... describe *practices* and *procedures* for ... practical application'.[12] And, to a very real degree, single-service doctrine statements such as field manuals exist to do just that. As a result, the earliest and hence most formative perception of doctrine amongst many service personnel is precisely as a guide to specific procedures and practices rather than anything more abstract.

There exist, therefore, both a deeply indoctrinated expectation of procedural guidance from doctrine and a measure of uncertainty amongst many participants about the exact level of hierarchy at which doctrine ought to be *conceptual* instead.[13] Consequently, throughout the production of JDP 2-00 perhaps the most fundamental difference between the 'radicals' and 'old guard' was whether the Intelligence Cycle was supposed to represent a series of standard operating procedures (SOPs) or a conceptual framework that might subsume many different specific SOP schemata under the auspices of an ambient rather than prescriptive logical structure. As we shall see shortly, the distinction between what might be called the *conceptualist* and *proceduralist* views of the Intelligence Cycle infuses civilian discussion of the Intelligence Cycle as well. But for the armed services, the need for procedural clarity has an urgency very different from that of any civilian enterprise, and consequently the dispute between conceptual and procedural concepts of the Intelligence Cycle likewise acquired an amplified sense of urgency and intensity of feeling amongst the disputants.

That need for clarity and prescription has long prompted the chronic concern amongst doctrine writers that, in J. F. C. Fuller's oft-quoted words, 'the danger of a doctrine is that it is apt to ossify into dogma'.[14] And herein lies the critical issue with which the JDP 2-00 team had to reckon, and of which the dispute between the conceptual and procedural 'camps' is essentially a restatement. Should the Intelligence Cycle articulate a descriptive account of 'doing' intelligence? Or should it be a general conceptual expression of basic functions of which the numerous institutional frameworks, such as RPSI or CCIRM (now confusingly IRM&CM) in the UK, and KIQs, NITs and 'Needs'[15] in the USA, are just specific cases and applications? As noted above, the view taken by the British military generally, and the JDP 2-00 team in particular, was that doctrine, and especially high-level joint doctrine, is about general principles, and low-level doctrine and field manuals are about procedure. With this in mind, the resulting approach was to try to defuse the Intelligence Cycle debate by making the concept–procedure distinction as explicit as possible and dealing with each concern separately. But to do so the JDP 2-00 team needed to reckon with a significant legacy of wider debate regarding the virtues or not of the Intelligence Cycle, a debate not confined to defence circles.

Conceptual background: the Intelligence Cycle debate

The value or otherwise of the Intelligence Cycle is now a standard item in the literature of intelligence theory (in Peter Gill's sense of 'theory for intelligence' rather than 'theory about intelligence'),[16] and it is possible to distinguish much the same division between conceptualist and proceduralist approaches to the Intelligence Cycle in the civilian intelligence discourse. Unsurprisingly, the conceptual camp tends to be less trenchantly dissatisfied with the Intelligence Cycle than the procedural school, although both sides have sought to clarify and improve the schema one way or another. Indeed, one could even argue that we all employ the same four functions when we plan our own personal research/ investigation and reporting activities. An academic 'tasks' himself or herself through a research plan, then 'collects' in the archives or through interviews, 'processes' the documents and transcripts to understand his object of study, and 'disseminates' that understanding through writing and publication. Sometimes a scholar farms out fieldwork or data processing to research assistants, but this does not alter the basic logic of the process.

Michael Herman has famously described the Intelligence Cycle as being a 'metaphor' based on the classic cybernetic concept of a feedback loop.[17] This is actually a very apt expression of the conceptual approach to the Intelligence Cycle, especially if one has actually done any software programming or built hardware sensor–actuator loops. In software terms, a feedback loop that appears as a straightforward drawing at the flow-charting stage can easily turn into hundreds or thousands of lines of intricately interwoven code. Printed out and laid across a desk (or several desks), the finished program bears little resemblance to the neat flow-chart diagram pinned to the wall. Thus, taking commentators such as Berkowitz and Goodman,[18] Loch K. Johnson,[19] Sir David Omand[20] and, indeed, Herman, they look at the cycle as an abstract statement of principles and then deliberate whether this is an accurate or appropriate representation of those principles. Berkowitz and Goodman and Johnson both use it as a diagnostic tool to interrogate specific institutional arrangements and processes but not as a representation of those processes, while Omand and Herman rethink sequencing and basic premises.

The procedural approach tries to correlate specific institutional entities into the steps of the Intelligence Cycle. The Church Committee allocated tasking to intelligence consumers, with senior agency managers receiving those requirements and priorities before passing them on to the working-level collectors who would then pass what they collected on to specific cohorts of analysts, and so forth. Senator Church's team then became acutely exercised about the fact that 'in reality this pattern is barely recognizable'.[21] Rob Johnston has sought to 'test' whether the Intelligence Cycle describes what CIA analysts do at their desks and in their teams (unsurprisingly judging that it does not).[22] Likewise both Arthur Hulnick[23] and Mark Lowenthal[24] have elaborated in some detail how the simple framework of the Intelligence Cycle fails to describe actual processes on the ground in US national intelligence. Given the simplicity of the Intelligence Cycle formula, descriptive and procedural interpretations are naturally more likely to find substantial asymmetry between the neatly drawn flow-chart and the thousands of lines of entangled institutional 'spaghetti code'.

The kind of dissatisfaction felt in military quarters has been articulated by Geraint Evans, an officer in the UK's Intelligence Corps, in a 2009 *Defence*

Studies article, published just as the JDP 2-00 re-write was in its infancy. While acknowledging that the Intelligence Cycle is 'composed of fundamental principles' rather than specific institutional entities or groups, he also views the relationships between those 'principles' as rigidly prescriptive procedural steps 'upon which the outcome of all ensuing action is determined'.[25] Although Evans acknowledges the conceptual nature of the Intelligence Cycle, his explicit goal appears to be to find a framework which can then be implemented explicitly, rigidly and in a manner that suggests (despite invoking Fuller's warning about ossified doctrine[26]) a certain procedural dogmatism.

Evans then argues that the Intelligence Cycle is currently under pressure to change as a result of a range of exogenous factors. The first problem is the immediacy of consumer demands and consumer expectations with which a step-by-step implementation of the cycle cannot keep pace in practice.[27] This is exacerbated by the information revolution in which intelligence consumers use intelligence differently (although he specifies no exact properties or examples of how that information use is 'different'),[28] intelligence staffs are confronted with increased risks of information overload because of the volume of data increasingly available,[29] and the availability of information does not conform to putatively 'traditional military staff silos' or chains of command.[30]

Evans's proposed solution is to expand the Intelligence Cycle into what he calls the 'hub and spoke' model. In this formulation review, planning and direction are broken out into separate functions, collection remains unaltered, and processing, analysis and production are also broken out from the 'P' function and dissemination, like collection, stands unaltered.[31] At the hub of this process would be the J2 cell, in receipt of information from all of the various functional stages and conducting a continuous and comprehensive review of the process.[32]

Evans acknowledges that the hub-and-spoke formula had already been 'tested on exercises and operations',[33] which is unsurprising because a version of the hub-and-spoke formula had actually been formulated some four years earlier for the Cabinet Office by Stuart Jack. Stuart Jack is a career Foreign and Commonwealth Office official who had, *inter alia*, headed the FCO Research and Analysis Department (RAD, the UK equivalent of the US Bureau of Intelligence and Research) in the late 1990s. In 2004 and 2005 he was head of the Butler Study Team and had authored a paper entitled 'Towards Better Analysis', colloquially known as the Jack Report. As part of this paper, Jack presented a version of the Intelligence Cycle which placed the analyst in the centre of a DCPD cycle, responsible not only for 'processing' but also taking a role in the 'collection' phase where raw data requires collating with other sources, and even feeding into the tasking process to facilitate consumers' understanding of what they can reasonably ask of intelligence (Figure 4.2).[34] In short, Evans's J2 'hub' is a military emulation of Jack's central, facilitating analysts, and is therefore representative of a direction in which wider intelligence thinking was already going in British government circles.

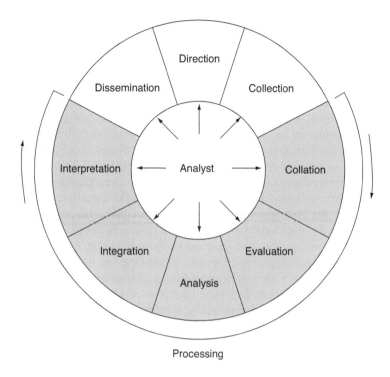

Processing

Figure 4.2 Jack Report intelligence cycle (reprinted in JDP 2-00 3rd edition).

The core functions paradigm

The initial case for the new doctrine explicitly adopting a conceptualist stance as a point of departure for addressing and taking on board proceduralist objections to the Intelligence Cycle was made in a BCISS memorandum to DCDC circulated in December 2009.[35] A number of the key arguments developed in that memorandum were subsequently carried forward by DCDC and published in a 2010 Joint Doctrine Note, JDN 1/10 *Intelligence and Understanding*. Joint Doctrine Notes 'do not represent a fully agreed or staffed position, but are raised in short order ... to establish and disseminate current best practice' and 'provide the basis for further development and experimentation'.[36] The explicit intention behind JDN 1/10 was that it should be a slightly contentious discussion piece, aimed at flushing out lines of dispute and uncertainty rather than trying to identify an easy consensus. Described in its preface as 'aspirational in nature' and requiring 'honest scrutiny appraisal and debate to ensure that it meets its purpose', JDN 1/10 did just that and was hotly debated in a number of defence quarters.

In JDN 1/10 a case was made for the core functions paradigm through a series of preliminary steps. The Intelligence Cycle, it was noted, 'is (and always was) a heuristic concept that describes a set of logical inter-relationships between several

types of classes of activity' and therefore 'cannot usefully be turned into a procedural clockwork that serves as a "quick win for busy analysts"'. Indeed, it was
further argued, it was precisely when people tried to use the cycle as 'procedural
clockwork' that the weaknesses of thinking of it as a mechanistic cycle were
mostly like to be exposed. While a steady, regular cycle application of the basic
activities of direction, collection, processing and dissemination might work for
'long-standing problems' where 'decisions are not required quickly' or are likely
to take unexpected forms, such an approach lacked agility. It was, therefore, ill-
suited to the 'contemporary or anticipated operating environments'. While the
four components of the Intelligence Cycle were essential activities, the 'cycle' or
'process' model 'does not fully represent their role or functionality'.[37]

It is important to appreciate that the goal was not to suggest that the 'core
functions' did not or could not have the properties of a cycle under certain circumstances. Rather, the idea was that the core functions paradigm was *more
than* a cycle, and that the traditional Intelligence Cycle could be subsumed by it.
Therefore, the next question was how to most usefully represent the 'logical
inter-relationships' between direction, collection, processing and dissemination.
The Brunel team argued that what was required was an alternative *topology*, and
that the most useful topological representation was as an *all-channel network*. In
practical terms, direction, collection, processing and dissemination continuously
communicated back and forth and across the 'cycle' more like subroutines
calling one another in computer software than the prevailing metaphor of an
electromechanical feedback system. The resulting core function topology was
originally represented in rough-and-ready graphical terms (see Figure 4.3).[38] It
was in response to the new topology that one of the current authors (Rigden) in
his role as head of the JDP 2-00 process coined the term 'core functions of intelligence' to replace the limited and evidently obsolescent notion of an intelligence
'cycle'. This was the topology presented to the UK's defence intelligence community in JDN 1/10.[39] An early promising omen for the core functions topology
was a number of senior officials responding in various forms of words equivalent
to 'that's what I have been doing throughout my career'.

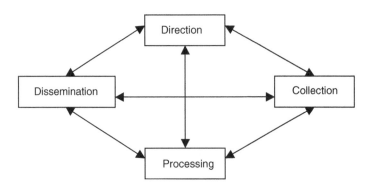

Figure 4.3 The original core functions network topology.

Under this formula, rather than steps in a sequence, the relationships between the various principal intelligence activities were best visualised as a network of dialogues and sometimes short-circuits across the DCPD framework. Any two, three or even all four functions could be 'wired together' in different, often spontaneous ways. Such cross-connections include:

From Collection to Direction: The conventional feed-forward role of direction-setting requirements and priorities for the collection process is generally viewed as straightforward, but the feedback and dialogue between the two is also essential. There are many situations where collection can and must 'push' information to the decision-makers to task it. The collection process can often provide opportunities for collectors to detect activities that are of significance to or threaten the concerns of the consumer and which it may not have occurred to the decision-maker to include in their requirements and priorities. Warning intelligence often takes this form. Under these conditions there needs to be the opportunity either for collection to short-circuit the processing and dissemination phases to present the evidence to the decision-maker, *or* for the collector to initiate the processing and dissemination cycle on their own authority to ensure that the decision-maker receives a properly assessed product instead of raw reporting which may be misunderstood or taken out of context. This also conforms to Michael Herman's alternative to the Intelligence Cycle[40] in which 'entrepreneurial' intelligence collectors anticipate decision-maker needs and seize the initiative to push product to decision-makers. Even the basic tasking relationship requires a real-time dialogue between consumer and collector concerning what *can* be acquired, at what risk, and at what direct cost or indirect opportunity cost to other requirements. If not, then requirements become an unrealistic wish-list and collectors are overcome with tasks, some of which must be allowed to lapse or none of which can be fulfilled effectively.[41]

From Processing to Collection: Although typically the Intelligence Cycle represents tasking coming from the consumer and raw intelligence flowing to the analyst, the connection between analyst and collector is often reversed as the analyst has to reach back to the raw intelligence reporting to assist their assessment process. Raw intelligence reports generally include what the collector thinks the analyst needs to know from the source; however, processing the raw intelligence often throws up gaps, ambiguities, uncertainties and conflicts in the raw reporting. In the first three cases, the analyst needs to reach back to the raw intelligence to clarify what has already been acquired but not necessarily circulated or recognised by the collector as in need of circulation, or to consult the raw intelligence in order to make a properly informed appreciation about what judgements can be made on the basis of the available intelligence. Where there are conflicts between the raw reporting the analyst will need to mine down into the validation and evaluation of the original sources to decide how to weight the relative credibility of the sources. By the same token, under such conditions the analyst may end up effectively driving and directing the collection phase, requiring collectors to go back to their sources to re-visit reporting already in hand or to re-task those sources to fill the gaps highlighted by the analyst.

From Dissemination to Processing: Much as the analyst may need to talk to the collector, so the drafter or briefer may need to delve into the analytical judgements and reasoning undertaken in the processing stage. Often, of course, the analyst is also the person drafting the disseminated product where written reports are concerned, but in verbal briefings the briefing officer may often be presenting a summary or amalgamation of finished materials received from other quarters. Under these conditions, some degree of dialogue with the processing phase and the relevant personnel and/or institutions will be necessary. It is also worth keeping in mind that consumer response to disseminated product will come back to the briefer in the first instance, and find its way to the analytical team via the dissemination team (as opposed to via revised direction and tasking as in the classic clockwork view of the Intelligence Cycle, with feedback taking the form of revised requirements fed forward to the collectors and analysts).

Between Dissemination and Collection: Much as the analyst may often need to dig into raw intelligence, the same may be true of the dissemination phase needing to consult with raw intelligence in order to aid the formulation and delivery of the finished intelligence product to the consumer. In this case, there must be provision for direct links *from* Dissemination *to* Collection as and when required. By the same token, collection elements should ideally have a running brief to provide urgent current reporting to the processing and dissemination phases throughout the process. Consequently, if a report received at the last is significant to presentation of a finished product to the consumer the collector must be in a position to forward that urgently and directly. This could well be a direct Collection *to* Dissemination short-circuit bypassing routine processing. However, if the product were not completely self-explanatory (such as technical product or a human source with significant attendant validation concerns attached), this might instead take the form of a three-point short-circuit running *from* Collection *to* Processing *to* Dissemination.

Between Processing and Direction: The history of intelligence is replete with examples of consumers not merely passively receiving finished intelligence products but insisting on being able to unpack and examine the analytical process and the combination of reporting and judgements that prompted the appreciation presented to them. It is also worth keeping in mind that in division-of-labour terms, the separation between dissemination and analysis often collapses when analysts double as drafters and briefers on the basis of their own work or that of their team. Likewise, the distinction between direction and analysis can collapse where commanders factor interpreted raw intelligence into their operational decision-making instead of having it cycled through a separate assessment phase. A more widespread example here is probably the most common: that most Intelligence Requirements are actually for fully assessed, finished intelligence. Consequently, in real terms, most collection tasking results from a three-cornered sequence running *from* Direction issuing requirements *to* Processing followed by analysts forwarding their information needs *to* Collection operators.

From Direction to Dissemination to Processing to Collection: While it might seem counter-intuitive, the DCPD cycle can actually run backwards, and often does. Much of the literature on the intelligence-producer/policy-maker relationship is replete with the actual feedback to finished intelligence taking the form of comments and directions from the consumer directly back to the disseminators/briefers. The briefers in turn then take that feedback to the analysts (where they are not one and the same person or entity) asking for the gaps, questions and inadequacies expressed by the consumers to be filled by the processing entity. And the analysts themselves more often than not find themselves reaching back to the collectors to fill those gaps – and the collectors themselves may find themselves having to go back to the consumers requesting clarification or further articulation of the requirements and priorities that started the whole process with which the consumer was so dissatisfied in the end.

Ironically, the only real objections to the core functions paradigm as it was now taking shape were from the defenders of the conventional DCPD formula who could not locate the traditional cycle within the new model. An alternative version was, therefore, presented which superimposed the traditional cycle on top of the new topology, not so much as an additional layer but as a kind of route map through the network (Figure 4.4).[42] Once the 'latent' traditional cycle was made explicit most of the resistance from members of the 'old guard' Intelligence Cycle advocates abated, apart from occasional grumbling about unnecessary extra complication.

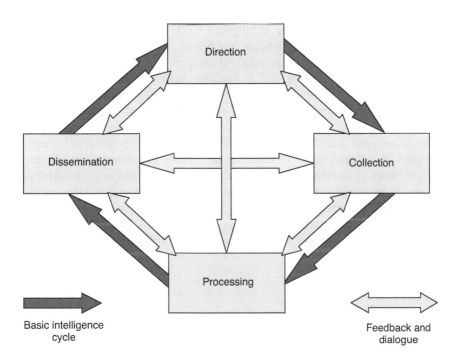

Figure 4.4 The core functions plus latent intelligence cycle.

Venn diagram of functional overlap

There then followed a series of 'thought experiments' on how to represent the 'core functions' of intelligence. The first was an effort to represent the core functions in terms of a Venn diagram of their logical and functional relationships. One of the chronic problems with the classic cycle formula has been the fuzzy boundaries of the various Intelligence Cycle stages, one of the reasons why there is such a wide assortment of intelligence cycles with slightly different constituent parts. Is collection management a direction or collection function? Are imagery analysis and cryptanalysis collection, processing, analysis or what? To make matters still more uncertain, although Freeman distinguishes between analysis and assessment as logically distinct tasks, he also asserts that 'assessment may be conducted separately from analysis or as an almost parallel process in the mind of the analyst'.[43] Given the fact that traditionally most assessments have taken the form of written reports given to consumers, is drafting an analytical or dissemination function? This latter problem has been particularly brought to light by Sherman Kent's classic problem of 'words of estimative probability'.[44]

The resulting diagram (Figure 4.5)[45] was not expected to appear in any final doctrine text. It was, rather, aimed at helping the drafting team try to work out how to articulate processes and principles along the fuzzier boundaries of the DCPD functions. It is worth acknowledging that the Venn diagram formulation helps understand the considerations underlying some of the more finely divided versions of the Intelligence Cycle such as Evans's 'hub and spoke' model. There is a significant number of functions that lie within the intersection sets between the main DCPD categories. Any or all of these could quite reasonably be 'broken out' as separate functions along the traditional loop. And that does give an additional insight into the resilience and longevity of the cycle despite its widespread unpopularity. It offers simplicity and even elegance that more elaborate alternatives do not. The Venn diagram schema suggests that Evans's outwardly reasonable formulation is actually the start of a slippery slope of breaking out distinct functions that would lead all too easily to Intelligence Cycle formulations of a dozen or more items or stages. Indeed, one can imagine subdividing the marginal functions on the intersections between the basic four (or five) core functions even more finely. Such an approach would likely introduce more confusion rather than less, and make the resulting schema more rigid and prescriptive rather than more flexible and adaptable.

Nested intelligence cycles

If the traditional, doctrinal Intelligence Cycle could be described as an oversimplification this could hardly be said of the doctrinal attempts to formulate collection management. Most attempts to articulate the processes and procedures necessary to manage the tasking of collection activities and assets might be

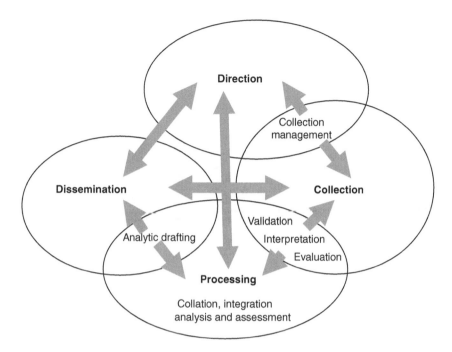

Figure 4.5 Venn diagram of core functions (revised).

kindly described as plumbers' nightmares. There was also the sense, in some quarters (typically from members of the 'clockwork' school), that there wasn't a *single* Intelligence Cycle occurring in a single institutional locus but many others spinning away at multiple different levels in different locations. Terms fielded for discussion on the working groups included a notion of 'wheels within wheels' and that intelligence exhibited a 'fractal structure' in which each phase of the intelligence process replicated the topological properties of the whole. The question was how to articulate this much more subtle and fluid concept. As one of the thought experiments, the BCISS team proposed the idea of 'nested' intelligence cycles, or, more accurately, nested core functions. According to this formula, one could 'break out' a core functions process from within each individual DCPD element. The resulting scheme (Figure 4.6) was intended to help represent this approach.

DCPD within collection

The idea of nested DCPD functions is most readily illustrated in 'Collection' and 'Processing', where the internal dynamics are most systematically examined and described. Collection management, for example, can be seen in terms of its own DCPD cycle:

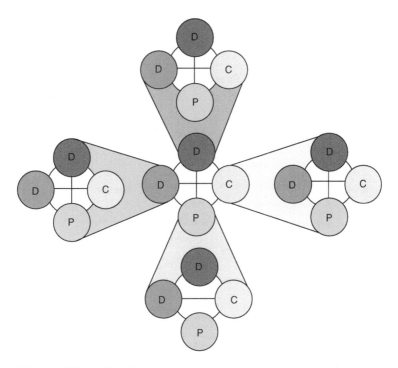

Figure 4.6 Nested intelligence cycles.

a   Direction = *Selecting and prioritising* the available databases, platforms, sensors and sources for direction to a particular target, or setting a human source with a particular matter to inquire into or report upon;

b   Collection = *Operating* in the sense of actually deploying the platform/sensor or contacting the agent and exfiltration or retrieval of the resulting information or 'raw' intelligence;

c   Processing = *Interpretation* in the sense of validation, and, in Freeman's sense, analysis of the generated raw intelligence e.g. imagery analysis of imagery from an unmanned aerial vehicle or satellite; decryption, translation and interpretation of an intercept; or debriefing the agent to generate a 'contact note' HUMINT;[46]

d   Dissemination = *Collating* the raw intelligence with other reporting and background context to turn the imagery analysis, intercept data into SIGINT or contact notes from an agent meeting into a source report.

It is easy to imagine the collection phase's own subordinate cycle, such as in a HUMINT operation where 'direction' is formulating the plan to contact the agent; 'collection' is the actual meet, clearing the letter drop or what have you; processing is generating the 'contact notes', treating secret writing to make it visible; and 'dissemination' is the generation of the source report or equivalent.

DCPD within processing

In the same way, 'Processing' can be broken down into DCPD steps, for example a JIC national assessment by the Assessments Staff consists of:

a   Direction = Identifying the requirement in question and target audience who have likely laid the requirement, formulating the paper's terms of reference;
b   Collection = Requesting and receipt and collation of supporting papers in the form of intelligence reports (e.g. SIS CX reports) and departmental views from other government departments such as Defence Intelligence, the Foreign and Commonwealth Office, the Home Office and others.
c   Processing = Collation of raw intelligence reports and departmental views, then forming an estimative judgement by weighing the evidence through traditional or structured analytical methodologies; then
d   Dissemination = writing the preliminary draft; challenge and review by Joint Intelligence Organisation Challenge team as well as at Current Intelligence Group(s) followed by revision to produce the final paper (which is then forwarded for publication and distribution under the conventional 'Dissemination' phase one level up).

DCPD within direction and dissemination

Much the same processes go on at the Direction level, with the commander or decision-makers deciding what decisions need to be made and what information is needed to make that decision; conducting an audit of their existing knowledge base; effectively conducting a gap analysis of that information and then, on the basis of the gap analysis, issuing intelligence requirements.

And, likewise, in the classic Dissemination phase at, for example, the national level the JIC's Secretariat would maintain a schedule for reports to be produced (direction), receive the final draft from the assessment staff (collection), proof and typeset the paper (processing) and then actually print the reports and send them out to their readers (dissemination).[47] The briefing officer preparing to present an intelligence summary to his or her commander would follow similar steps (perhaps substituting working with PowerPoint for the desktop publishing work of their 'processing' phase), then actually presenting the information verbally to the commander.

The implication of the nested approach was, of course, that one could mine down still further, right down to the level of the individual officer at a desk asking themselves 'what do I need to know?', finding that information, making sense of it individually, and then communicating it as required to whomsoever might need it (potentially just themselves). The goal was not some bewilderingly complex scheme of Copernican epicycles but, rather, to detach the DCPD heuristic from institutional and procedural specifics.

Conclusion: a higher common denominator

With JDN 1/10 in circulation the notion of a core functions paradigm, including the network topology, rapidly secured a viable level of consensus and cross-community 'buy-in'. The 'nested intelligence cycle' concept received a limited trial in the Study Draft of JDP 2-00 but was quickly abandoned as being far too abstract for doctrine-writing purposes. The principle remained, however, with the final version of JDP 2-00 warning the reader that:

> While the intelligence cycle outwardly appears a simple process, in reality it is a complex set of activities. It is a continuous process comprising many cycles operating at different levels and speeds. Although the 4 individual tasks are discrete, as information flows and is processed and disseminated as intelligence, the tasks overlap and coincide so that they are often conducted concurrently, rather than sequentially.[48]

The final visual representation of the core functions paradigm presented in JDP 2-00 was essentially the enhanced core functions topology given in Figure 4.4, that is, with the 'latent', traditional Intelligence Cycle marked out separately and the newer core functions topology inscribed within the cycle. The only notable alteration to the network topology was the superimposition of the Jack Report's continuous review process over the horizontal and vertical cross-connections in the centre of the diagram (Figure 4.7).

On the whole the JDP 2-00 Third Edition has been well received across the defence community, the most common point of dissent being its length (arising chiefly from the number of relatively detailed 'vignettes' or illustrative examples). It is not, of course, a perfect fix. While the 'core functions of intelligence' paradigm effectively addresses most of the substantive dissatisfactions with the old Intelligence Cycle formula it has done so at the potential cost of being a much more abstract conceptual exercise. The new doctrine is intentionally, one might even say *pointedly*, conceptual rather than procedural. Indeed, it is so much an exercise in abstract general principles that no need was seen to subject it to protective document marking and consequently it is the first British military intelligence doctrine to have been published unclassified. The need for both procedure and for a doctrine to speak to more sensitive methods and examples has not been negated. Instead, specific and sensitive matters are being addressed in a series of sub-doctrine statements on matters such as HUMINT, SIGINT, GEOINT and so forth,[49] many of which will be produced at higher levels of classification. This formulation satisfied the 'old guard' Intelligence Cycle advocates while also meeting the concerns of 'radical' critics by making the difference between principle and practice explicit, and providing for separate articulation of procedural specifics at a different (and more appropriate) doctrinal level.

Despite its acceptance across defence and favourable reception in most quarters there is a definite sense amongst those who produced the new intelligence doctrine that it is very much an experiment in progress. The case for DCPAD is

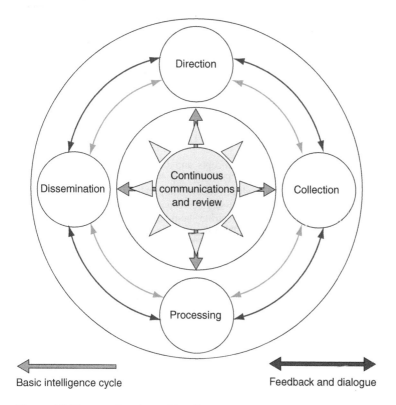

Figure 4.7 The core functions of intelligence (JDP 2-00 3rd edition).

still a strong one, and collection management remains a plumber's nightmare.[50] Doctrine is, as it were, always a moving target and whether or not the third iteration of the UK's Joint Intelligence Doctrine is at least moving in the right direction will be a matter for close scrutiny during the next comprehensive doctrine review round, due in the second half of this decade.

Notes

1 BCISS, 'BCISS Comments on JWP 2-00 Re-Write Arising from DCDC Intelligence Seminar', 3 December 2009.
2 Formerly known as the Defence Intelligence Staff (DIS).
3 The distinction is not merely a formal one; arguably ISTAR reflects a potential fusion of J2 analytical deliberations and nominally J3 targeting functions that in other national armed services are often kept nominally separate.
4 See, for example, Philip H. J. Davies, 'Twilight of Britain's Joint Intelligence Committee?' *International Journal of Intelligence and CounterIntelligence*, Vol. 24 No. 3, 2011, pp. 427–46.
5 Walter Laqueur, *A World of Secrets: The Uses and Limits of Intelligence* (New York: Basic Books, 1985) pp. 20–21.

6 See, for example, Central Intelligence Agency, *A Consumer's Guide to Intelligence* (Washington, DC: National Technical Information Service, 1993), pp. viii–4.

7 House of Commons Select Committee on Defence, *The Contribution of ISTAR to Operations: Eighth Report of Session 2009–10* (London: TSO, 2010), pp. 3, 8, 9–11 and *passim.*

8 John Hughes-Wilson, *Military Intelligence Blunders and Cover-Ups* (London: Robinson, 2004), pp. 4–5.

9 Lord Butler, *Review of Intelligence of Weapons of Mass Destruction* (London: TSO, 2004), p. 10.

10 Ibid., pp. 10–11.

11 John Kiszely, 'Thinking about the Operational Level', *RUSI Journal*, December 2005, p. 39.

12 Ministry of Defence Development, Concepts and Doctrine Centre (DCDC), *Army Doctrine Primer* (Shrivenham, UK: DCDC, 2011), p. 3.

13 The *Army Doctrine Primer* was produced roughly in parallel with JDP 2-00 and can, in many respects, be seen as a single-service response to this problem, spending roughly five pages on which levels of doctrine should be practical, conceptual or philosophical – then confusingly putting *joint* doctrine on its own separate level above 'philosophical' (*Army Doctrine Primer* p. 5).

14 J. F. C. Fuller, *The Foundations of the Science of War* (London: Hutchinson, 1926), p. 254.

15 In order of appearance: Requirements and Priorities for Secret Intelligence; Coordination of Collection and Intelligence Requirements Management; Intelligence Requirements Management and Coordination of Collection; Key Intelligence Questions; National Intelligence Tasks; while the 'Needs process' was an attempt to articulate a real-time requirements and priorities process within the constraints of President Bill Clinton's Presidential Decision Directive 35 (PPD-35). Roughly speaking, RPSI and CCIRM have historically operated with relatively little difficulty and KIQs, NITs and 'Needs' with comparatively little success. See Philip H. J. Davies *Intelligence and Government in Britain and the United States: a Comparative Approach* (Santa Barbara, CA: Praeger Security International 2012), *passim.*

16 Gregory F. Treverton, Seth G. Jones, Steven Boraz and Philip Lipscy, *Toward a Theory of Intelligence: RAND Workshop Report* (Santa Monica, CA: RAND, 2006), p. 4.

17 Michael Herman, *Intelligence Power in Peace and War* (Cambridge: Cambridge University Press, 1996), p. 293.

18 Bruce D. Berkowitz and Allan E. Goodman, *Strategic Intelligence for American National Security* (Princeton, NJ: Princeton University Press, 1989), pp. 30–39, 185–92.

19 Loch K. Johnson, 'A Framework for Strengthening US Intelligence', *Yale Journal of International Affairs*, Vol. 1 No. 2, 2006, pp. 116–31.

20 David Omand, *Securing the State* (London: Hurst, 2010), pp. 117–20.

21 Senate Select Committee to Study Governmental Operations With Respect to Intelligence Activities (hereafter referred to as the Church Committee), *Final Report Book 1: Foreign and Military Intelligence* (Washington, DC: United States Government Printing Office, 1976), pp. 17–18.

22 Rob Johnston, *Analytic Culture in the US Intelligence Community* (Washington, DC: Center for the Study of Intelligence, 2005), pp. 45–60.

23 Arthur S. Hulnick 'What's Wrong with the Intelligence Cycle', *Intelligence and National Security* Vol. 21 No. 6, 2006, pp. 959–79.

24 Mark M. Lowenthal, *Intelligence: From Secrets to Policy* (3rd edn, Washington, DC: CQ Press, 2006), pp. 65–7.

25 Geraint Evans, 'Rethinking Military Intelligence Failure – Putting the Wheels Back on the Intelligence Cycle', *Defence Studies* Vol. 9 No. 1, 2009, p. 23.

26 Ibid., p. 28.
27 Ibid., pp. 26–7.
28 Ibid., p. 28.
29 Ibid., p. 29.
30 Ibid.
31 Ibid., pp. 41–2.
32 Ibid., p. 42.
33 Ibid., p. 41.
34 Parts of the Jack Report were released by the Cabinet Office in 2009 and can be found as appendices to Paul Brelsford, 'The Professional Head of Intelligence Analysis', unpublished dissertation for MA in Intelligence and Security Studies, Brunel University, March 2010.
35 BCISS, 'BCISS Comments on JWP 2-00 Re-Write Arising from DCDC Intelligence Seminar', 3 December 2009.
36 JDN 1/10, p.iii.
37 JDN 1/10, pp. 2–4. The idea of 'anticipated' operating environments refers to a pair of horizon-scanning documents produced by DCDC to guide thinking on matters with medium- or long-term ramifications. These are DCDC, *Future Character of Conflict* (Shrivenham, UK: DCDC, 2010) and *Global Strategic Trends out to 2040* (Shrivenham, UK: DCDC, 2010).
38 Brunel Centre for Intelligence and Security Studies, 'BCISS JDP 2 Note 1', 17 February 2010.
39 JDN 1/10, pp. 2–4.
40 Herman, *Intelligence Power in Peace and War*, pp. 294–5.
41 This has been examined in the case of the Secret Intelligence Service (SIS or MI6) with reference to the public choice concept of 'overgrazing'. See Philip H. J. Davies, *MI6 and the Machinery of Spying* (London: Taylor & Francis, 2004), pp. 342–3.
42 BCISS, 'BCISS JDP Note 5', 14 April 2010.
43 Butler, *Review of Intelligence on Weapons of Mass Destruction*, p. 10.
44 Sherman Kent, 'Words of Estimative Probability', *Studies in Intelligence*, Fall 1964.
45 BCISS, 'BCISS JDP Note 11', 21 May 2010. Note that the version presented here is slightly altered from the original 2010 document to reflect later work, especially on collection management.
46 The contact note-source report-intelligence report referred to here is MI5 HUMINT practice disclosed during the Matrix Churchill trial in the early 1990s; see David Leigh, *Betrayed: the Real Story of the Matrix Churchill Trial* (London: Bloomsbury, 1993), p. 133.
47 For an account of the JIC Secretariat's work, see Michael Herman, *Intelligence Services in the Information Age* (London: Frank Cass, 2001), pp. 164–79.
48 Ministry of Defence Development, Concepts and Doctrine Centre, *JDP 2-00 Understanding and Intelligence Support to Joint Operations* (3rd edn, Shrivenham, UK: DCDC, 2011), pp. 3–4.
49 DCDC JDP 2-00, p. v.
50 DCDC JDP 2-00, pp. 3–12.

5 Defining the role of intelligence in cyber

A hybrid push and pull

Aaron Brantly

"If ignorant both of your enemy and yourself, you are certain to be in peril."[1]

Sun Tzu

Information is the lifeblood of modern states. Intelligence is increasingly facilitating information superiority through an understanding of the cyber domain. The US Department of Defense Joint Vision 2020 establishes the goal of information superiority on the battlefield.[2] This information superiority enables decision superiority and favorably tilts the strategic and tactical balance.[3] Information superiority is built on cyber power, scale and complexity of attacks, robustness of defense, policy positions, systemic vulnerabilities and dependencies, and actor anonymity and attribution issues. Intelligence plays a mission-critical role in assessing these characteristics. This chapter examines the role of intelligence in identifying these characteristics within the cyber domain and examines how it influences the decision-making of policy-makers. Specifically, this chapter focuses on how intelligence increases the effectiveness of identifying potential attackers within the cyber domain and informs the decision-making of policy-makers when engaging in covert cyber action directed against a potential adversary. This chapter is designed to serve as a strategic framework in which to understand the role of intelligence within the cyber domain.

Is it really necessary to treat the role of intelligence within the cyber domain as contextually different from its role in a conventional domain? The short answer is yes. Cyber necessitates independent examination because it is characteristically different, and yet at the same time it is a pervasive feature affecting outcomes within other domains. What differentiates cyber from land, sea, air, and space, are three fundamental attributes relevant to intelligence practitioners. First, the cyber domain is a man-made domain. Second, military capabilities across the other domains are managed through the cyber domain. Third, military and civilian aspects of the cyber domain are often intertwined and difficult to differentiate. These attributes pose unique opportunities and problems for intelligence officials.

The man-made nature of the cyber domain makes it a largely virtual domain with its value corresponding to the speed and volume of information contained within it. However, the cyber domain is not entirely virtual and has numerous real-world connection points to everything from industrial control systems of power and water management facilities to the weapon systems of drones flying above distant battlefields.

Cyberspace is not tangible in the same way as more conventional domains and therefore necessitates a new form of dynamic intelligence evolving from all-source collection of conventional and novel intelligence sources. A recent National Research Council report states that intelligence in the cyber domain is useful for both strategic and tactical purposes.[4] The strategic and tactical importance of intelligence's role in influencing the cyber domain falls within the concept of all-source intelligence. Loch Johnson defines all-source intelligence as one of the fundamental propositions of a theory of strategic intelligence.[5] More importantly, for the purposes of understanding the operational and political environments within which offensive and defensive actions in cyberspace can occur, it is necessary to understand what intelligence is within, and how intelligence influences, decisions regarding the cyber domain.

Defining intelligence

There are dozens of different definitions of intelligence, each of which is in some way applicable to understanding cyber action. One of the more succinct and conceptually ordered comes from Michael Warner. Warner defines intelligence as a "secret, state activity to understand or influence foreign entities."[6] His definition establishes the fundamental premises of both collection and analysis, while including actions designed to influence. Intelligence is vital to the cyber domain because foreign entities are increasingly storing, managing, and directing their governmental, public, private, and military functions in a digitized world.

The traditional intelligence collection types (INTs) are still of immense value, yet they must be combined with aspects of the digitized target spectrum to provide a holistic view of both threats and opportunities. At present the majority of studies in the public domain have focused on defense.[7] This defensive posture is made clear by General Keith Alexander, the Director of the National Security Agency and Commander of United States Cyber Command when he writes:

> US Cyber Command's efforts and planning aim to ensure that the DoD [Department of Defense] has done all it can to defend and deter determined adversaries, mitigate dangerous threats, and address nagging vulnerabilities, so that even our most capable opponents will know that interfering with our nation's equities in cyberspace is a losing proposition.[8]

This defensive and deterrent reliant posture is limiting and prone to inadequacies. Echoing Machiavelli and, to some extent, Sun Tzu, the adage "the best defense is a good offense" offers a novel way of considering action and intelligence within cyber. More accurately, it allows for a systematic approach to both national cyber defensive and offensive resource allocations. Beyond the efficiency argument for shifting the focus from solely defense to a balance between defense and offense, intelligence collection can help to inform offensive strategies and the decision to use cyber as a weapon. The role of intelligence within cyber becomes increasingly important when considering the difficulty of achieving any significant measure of deterrence within the cyber domain.[9]

The defensive orientation of the majority of cyber literature has a constraining effect on decision-making processes for the use of offensive cyber weapons. This defensive focus is largely due to both the alarmist calls of some scholars and policy-makers and an information communications technologies (ICT) industry orientation offering many more strategies for defense than for offense. While not disputing the need for defense, this defensive focus leads the national security establishment down a path of attempting to create an impenetrable system. If there is one thing that is abundantly clear in the cyber domain it is that the only impenetrable system is the one that has not been made. Cyber is based on physics and algorithms. The mathematics and science behind security measures can be immensely complex and take massive computing power to penetrate, but that does not make them impenetrable.

Instead of focusing on a solely carte blanche defensive posture towards cyber security, intelligence can provide both an offensive and a defensive picture more effective at safeguarding national security. Taking a step back from the conventional cyber security literature, intelligence can direct cyber security efforts to not merely safeguard national security, but also provide an offensive tool for use against other states. The vast literature on intelligence, ranging from the way intelligence influences the policy-making process, to how it helps to understand aspects of the development of utility for actions, serves as a guide in defining the role of intelligence within the cyber domain.

Reflecting on Warner's definition of intelligence, the spectrum of intelligence collection methods from Human Intelligence (HUMINT) to the more technical collection methods of Signals (SIGINT), Measurement and Signatures (MASINT), Geospatial (GEOINT), and Open Source (OSINT), all work together in an all-source environment to provide an accurate understanding of foreign entities. (Table 5.1 provides a definitional reference for the various intelligence collection types.) The understanding provided by intelligence has largely been focused in the conventional domains and in political decision-making. However, as decisions in conventional domains increasingly migrate towards cyberspace, and the systems controlling the tools used in these domains increasingly become digitally connected, the importance of understanding the technical schematics and decision processes becomes vital to national security.

Nick Cullather in an article on digital connections on the battlefield indicates significant advances in the development of network-centric warfare. He notes that the rise of a "revolution in military affairs" has largely not been matched by the intelligence community's ability to keep up.[10] This is of particular importance when looking beyond the network-centric battlefield of conventional weapons to the new zone of confrontation within cyberspace itself. Similarly, Michael Herman finds that counter-terrorism intelligence

Table 5.1 Intelligence collection methods[a]

Intelligence source type	Definition
Open Source (OSINT)	Overtly available information found, selected, and acquired from publicly available sources.
Measurement and Signatures (MASINT)	Intelligence detected and classified from targets, that identifies or describes signatures (distinctive characteristics) of fixed or dynamic target sources.
Human (HUMINT)	Intelligence collected through interpersonal contact via human collection officers.
Geospatial (GEOINT)	The exploitation and analysis of imagery and geospatial information to describe, assess, and visually depict physical features and geographically referenced activities on the earth. Geospatial intelligence consists of imagery, imagery intelligence, and geospatial information.[b]
Signals (SIGINT)	Intelligence-collection by interception of signals through various communications technologies.
Cyber (CYBERINT)	Obtaining prior knowledge of threats and vulnerabilities to information communications systems through a variety of technical means. Also referred to as Computer Network Exploitation (CNE)[c]

a The definitions in Table 5.1 are largely adapted from Mark M. Lowenthal, *Intelligence: From Secrets to Policy* (4th edn., Washington, DC: CQ Press, 2009).
b US Code Title 10, §467.
c Based on Phil Williams, Timothy Shimeal, and Casey Dunlevy, "Intelligence Analysis for Internet Security," *Contemporary Security Policy* Vol. 23 No. 2, 2010, pp. 1–38. CYBERINT is considered independent of traditional SIGINT. However, as in many of the other types of intelligence collection, techniques and agencies often overlap.

analysis requires a broad spectrum of information sources brought together.[11] The use of ICT facilitates the mitigation of "stovepipes" and increases the efficiency in information transference.[12] Information transference has also been facilitated following the US Intelligence Reform and Terrorism Prevention Act of 2004 by the creation of "fusion centers."[13] There is a role for ICT to play not only in the conduct of war on the battlefield, but also in the management of a conventional traditional threat spectrum within the fusion centers and beyond in the wider intelligence community.

Terrorism is not commonly regarded as part of the conventional threat spectrum, yet in reality most terrorist acts take place in the physical world and require bombs and explosives. However, the information transference necessary to organize, plan, and conduct warfare or terrorist acts, and to plan political strategies, has largely shifted to cyberspace. Available open-source information provides only a limited focus on the ability to realistically size up threats and targets within cyberspace itself. Joel Brenner, a former Inspector General of the National Security Agency and head of US counterintelligence, indicates there is already an enormous threat emanating from within cyberspace that is not being adequately addressed.[14]

Modern warfare – command and control warfare (C2W) – is network based. Large swaths of national critical infrastructures in states that pose a conventional security and economic threat to the United States are controlled by digital systems. The literature is less focused on the need for understanding these vulnerabilities than it is on safeguarding them. The defensive focus, to a large degree, overshadows the development of offensive capabilities.

One work that makes the case for the defensive necessity of intelligence to inform national cyber security is that of Phil Williams and his colleagues, who make a well-reasoned argument for focused intelligence efforts on identifying threats to national cyber security.[15] Williams *et al.* make a valid point that needs to be and is being addressed by several national strategy documents on the topic, including the *National Strategy to Secure Cyberspace*[16] and the *International Strategy for Cyberspace.*[17] One report of particular importance, addressing many of the issues brought up by Williams *et al.*, is the October 2011 report by the Office of the National Counterintelligence Executive on cyber espionage.[18] A broad spectrum of federal strategies and reports has made identification and protection against vulnerabilities a top priority.

Currently cyber security is based on attacks in progress or attacks that have already occurred. It is difficult, if not impossible, to defend against an unknown attack. Much of the effort in the United States cyber community now seems to be equivalent to plugging the holes in the dyke after it floods. Most types of cyber attacks are repeat attacks and originate at the lower end of the threat spectrum. The strategy to begin filling in holes makes sense from the perspective of attempting to prevent further intrusions of the same types of attacks, but largely fails to address the more serious problem of accurately anticipating what the next type of attack is going to be. This strategy is referred to as a "Maginot Line" strategy and is one that is prone to failure in areas where technological and strategic capabilities rapidly evolve. The real challenge is to develop an intelligence strategy that prevents future attacks before they happen.

In a world of known unknowns and unknown unknowns, to paraphrase Secretary Rumsfeld, cyber security is likely the former rather than the latter.[19] How can intelligence be used to better the cyber security situation to not only protect the national infrastructure in a more systematic and logical manner, but also to use this information to inform the decision-making processes of policy-makers?

One problem associated with the US cyber community is proximity. Because the community develops, tests, and employs its own tools, it is unable to take into account methods of testing that have not yet threatened systems in the past. This is an in the box, out of the box problem. The designers of systems, software, and networks are talented and smart individuals, they lead the world in technical innovation, yet because they are inside their own systems it becomes intrinsically difficult to isolate unforeseen problems.

Solutions are best achieved by dividing the resources of the intelligence and technical community in several ways. First, the current orientation towards plugging holes must continue. While this post-hoc process is frustrating it prevents or at least slows further intrusions. The mentality of these individuals is one of defense. The objective is to secure and defend systems against all possible or known types of attacks. The most realistic approach is to defend against known types of attacks. The systems become fortified against repeat incidents or at least can minimize their severity.

Intelligence organizations must use all-source methods to collect as much intelligence on potential opponents as possible. This means profiling every aspect of other nations' cyber offensive and defensive capabilities. This requires a robust all-source collection methodology. Signals intelligence must look for transmissions and communications as well as spikes in internet traffic and geo-locate them using IP addresses. These geo-located IP addresses need to be analyzed using satellites and drones to provide accurate geospatial information on the areas in question. Open-source intelligence collection should attempt to gain as much publically available information on areas of interest as possible through legal means. Once all of this information has been compiled and assessed, targeted HUMINT operations should begin working on developing assets within these areas or with connections to these areas. These agents should be recruited for multiple purposes. First, they should be used to secure intelligence on the capabilities of potential adversaries. These capabilities will be defined in more detail below. Second, agents should also be recruited to become potential insider threats, a tool of particular importance on air-gapped systems.[20] Lastly, intelligence agencies should also place an emphasis on computer network exploitation and attempt to probe and map out network infrastructures, vulnerabilities, and strengths of adversaries. The last point is of importance both from an offensive and a defensive strategic orientation.

Another major problem with the cyber domain arises out of its systemic complexity. As Williams *et al.* accurately note, cyber defenders often do not have a realistic or accurate picture of their own systems, let alone the systems of adversaries who are attacking them.[21] Following their recommendations it is prudent for the national security community to make use of the principle of knowing yourself. This requires a consistent focus on domestic systems. However, only focusing on domestic systems leads to the "Maginot Line" tendency in which it is assumed networks are created to be impenetrable.

Intelligence and the cyber battlespace

The cyber domain is a modern battlespace and necessitates a holistic understanding. When defending against or engaging in hostile actions it is necessary to have an accurate understanding of the operational environment. Any battlespace, whether offensive or defensive, according to Edward Waltz requires a combination of dominant battlespace awareness (DBA) and dominant battlespace knowledge (DBK).[22] The process of identifying what is and is not important to understanding a particular battlespace largely falls to the discretion of policymakers within the Intelligence Cycle.

Stephen Marrin writes about intelligence and decision-making that:

> the intelligence cycle starts with decision-maker information requirements levied on intelligence collection capabilities, the processing of collected raw intelligence and transmission of this processed material to analysts who decipher its meaning, and relay that understanding back to the decision-makers...[23]

The decision-maker engages in tasking through a number of different "pull" mechanisms including governmental reports, hearings before Congress, Presidential directives, and executive orders. These tasking methods and others all combine to facilitate within the intelligence community an accurate understanding of what constitutes the battlespace in the eyes of the policy-maker. Often the planning and direction can be via informal requests from the Executive or from Congress and at other times it can be via official strategy documents.

Prior to 9/11 terrorism was a priority, but the planning and direction of resources had not yet reached a critical mass sufficient to prevent the terrible attacks on the World Trade Center and the Pentagon. Marrin and others find the intelligence process frequently fails to adequately define what constitutes a tasking priority for the intelligence community, necessitating a "push" from within the community outward. There are many instances in which policy-makers ignore, misinterpret, or misuse intelligence despite adequate tasking and intelligence production and dissemination.[24]

The push mechanism of the intelligence community can happen in several ways. Often it can follow what constructivists call "norm entrepreneurs." Entrepreneurs in the cyber domain include Richard Clarke,[25] John Arquilla, and David Ronfeldt[26] among others. These individuals bring to national policy-makers' attention issues of importance and help direct the intelligence community's efforts. If, however, they make outlandish claims and statements, their push for new norms can have a backlash and inspire counter entrepreneurs such as Thomas Rid, who writes that cyber war does not and will not occur.[27] Most traditional intelligence push comes from within the intelligence community itself.[28] Because the intelligence community is pushing intelligence not requested by the decision-makers the concept of the Intelligence Cycle can, as Marrin notes, become linear.[29] The reality is likely to be a combination of the two and the eventual decision-making process on what to do based on available intelligence is legally within the hands of the policy-maker.

For intelligence to adequately focus its sights on any battlespace, planning and direction from policy-makers must occur. Once policy-makers have established the importance of a battlespace the intelligence community must find ways to deliver accurate and reliable intelligence. The objective of intelligence collection is not solely to provide real-time information on the battlespace, rather it is best thought of as battlespace preparation or what Waltz refers to as "intelligence preparation of the battlespace" (IPB).[30] Although Waltz specifically refers to IPB in the context of coordinated conventional warfare and the use of information operations in network-centric warfare, the theoretical principles apply across all domains. According to Waltz, IPB includes providing an understanding of the "physical, political, electronic, cyber, and other dimensions of the battlespace."[31] Alan Campen reiterates the concept of IPB in *Cyberwar 3.0.*[32] Campen states that information warfare requires an accurate knowledge of the battlespace as well as real-time awareness of situations within the battlespace as they arise.

Before moving directly into how each collection type can add to a holistic picture of the battlespace, it is necessary to define what constitutes the battlespace in the cyber domain. The battlespace according to Waltz constitutes "all decision-relevant elements within a defined battlespace, and the ability to predict with very high confidence near-term enemy actions and outcomes."[33] More specifically this requires an understanding of capabilities in their human, material, and technical forms and the relationship of these capabilities within themselves and to other aspects of the operational environment. It is also important to understand the political implications of alterations in capabilities and the environment over time. A battlespace for cyber can be domestic or foreign. Intelligence must inform policy-makers on both.

Capabilities can be broadly defined as including mechanisms of offensive and defensive military strength such as size and number of offensive cyber units, and it can include doctrinal measures or indicators such as official cyber security and warfare doctrines. The capabilities can include the size and complexity of systems and their connections to other systems of importance. And it can include technical capabilities such as programming skill within the environment.

The capabilities matrix included here is overly simplified, yet it indicates a host of areas where the intelligence community can provide significant assistance to decision-makers. What is important to consider is that these capabilities are not limited to the United States or its allies. Capabilities need to be assessed on a nation-by-nation basis and likely on a sub-state basis as well. Together these and many other unmentioned cyber capabilities combine to provide an accurate picture of the battlespace.

Identifying the capabilities and political situation of a new battlespace is difficult under the best of circumstances. Cyber is immensely complicated and therefore necessitates a logical template within which to examine capabilities. There is a need for a differentiation between the domestic (defensive) and the foreign (offensive) battlespace. This distinction is important for both tasking and decision-making. By logically separating the two battlespaces they are able to inform one another. Table 5.2 highlights many of the primary areas for consideration within the two battlespaces necessary for DBA and DBK.[34]

The INTs from the previous section of this chapter can and should be focused on these and related areas within the cyber domain. A holistic picture of the above components of the domain will provide decision-makers with a clear visualization of the battlespace. Again, following Waltz, a visualization of any battlespace includes:[35]

1   Developing a clear understanding of the state with relation to the enemy and environment;
2   Envisioning a desired goal or objective representing the successful completion of the mission;
3   Visualization of the sequence of activities that move the current state to the desired state.

Edward Amoroso argues the intelligence community should focus on creating an addition to the conventional intelligence briefs that consists solely of information

Table 5.2 Components of cyber DBA and DBK

Domestic (Defense Oriented)	*Foreign (Offense Oriented)*
Policy considerations (offensive and defensive)	Policy considerations (offensive and defensive)
Domestic network mapping	Foreign network mapping
Budget allocations	Budget allocations
ICT collaboration (alliances, partnerships)	Offensive unit size and training
Defensive unit size and training	Defensive unit size and training
Critical infrastructure	Critical infrastructure
Insider threats for defensive purposes	Insider threats for offensive purposes
Threat spectrum capabilities	Historical record of attack and defense
Known vulnerabilities	Threat spectrum capabilities
Time to attack recognition	Known vulnerabilities
Time to attack attribution	ICT collaborations (alliances, partnerships)
Systemic dependencies	Time to attack recognition
Monitoring	Time to attack attribution
	Systemic dependencies
	Surveillance
	Reconnaissance

pertaining to cyber.[36] Amoroso indicates such a report should focus on current security posture, top and new security risks, automated metrics, and human interpretation. Amoroso's case for the creation of a cyber-specific intelligence brief is sound and works towards promoting an accurate and realistic understanding of the threats and opportunities within this new and evolving domain relevant to national security.

Policy considerations

The Joint Chiefs of Staff have placed an increasing emphasis on the cyber domain within various joint doctrine publications. Joint doctrines provide insight into the needs of both the services and policy-makers in the employment of and defense against cyber attacks. Documents also include many of the ways cyber has come to rely heavily on intelligence assets. Information superiority has become a mission-critical aspect of defending national security. The Joint Doctrine for Command and Control Warfare dating back to 1996 highlights the importance of intelligence products in support of C2W. The document indicates the use of intelligence assists in the conceptualization of all aspects of a battlespace.[37]

Comprehension of any battlespace, including the cyber domain, requires understanding the policy environment in which an action occurs. Is there a national cyber defense strategy within the targeted country? How have they publicly or privately declared they would respond to hostile actions within the cyber domain? An example of the policy environment can be found in the *Department of Defense Strategy for Operating in Cyberspace*. The strategy outlines five strategic initiatives in its declassified report:[38]

> **Strategic Initiative 1:** Treat cyberspace as an operational domain to organize, train, and equip so that DoD can take full advantage of cyberspace's potential.
>
> **Strategic Initiative 2:** Employ new defense operating concepts to protect DoD networks and systems.
>
> **Strategic Initiative 3:** Partner with other US government departments and agencies and the private sector to enable a whole-of-government cybersecurity strategy.
>
> **Strategic Initiative 4:** Build robust relationships with US allies and international partners to strengthen collective cybersecurity.
>
> **Strategic Initiative 5:** Leverage the nation's ingenuity through an exceptional cyber workforce and rapid technological innovation.

The classified sections of the report cited in the media indicate a doctrinal shift in the way the DoD approaches the cyber domain. Journalistic accounts indicate that the DoD considers that some instances of cyber attacks can constitute an act of war.[39] The understanding of the policy positions within the domestic battlespace and in the foreign battlespace will help to alleviate information asymmetries and establish clearly identifiable patterns for response. Whether it is the knowledge that Germany and the Netherlands both have official cybersecurity doctrines or that China has begun implementing a policy of making offensive cyber capabilities a strategic priority, the overt and covert collection of policy positions provides policy-makers with a foundation upon which to understand intelligence related to cyber.

Policy platforms also help to codify international law, to create zones of norms or an identifiable policy framework within which states will interact or respond to incidents emanating from cyberspace.[40] While both the United States and Russia have made known that a cyber attack could constitute an act of war, there has been little elaboration on the specific characteristics of such an attack. Often states will intentionally leave room for policy ambiguity as a mechanism of deterrence.[41] Understanding ambiguity, information gaps, and information asymmetry is crucial particularly in comprehending how leaders arrive at decisions. As such, just as in conventional warfare, in cyber conflict knowledge about what a potential adversary will do in a given situation provides a strategic edge.

CNE – network mapping, systemic dependencies, and historical records

Understanding the policy environment both domestically and among foreign adversaries is only part of the larger intelligence process. Computer network exploitation (CNE) constitutes a series of technological and analytical approaches to cyber-specific espionage. For the purposes of conventional intelligence collection CNE can include the penetration of foreign networks to secure information on weapons systems, policy positions, and much more. It is invasive, yet does not disrupt, deny, or destroy data, it collects. When CNE operations focus intelligence on the cyber domain for offensive and defensive purposes the objective is to understand the systems themselves. The goal becomes identifying the strengths and weaknesses of systems, the connectivity of systems to points of interest, and the interaction of those systems with strategic and tactical objectives.

There are numerous methods of CNE; for the purposes of simplicity only a few will be examined. Network mapping is a form of CNE that studies the physical connectivity of networks or the availability of insecure ports. This type of mapping provides information on what types of systems and servers operate on different networks and identifies the characteristics of the various component parts these systems constitute. Network mapping can drill down to very low levels on particular networks and provide significant information. This information can then be used to isolate portions of networks to pick at vulnerabilities.

Network mapping is also useful for illustrating the potential for any particular targeted attack to extend beyond its directed target and result in collateral damage or blowback. Conceptually network mapping is not dissimilar from attempting to map radar or surface-to-air missile locations prior to a bombing campaign. The intent of network mapping is to gain operational knowledge of an adversary's systems prior to engaging in hostile actions.

Forensic analysis of the Stuxnet worm which targeted the Iranian uranium enrichment program found that the worm partially employed network mapping to target its attacks, focusing on isolated networks using memory sticks as the initial method of transmission.[42] Once in, Stuxnet focused its attack on networks with programmable logic controllers (PLCs) of a specific type[43] and caused uranium enrichment centrifuges to malfunction.[44] The level of sophistication required to drill down to get to this level of detail to plan an attack is remarkable, particularly considering the complexity and number of overall systems and the air-gapped nature of the systems.

Network mapping is both an offensive and defensive intelligence endeavor. To adequately prepare both the defensive and offensive battlespaces, an accurate picture of systems is needed. Arguably the dual domestic–foreign pictures are complimentary and help to avoid violating part 2.13 of Executive Order 12333, which prevents any covert action from influencing US political processes, public opinion, policies, or media.[45]

Network mapping and monitoring is a double-edged sword. Legally, network mapping can be considered CNE and therefore domestic network mapping by US intelligence agencies without a warrant would be prohibited. However, network mapping is of critical importance to the maintenance of national security infrastructures. Thus far the intelligence community does not have a formal commitment from the White House or the Justice Department to engage in any domestic CNE operations.[46] Currently in the United States there is an uneasy and inefficient public–private commitment to providing information on network security across critical infrastructure. A thorough understanding of domestic and foreign networks assists in visualization for both offensive and defensive purposes and the effort to push reasoned analysis of threats has begun to make its way into Congress.[47]

Network mapping assists in the identification of network components. Once network components are known it becomes necessary to explore vulnerabilities within systems. Most damaging are zero-day vulnerabilities. Zero-day vulnerabilities are vulnerabilities in computer applications of which even system administrators are unaware. The Stuxnet attack exposed several zero-day vulnerabilities in the Windows software controlling/monitoring the programmable logic controllers, causing the attached centrifuges to spin outside of their safe operational standards.

Systemic vulnerabilities necessitate a thorough understanding of the historical record of different types of attacks and exploits. The identification of zero-day vulnerabilities should lead network administrators to immediately patch these gaps. Intelligence plays a role in identifying what types of attacks have been used in the past and what vulnerabilities these attacks attempted to exploit. Historical accounting is important for both offensive and defensive preparation of the battlespace. For obvious reasons it is important to prevent repeat attacks on domestic systems, while at the same time it is important not to engage in repeat attack methods once a vulnerability on an opposing system has been fixed. Such an attack would likely be ineffective and lead to anonymity-attribution problems.

The historical accounting of attack types by countries and sub-state actors also alerts operators within the intelligence community to the threat spectrum capabilities of a particular cyber adversary. Understanding the threat spectrum capabilities of states facilitates an accurate conceptualization of their power to operate within the domain. Table 5.3 is a representation of known threat spectrum capabilities.

The above areas of consideration within CNE are only a small sampling of the overall tasking priorities for intelligence using CNE methods. They hint at a broad applicability for CYBERINT methods in the preparation of the battlespace.

Conventional intelligence

Intelligence collected on budgetary allocations, offensive and defensive cyber unit sizes, and training methodologies provides the clearest parallel to conventional intelligence. As in conventional intelligence, most countries are frequently unwilling to release data on absolute military expenditures or the sizes and structures of forces within their military. Military capabilities are a closely guarded secret in many countries. Capabilities are particularly secretive in the cyber domain. Often, if cyber capabilities are exposed they cease to be capabilities.

An example of a diminished capability comes from Stuxnet. Once Stuxnet was discovered by the Iranians defensive measures were taken to "plug" the holes the Stuxnet attack employed. This dramatically reduces the effect a repeat Stuxnet attack would have on any other nation. Whereas missiles can be launched with repeated success because the ability to defend against a moving projectile is difficult, a similar cyber weapon is more easily defended against once it has been identified. Anti-virus software can be reprogrammed to identify and isolate repeat threats, and zero-day vulnerabilities can be patched.

An excellent example of an open-source analysis of cyber capabilities comes from Stokes et al.[48] They examine in explicit detail the construction, location, leadership, and mission of many aspects of the Chinese People's Liberation Army information warfare programs. Their report is an example of a high-value detailed analysis that could be supplemented by conventional intelligence to enhance policy-maker and combatant commander comprehension of the battlespace.

The implications for conventional intelligence collection methods indicate that intelligence on cyber does not necessarily need to remain cyber-bound or exclusively within the realm of CNE. Many metrics such as force size matter in

Table 5.3 Cyber threat spectrum

Levels (types) of attack	Description	Feasibility	Complexity
		High	Low
		↑	↑
Propaganda	The propagation of information via the internet to affect public, private or governmental opinion. This can be combined with web vandalism.		
Web Vandalism	The defacement of websites either official or private for non-political or political purposes.		
Denial of Service Attack (DOS)	The denial of service to a user or users of a computer, server, website, network, or system.		
Distributed Denial of Service Attack (DDOS)	The denial of service to a user or users of a computer, server, website, network, or system – this type of attack is similar to a DOS attack but is distributed across a botnet or other computer systems remotely activated.		
Computer Network Exploitation	The secret collection and reproduction of digital data from computers or networks.		
Equipment Disruption	The disruption or interception of communications or information flow from systems.		
Critical Infrastructure	The targeted disruption of systems designed to provide for or maintain critical infrastructures of vital importance – systems include power, water, fuel, communications, commercial, and transportation.		
		↓	↓
Compromised Hardware Systems	The implantation of malware designed to affect systems in the production phase of a product.	Low	High

NB: This is not an all-inclusive threat spectrum.

cyber and can be examined to create a better assessment of potential adversaries. Cyber force size is particularly important from a malware development perspective. Complex coding scripts typically take large numbers of programmers to develop and test. It is possible for an individual to accomplish highly complex attacks, but less likely than a large cyber warfare unit working with the same objective.

Likewise, knowing where a unit is located or how they were trained can help planners determine the best response to a particular attack, or how best to manipulate their organizational structure. Derek Clark and Kai Konrad refer to this as identifying the weakest link.[49] The identification of the weakest link is particularly important in cyber defense and offense. There are multiple fronts (systems) needing defense. All it takes is one "best shot" to achieve significant damage. While this weakest link can be identified through CNE operations outlined in the previous section, it can also be identified within the training, command, and organizational structure of units charged with conducting or protecting against cyber attacks.

Closely related to the conventional military metrics above, yet likely unique to the cyber domain, are public–private ICT collaborations. Although most countries have programs for military public and private collaborations with universities and businesses for research and development, within the cyber domain the importance of this relationship is magnified for multiple reasons. First, much of the training and education necessary to conduct offensive or defensive CNO within cyberspace is, or can be, learned at public institutions, or can be crafted for private sector use. This extends far beyond the development of technology to the actual training of the warfighter, the development of the platforms upon which the domain rests, and more. Second, these collaborations spread out, but do not diffuse potential vulnerabilities.

Collaborations can serve as a foundation for educating cyber warriors within offensive and defensive units and through mutual development can train, equip and prepare states for CNO in ways far different from conventional military means. Most countries have a balance between civilian and military protection of their national cyber infrastructures based largely on the development of Computer Emergency Response Teams (CERTs). An intelligence assessment of the strength and quality of ICT collaborations is of critical importance in understanding the cyber battlespace.

Such ICT collaborations are not necessarily official and do not need to be highly structured and regimented. Alexander Klimburg provides evidence that Russia and China have created groups of plausibly deniable cyber attackers.[50] Creating an accurate open-source measure of unofficial collaborations is difficult. An intelligence focus on unofficial collaborations with entities can contextualize cyber incidents such as the 2007 cyber attacks against Estonia.[51] The 2007 attacks were directed at Estonian governmental, bank, and communications websites.[52] The attacks were motivated by a decision to move a Russian war memorial from central Tallinn. While initial reports indicated Russia was the culprit, Russia denied any participation in the cyber attacks.[53] The reality is somewhat murkier and more akin to an unofficial sanction or condoning of cyber attacks by the Russian government.[54]

The collection and production of intelligence on more conventional attributes of pertinence to the cyber domain are a role the intelligence community is likely already engaged in. Occasionally reports on issues relating to this category of intelligence are published for public consumption. A recent report of this type was produced for the US–China Economic and Security Review Commission to examine China's capability to conduct cyber warfare and computer network exploitation.[55] Knowledge of capabilities is still applicable to the cyber domain and is greatly influenced by conventional intelligence collection methods and subsequent analysis, which contextualizes the meaning of raw intelligence.

HUMINT and cyber

Human intelligence (HUMINT) stands out in cyber for two particular reasons. First, HUMINT agents can provide accurate internal information on systems and access to those systems unavailable through CNE and other intelligence collection methods. Second, human assets can serve as a bridge between the external world and air-gapped or other forms of secure networks. As was indicated above, it is likely that the Stuxnet virus was distributed using a thumb drive, which needed to be inserted into a machine within an air-gapped network. Thus HUMINT agents can serve as a vulnerability most network administrators will be unable to provide significant protection against.

The role of a HUMINT asset with access to information on networks can be extremely damaging. Even if the agent is on a lightly classified network, the repercussions of his or her actions can be enormous. The WikiLeaks scandal caused by Bradley Manning leaking more than 260,000 diplomatic cables is illustrative of the problem posed by internal threats.[56] Threats using HUMINT need to be developed and enhanced for offensive intelligence and protected against for domestic national security counterintelligence. Gaining access to the technical schematics, documents, information, login procedures, or any of a multitude of other targets of intelligence, a HUMINT asset provides a critical tool added directly by intelligence to further the understanding of the cyber domain.

Beyond the collection of intelligence from HUMINT sources, these insiders can assist in the implementation of cyber actions. A 2005 report by the United States Secret Service in cooperation with Carnegie Mellon indicated that up to 29 percent of all attacks against a surveyed group of critical infrastructure stakeholders were initiated by insiders.[57] The majority of motivations behind these attacks were not intelligence or covert action related. This, however, does not preclude the possibility of using insiders to affect or gain information/access on adversary systems. The recruitment and maintenance of insider threats by the intelligence community should be a top priority. These agents can offer a mission-critical component, often during times when more lengthy intelligence collection processes are constrained by events.

Time to attack recognition, completion, and attribution

Attack recognition and attribution are also critical for both defensive and offensive battlespace planning. All of the intelligence collection methods and the focus of the Intel process of trying to comprehend the cyber domain culminate in understanding, from a mission-critical orientation, the progression of cyber attacks. Figure 5.1 is a simplified model for understanding attack planning and progression within a battlespace modeled loosely on the JP 3-51 electronic warfare-planning model.[58] This model is informed by intelligence collection. Line one of the figure indicates a policy-maker's perspective on the process of engaging in conflict. A conflict initiation is (0) planned, (1) implemented, and (2) completed. Policy-makers want to know what resources any given action will take and how long it will take to complete it. In cyber a more accurate timeline for action in cyberspace requires (0) intelligence collection, (1) operational planning of the attack with an informed knowledge of the battlespace, (2) understanding of the time it takes for the attack to be completed, (3) how long until the attack is recognized as an attack by the adversary, (4) how long until that adversary can do something about the attack, and (5) how long until the adversary assigns attribution for the attack. The ordering of the items listed above greatly affects the ability for an attack to be conducted successfully.

Intelligence informs the policy-maker and commander as to the feasibility of a particular type of attack and the probability of success. If recognition of an attack occurs early in the timeline of events the probability of success is diminished.

The timeline can be tested in much the same way conventional weapons are tested. It would be absurd to send a bomber over a potential target with a completely untested bomb, or to send a soldier into battle with an untested model of rifle. Just as weapons are tested in the physical world they need to be tested in the cyber domain as well. This testing provides added information to both the policy-maker and the combatant commander as to the effectiveness of the weapon and the timeline of events above. If a cyber weapon is slow and easily detectable, its probability for success is diminished. This lowered probability for success does not nullify its use but it does condition it.

One aspect of this phase of IPB is that it is extremely beneficial to both the offensive and defensive strategic and tactical operations. By planning and testing potential attacks against theoretical adversarial systems, the intelligence community provides an out-of-the-box perspective necessary to prevent similar

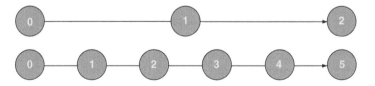

Figure 5.1 Timeline for attack implementation.

attacks against domestic targets. This logic would indicate that an attempt to use a worm like Stuxnet against the US infrastructure would run into greater problems than if the weapon had been developed first elsewhere.

IPB and its impact on cyber

The role of intelligence in cyber is not dissimilar from its role in the conventional domains. There are new areas in which collection and analysis need to occur, yet its overall objective remains the same. Returning to Waltz's concept of information preparation of the battlefield, Figure 5.2 illustrates intelligence's influence on operations originating within the cyber domain. The role of intelligence in cyber is to accurately facilitate an understanding of and the possible tools by which to influence those entities. The cyber domain is surrounded with hype and hysteria. Many of the claims are accurately based in reality. But the known unknowns are still enormous within this evolving domain and it is incumbent on intelligence to provide an accurate assessment of the current state of affairs.

All-source intelligence for cyber requires the intelligence community to think beyond domestic system defense. The focus should be balanced between foreign and domestic intelligence, thereby mutually informing one another and creating

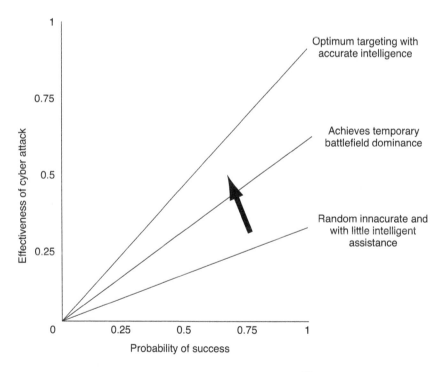

Figure 5.2 The influence of intelligence on cyber operations.[59]

a systemic defense for national assets in addition to providing decision-makers with a more accurate picture of how a potential cyber attack might succeed or fail.

Cyber as covert action

To further define the role of intelligence in cyber, it is necessary to look more deeply into the laws codifying the conduct of the intelligence community. All of the above sections provide a framework for defining the role of intelligence with regards to IPB. Cyber conflict is, by its very nature, covert. Even if the attack is discovered it is often unattributable. Attacks can be designed to go unnoticed and affect changes to systems and their components for days, weeks, or months without detection. Even in instances where groups such as Anonymous publically take credit for attacks, responsibility is typically claimed post hoc. Nearly all examples of state-on-state cyber attacks have been covert.

The covert nature of cyber brings this chapter full circle to Warner's definition of intelligence as attempting to influence. Covert action is a secret operation to influence a foreign entity. At least in theory, most, if not all, cyber attacks begin covertly. Section 1.7(a)(4) of Executive Order 12333 regarding intelligence community elements and covert action states that the Central Intelligence Agency (CIA) shall:

> Conduct convert action activities approved by the President. No agency except the Central Intelligence Agency (or the Armed Forces of the United States in time of war declared by the Congress or during any period covered by a report from the President to the Congress consistent with the War Powers Resolution, Public Law 93-148) may conduct any covert action activity unless the President determines that another agency is more likely to achieve a particular objective.[60]

It is already evident in the structuring of the governmental response to cyber covert action that the Department of Defense has taken the lead, with General Keith Alexander as the head of both the National Security Agency (NSA) and Cyber Command. This indicates that the President has established an agency other than the CIA as the primary covert operator within this domain. While the logic behind having a military intelligence organization commander and an organizational structure that falls under STRATCOM runs counter to EO 12333, the institutional capacity of the DoD in the technical domain and the scale of the problem being faced within this new domain make the assignment appropriate.

Conclusion: summarizing the role of intelligence within the cyber domain

In defining the role of intelligence within the cyber domain it is necessary to take a holistic approach. From a collection perspective, the intelligence community should work and has been working in coordination with a hybrid push-and-pull intelligence cycle to both elevate the importance of this domain and to facilitate collection within it. The emphasis has been heavily defensive up to this point and largely focused on countering threats rather than anticipating them. This needs to change. The only way it can change is if the intelligence community begins to actively turn its sights on adversaries and develop more rigorous all-source intelligence combining novel CYBERINT technologies with augmented reporting on this domain. Parroting Amoroso's assertion, cyber should be included on the daily intelligence briefs of policy-makers. The inclusion would likely start the process of demystification of this immensely complicated domain.

Cyber is a domain that can be used to fulfill all aspects of Warner's definition of intelligence to some degree. It is a domain in which it is possible to gain understanding about other states beyond and within the domain itself, but it is also a domain that can serve to influence other states' policy decisions as well as perceptions. In particular, accurate intelligence on both sides of the domestic–foreign divide can mutually inform decision-makers about vulnerabilities and the eventual decision to use cyber as an offensive weapon or how best to defend against attacks. Furthermore, intelligence can reign in the debate on cyber to a more realistic area of operations predicated on sound estimates rather than on grandiose speculation.

The intelligence community itself is and rightly should be the point of origin for hostile actions emanating from the domain and will likely serve as a force multiplier in instances where a combined conventional cyber attack is necessary. To engage in cyber conflict, just as in conventional conflict, intelligence is needed to prepare the battlespace and facilitate an accurate assessment of the probability for success and utility for any type of operation. This preparation hones the weapons, decisions, and effect of a potential attack. More importantly for national security, a thorough and accurate preparation of both the foreign and domestic battlespaces will serve to inform one another and enhance cyber security.

Notes

1 Sun Tzu, *The Art of War* (Berkeley, CA: Ulysses Press, 2007).
2 *Joint Vision 2020* (Washington, DC: US Government Printing Office, 2000).
3 Ibid.
4 William A. Owens, Kenneth W. Dam and Herbert Lin, *Technology, Policy, Law, and Ethics Regarding U.S. Acquisition and Use of Cyberattack Capabilities* (Washington, DC: National Academies Press, 2009).
5 Loch K. Johnson, "Sketches for a Theory of Strategic Intelligence," in Peter Gill, Stephen Marrin, and Mark Phythian (eds.), *Intelligence Theory: Key Questions and Debates* (London; New York: Routledge, 2009), pp. 33–53.
6 Michael Warner, "Wanted: A Definition of 'Intelligence'," *Studies in Intelligence* Vol. 46 No. 3, 2002, https://www.cia.gov/library/center-for-the-study-of-intelligence/csi-publications/csi-studies/studies/vol46no3/article02.html, last accessed November 25, 2012.

7 Keith B. Alexander, "Building a New Command in Cyberspace," *Strategic Studies Quarterly* Vol. 5 No. 2, 2011, pp. 3–12; CSIS Commission on Cybersecurity for the 44th Presidency, *Securing Cyberspace for the 44th Presidency* (Washington, DC: CSIS, Dec. 2008); Wesley K. Clark and Peter L. Levin, "Securing the Information Highway," *Foreign Affairs* Vol. 88 No. 6, 2009, pp. 2–10; Daniel E. Geer, Jr. "Cyber-security and National Policy," *Harvard National Security Journal* Vol. 1, 2010, pp. 203–15.

8 Alexander, "Building a New Command in Cyberspace."

9 Martin C. Libicki and Project Air Force (U.S.), *Cyberdeterrence and Cyberwar* (Santa Monica, CA: RAND, 2009).

10   Nick Cullather, "Bombing at the Speed of Thought: Intelligence in the Coming Age of Cyberwar," *Intelligence and National Security* Vol. 18 No. 4, 2006, pp. 141–54.

11 Michael Herman, "Counter-Terrorism, Information Technology and Intelligence Change," *Intelligence and National Security* Vol. 18 No. 4, 2003, pp. 40–58.

12 Ibid.

13 Edward G. Amoroso, *Cyber Attacks: Protecting National Infrastructure* (Oxford: Butterworth-Heinemann, 2010).

14 Joel Brenner, *America the Vulnerable: Inside the New Threat Matrix of Digital Espionage, Crime, and Warfare* (New York: Penguin Press, 2011).

15 Williams *et al.*, "Intelligence Analysis for Internet Security."

16 *National Strategy to Secure Cyberspace* (Washington, DC: United States Department of Homeland Security, 2003).

17 *International Strategy for Cyberspace: Prosperity, Security, and Openness in a Networked World* (Washington, DC: White House, 2011), www.whitehouse.gov/sites/default/files/rss_viewer/international_strategy_for_cyberspace.pdf, last accessed November 25, 2012.

18 *Foreign Spies Stealing U.S. Economic Secrets in Cyberspace: Report to Congress on Foreign Economic Collection and Industrial Espionage, 2009–2011* (Washington, DC: Office of the Director of National Intelligence, 2011).

19 Secretary of Defense Donald H. Rumsfeld, "DoD News Briefing – Secretary Rumsfeld and Gen. Myers," 2002, www.defense.gov/transcripts/transcript.aspx?transcriptid=2636, last accessed November 25, 2012.

20 An air gap is a security measure often taken for computers and computer networks that must be extraordinarily secure, ensuring that a network is physically, electrically, and electromagnetically isolated from insecure networks, such as the public Internet or an insecure local area network. This often includes creating a network with electric supplies independent from public utilities.

21 Williams *et al.*, "Intelligence Analysis for Internet Security."

22 Edward Waltz, *Information Warfare: Principles and Operations* (Boston, MA: Artech House, 1998).

23 Stephen Marrin, "Intelligence Analysis and Decision-Making: Methodological Challenges," in Gill, Marrin, and Phythian (eds.), *Intelligence Theory*, pp. 131–50.

24 Paul R. Pillar, *Intelligence and U.S. Foreign Policy: Iraq, 9/11, and Misguided Reform* (New York: Columbia University Press, 2011).

25 Richard A. Clarke and Robert K. Knake, *Cyber War: The Next Threat to National Security and What to do About It* (1st edn., New York: Ecco, 2010).

26 See Chapter 2: "Cyberwar is Coming," in John Arquilla and David Ronfeldt, *In Athena's Camp: Preparing for Conflict in the Information Age* (Santa Monica, CA: Rand Coporation, 1997).

27 Thomas Rid, "Cyber War Will Not Take Place," *Journal of Strategic Studies* Vol. 35 No. 1, 2012, pp. 5–32.

28 See Marrin, "Intelligence Analysis and Decision-Making."

29 Ibid.

30 Waltz, *Information Warfare.*

31 Ibid.
32 Alan D. Campen and Douglas H. Dearth, *Cyberwar 3.0: Human Factors in Information Operations and Future Conflict* (Fairfax, VA: AFCEA International Press, 2000).
33 Waltz, *Information Warfare*.
34 Dominant Battlespace Awareness (DBA) and Dominant Battlespace Knowledge (DBK).
35 Waltz, *Information Warfare*.
36 Amoroso, *Cyber Attacks*.
37 Joint Chiefs of Staff, *Joint Doctrine for Command and Control Warfare (C2W)* (Washington, DC: Department of Defense, 1996).
38 Department of Defense, *Department of Defense Strategy for Operating in Cyberspace* (Washington, DC: Department of Defense, 2011).
39 Siobhan Gorman and Julian E. Barnes, "Cyber Combat: Act of War," *Wall Street Journal*, May 11, 2011, http://online.wsj.com/article/SB10001424052702304563104576355623135782718.html, last accessed November 25, 2012.
40 Susan W. Brenner, "'At Light Speed': Attribution and Response to Cybercrime/Terrorism/Warfare," *The Journal of Criminal Law and Criminology* Vol. 97 No. 2, 2007, pp. 379–475.
41 Brian M Mazanec, "The Art of (Cyber) War," *The Journal of International Security Affairs* 16, Spring 2009, www.securityaffairs.org/issues/2009/16/mazanec.php, last accessed November 25, 2012.
42 Nicolas Falliere, Liam O. Murchu and Eric Chien, *W32.Stuxnet Dossier* (Symantec Security Response, 2011), www.symantec.com/content/en/us/enterprise/media/security_response/whitepapers/w32_stuxnet_dossier.pdf, last accessed November 25, 2012.
43 The PLCs affected were Siemens S7-315 and S7-417.
44 Paulo Shakarian, "Stuxnet: Cyberwar Revolution in Military Affairs," *Small Wars Journal*, 2011, http://smallwarsjournal.com/blog/journal/docs-temp/734-shakarian3.pdf, last accessed November 25, 2012.
45 United States Intelligence Activities, "Executive Order 12333," December 4, 1981, https://www.cia.gov/about-cia/eo12333.html, last accessed November 27, 2012.
46 Ellen Nakashima, "White House, NSA weigh cybersecurity, personal privacy," *Washington Post*, February 27, 2012.
47 Ibid.
48 Mark A. Stokes, Jenny Lin and L. C. Russell Hsiao, *The Chinese People's Liberation Army Signals Intelligence and Cyber Reconnaissance Infrastructure* (Arlington, VA: Project 2049 Institute, 2011).
49 Derek J. Clark and Kai A. Konrad, "Asymmetric Conflict: Weakest Link against Best Shot," *The Journal of Conflict Resolution* Vol. 51 No. 3, 2007, pp. 457–69.
50 Alexander Klimburg, "Mobilising Cyber Power," *Survival* Vol. 53 No. 1, 2011, pp. 41–60.
51 Mark Landler and John Markoff, "Digital fears emerge after data siege in Estonia," *New York Times*, May 29, 2007.
52 "Europe: A Cyber-Riot; Estonia and Russia," *The Economist*, May 12, 2007.
53 Ian Traynor, "Russia accused of unleashing cyberwar to disable Estonia," *The Guardian*, May 17, 2007, www.guardian.co.uk/world/2007/may/17/topstories3.russia, last accessed November 25, 2012.
54 Klimburg, "Mobilising Cyber Power."
55 Bryan Krekel, *Capability of the People's Republic of China to Conduct Cyber Warfare and Computer Network Exploitation* (Mclean, VA: Northrop Grumman Cooporation 2009), www.uscc.gov/researchpapers/2009/NorthropGrumman_PRC_Cyber_Paper_FINAL_Approved%20Report_16Oct2009.pdf, last accessed November 25, 2012.
56 Brenner, *America the Vulnerable*.

57 Michelle Keeney Eileen Kowalski, Dawn Cappelli, Andrew Moore, Timothy Shumeall and Stephanie Rogers, *Insider Threat Study: Computer System Sabotage in Critical Infrastructure Sectors* (Washington, DC: United States Secret Service and Carnegie Mellon Software Engineering Institute, 2005), www.secretservice.gov/ntac/its_report_050516_es.pdf, last accessed November 25, 2012.
58 Department of Defense, *Joint Doctrine for Electronic Warfare Joint Publication 3-51* (Washington, DC: 2000).
59 Modified from Waltz, *Information Warfare*.
60 United States Intelligence Activities, "Executive Order 12333," Section 1.7(a)(4).

6 To go beyond the cycle of intelligence-led policing

James Sheptycki[1]

Introduction

There is a case to be made for moving beyond the Intelligence Cycle in the policing sector and it lies in a critical appraisal of the contemporary practices of intelligence-led policing. This chapter provides a critique of the Intelligence Cycle under several headings: management mythology, the rhetoric of realism, the data delusion, the panoptic promise, covert policing and antitrust, and war fever. Practical considerations about what lies beyond the Intelligence Cycle in policing rest upon the foundations of a sure understanding of present practice.

The context

In 2011 the UK Home Office impressively announced that it was launching a new National Crime Agency.[2] According to the document setting out the priorities of the new agency:

> Cutting crime is the sole objective that the Government has set for the police. Serious and organised crime is a national threat. It requires a multi-agency response. The current response remains patchy, with serious and organised criminality causing harm to communities up and down the country and beyond, every day of every year. It is time for a fresh start.[3]

The new agency was to be a "powerful body of operational crime fighters" which would "set the national operational agenda for fighting serious and complex crime and organised criminality."[4] It would "have strong two-way links with local police forces and other law enforcement agencies" and would be "home to a significant multi-agency intelligence capability."[5] With its presumed control over the Intelligence Cycle it would also "have the authority to undertake tasking and coordination of the police ... to ensure networks of organised criminals are disrupted and prevented from operating."[6] Home Secretary Theresa May welcomed the establishment of the new agency as "a landmark moment in British law enforcement."[7]

Media commentators looked on skeptically. Simon Jenkins noted that:

> Government attempts to nationalize crime-busting began back in 1992 with the National Criminal Intelligence Service. In 1998 Blair inflated this into a National Crime Squad, with its own image-boosting BBC series *NCS Manhunt*. When this came to nothing, Charles Clarke remamed it the Serious Organised Crime Agency which was launched in 2006 with an identical remit – "to combat organised crime, Class A drugs, illegal arms dealing, human trafficking, computer and high-tech crimes, money laundering, extortion, kidnapping and murder". Macho title, macho minister.[8]

While Jenkins could, perhaps, be forgiven for getting some of the details wrong, he was correct in one important respect. There could be no doubt that the policing sector was in the midst of a prolonged and intense cycle of institutional restructuring that went back to the period just after the end of the Cold War and included both of the major intelligence agencies – MI6 (the Secret Intelligence Service, in charge of foreign intelligence operations) and MI5 (the Security Service, responsible for domestic intelligence). The policing sector in the UK was stuck in an interminable transformation cycle and the evidence suggested that this was part of an international trend.[9]

Here is how I looked at the UK situation when I was writing in 2007:

> In mid-2003, UK Prime Minister Tony Blair began to hint strongly that the structure of policing in the United Kingdom was due for a radical change. Amidst headlines foretelling of a "British FBI", Blair stated: "some have argued that the time has come to bring together some or all of the national law enforcement agencies ... and create a dedicated national agency". A "historic overhaul" of Britain's policing architecture was announced in early 2004 confirming government plans to create an FBI-style national force. More or less casual consumers of police current affairs might have thought that the gestation period for the new Serious and Organised Crime Agency was a mere seven months. But the merger of four pre-existing agencies (the National Criminal Intelligence Service [NCIS], the National Crime Squad [NCS], the investigative unit of Her Majesty's Customs and Excise [HMCE] and similar units from Her Majesty's Immigration Service [HMIS] was part of a much longer trend going back to at least the early 1990s. Nor was this organizational trend limited to the UK policing sector. Many countries, especially those centrally situated in the global system, exhibited similar tendencies to reconfigure their national policing apparatuses, and in every instance the explanation was the same. Police systems needed to be restructured so as to be more responsive to serious and organized crime, especially its transnational variants.[10]

Other scholars also noted the transformations in the architecture of police and law enforcement systems in a variety of jurisdictions, along with the rise of the intelligence-led policing paradigm.[11] Internationally, intelligence-led policing has been at the forefront of thinking within this rapidly transforming landscape of crime control institutions.

Police and law enforcement agencies have been undergoing more or less continuous restructuring and this has been carried out on the basis that proper organization is necessary in order to get the theory of policing with intelligence functioning properly. When the UK created NCIS in the early 1990s, it built upon the promise that better orchestration of the Intelligence Cycle would be decisive in the pursuit of organized and serious crime. When SOCA (Serious and Organised Crime Agency) was created scarcely a decade later, it was again premised on the need to get the functional logic of the Intelligence Cycle working properly. When the new NCA (National Crime Agency) was announced, it came with the expressed expectation of the need to get the Intelligence Cycle properly tasking and coordinating operational policing.

I have long been skeptical about this program of reform and restructuring. This is partly because I believe that policing has been erroneously and endlessly re-organized around notions of national security, when it would be more apt to think about policing in terms of human security.[12] The attempt to centralize policing intelligence systems at the national level has, I argue, distorted the delivery of policing services so they are not fit for the purpose of securing people's well-being in the communities in which they live and work. However, as I aim to make clear in the sections that follow, it is not just a preference of nomenclature – "human" over "national" security – important though that is. The way it is practiced, the cycle of intelligence-led policing is bound to fail on its own terms.

Currently the most cited article in the journal *Intelligence and National Security* is one which is very critical of the Intelligence Cycle paradigm, calling it a "highly flawed model" which, "nevertheless continues to be taught in the US and around the world."[13] For the article's author, Hulnick, the Intelligence Cycle model is wrong-headed partly because policy-makers do not make choices based on intelligence analysis. Rather they want intelligence analysis to justify their policy choices – a case of the cart before the horse. There are other problems to do with intelligence collection and analysis – it is imperfectly collected and analysis is usually rudimentary or incomplete. There are problems with intelligence dissemination – agents working "on the ground" complain equally about being inundated with information or not being given information in a timely manner. Lastly, the purveyors of the Intelligence Cycle model have not been very good at understanding the role, often confounding, of covert intelligence and secrecy in intelligence practice.

In this chapter I do not want to join the legion of commentators and experts propounding new models for "policing with intelligence." I agree that intelligence-led policing is better than its opposite. What I want to do instead is explore the institutional basics of the intelligence-led policing paradigm and shortcomings of Intelligence Cycle thinking. I am intrigued as to the reasons why, in spite of the evidence, policy-makers and practitioners in the policing sector have continued to make the same mistakes for two decades or more. Following the theme of this collection, in order for the police sector to move beyond the Intelligence Cycle, it is necessary to accept some very critical observations about what is involved in intelligence-led policing.

Management mythology

Back in the late 1990s I was engaged by the UK Home Office to do some research on intelligence-led policing and the, then new, National Intelligence Model.[14] Looking back over my field notes from that time I am struck by some of my descriptions of the NCIS HQ located in Spring Gardens, Vauxhall on the south bank of the River Thames. By that time the organization was more than five years old and so the degree of flux and chaos in the building itself was striking. Stacked high in the corridors were unpacked boxes of computer monitors waiting to be installed in offices, months-old yet out-of-date office organization charts were pinned haphazardly to staff bulletin boards and everywhere there was a sense of movement and change. Reportedly the annual staff turnover rate was upwards of 30 percent, but then it was supposedly a place for high-flyers. Perhaps that was why it had so many senior-ranking officers. The perceived need to meet the prestige requirements for international work meant there simply had to be a lot of senior positions, but they did not seem to stay in one post for long prior to redeployment. This staff flow-through was, reportedly, to facilitate better management through the infusion of new ideas and attitudes. The main thing was to produce good numbers for the key performance objectives and that was something the organization was good at. Outputs, outcomes, efficiency and effectiveness criteria – in spite of the evident organizational chaos, the numbers looked good.

My observations merely mirrored more official ones. According to Her Majesty's Inspectorate of Constabulary: "For an organisation of just over 500 personnel, the results represented a considerable return on investment, especially as the criminality involved was at the top end of the scale."[15] Those results were presented in the typical and time-honored fashion of police success. Thus

- Between 1 April and 31 December 1996 … 147 arrests had resulted from joint operations, with drugs seized worth over £49 million (street value) and property worth over £2.25 million had been recovered. Over £80,000 had been paid in rewards, resulting in 145 arrests and the recovery of property and drugs valued at over £12 million.[16]
- Between 1 April and 31 December 1996, 12,252 disclosures were received from financial institutions, with 11,212 disseminated and 7,362 replies received. Of these, 1,422 were under active investigation and 43 arrests had already resulted. The Drugs Unit had received 171 disclosures from chemical companies, all passed out to investigative agencies, with four significant arrests and ten illicit laboratories uncovered. The Football Unit received 4,260 intelligence reports and sent out 3,241 and the work of the Paedophile

Unit had contributed to 31 arrests in this period, targeting the activities of paedophiles within the UK and abroad.[17]

• Between 1 April and 31 December 1996, the International Intelligence Branch received 9,376 intelligence reports and disseminated 9,695. Its operations contributed to 551 arrests and the recovery of controlled drugs with a street value in excess of £698 million.[18]

These numbers may look impressive, but what do they mean? Klaus von Lampe notes that the "dark figure of crime"

> could be especially high for organized-crime related offenses given the absence of direct victims in most illegal markets and a potentially lower propensity to report offenses out of fear of retaliation. In turn, the greater the reliance on the active detection of crimes, the more susceptible the statistics become to differential priority setting and bias in tactical and strategic police work.[19]

Petrus van Dunye and Maarten van Dijck argue that assessing organized crime is an "impossible art," likening the UK Threat Assessment to an expressionist painting "approaching the gloomy colours of Munch's painting 'The Scream'."[20] Elsewhere, van Duyne compared the measurement of organized crime to "counting clouds": "the imprecise application of imprecise definition leads already to uninterpretable statistical outcomes."[21] With all this fuzziness regarding counting the actual "amount of organized crime," any statistics that purport to show effectiveness in terms of "arrests" and other types of "clear-up statistic" are bound to miss the mark. As has long been recognized, these kinds of statistics are open to manipulation by personnel anxious to provide evidence of their effectiveness and any claims made about "statistical results" are a function of organizational and personal self-interest rather than an objective measure of performance.[22]

Flash forward to more recent times. In 2006 NCIS was replaced by a bigger, better successor agency, SOCA, which I predicted would perform not much differently than its predecessor.[23] I was wrong: it was worse. A public storm soon engulfed the new agency. Rancorous media coverage described the agency as "cautious and bureaucratic, overburdened with managers and inexperienced at the sharp end."[24] Critics, including internal ones, described SOCA as "ineffective" and interested in "sexy" work rather than the "real nuts and bolts" of organized crime intelligence. *The Times* reported that it had abandoned the hunt for "organised crime lords" because it lacked operationally experienced staff. One hundred and forty eight former police officers – many of whom were cherry-picked to join the unit – retired or returned to policing within two years of moving to SOCA, complaining of a lack of enforcement activity.[25] After being "open for business" for only a few years the new agency had its budget slashed amidst criticism that it was plagued by a top-heavy management structure and engaged in "building a never-ending intelligence picture."[26] As one SOCA insider reported:

> Since SOCA started, I haven't taken on any new investigations and haven't been asked to develop any intelligence to move into an investigation. I am just purely performing email, admin tasks ... It is bureaucratic. Its management is top-centred ... In my section of the organisation, morale is probably the lowest I have ever known it, and it is low because people are under-utilised.[27]

Police organizations are in the grip of a management mantra that emphasizes counting results and the production of management information over actual functioning. This is not only true for British police institutions; it is an international phenomenon.[28] Internationally, the policing literature is replete with titles extolling the virtues of "management by objectives," "managing police effectiveness," "police management and practice," "policing performance culture" and the like. Observing all of this literature, Barry Loveday was moved to remark that:

> The evidence to date suggests that the application of a "performance culture" to policing may have unintended but serious consequences which both undermine quality of service and question its effectiveness. The use of management "techniques" more usually associated with the sale of double glazing, endowment mortgages or mobile telephones does not appear to have a great deal to offer what remains a vital and still highly valued public service.[29]

The managerialism that has swept through public policing, including the policing of organized crime and other "security threats," is reminiscent of the management fads that emanated from business schools in the early 1980s, which is not surprising because that is where and when the ideas first migrated into policing.[30] The central intellectual justification of managerialism concerns the application of the "principles of management information" to organizations with the aim of producing economic efficiency (i.e. maximum output with minimum input). Managerialism rests on the belief that institutions have more similarities than differences and that the performance of any organization can be optimized by the application of generic management techniques. The expectation is that there is little difference in the skills required to manage a research university, a national rail system, an advertising agency or a police service. The mistake is that there are huge differences, not least in the motivations of the people who work in these disparate spheres. The result of this assumption is that everything gets reduced to the common denominator: management by the numbers.

The effect of managerialism in the policing sector is, in effect, twofold. First, these organizations have come increasingly to be managed by high-flyers with generic management skills. The movers of the cycle of transformational change, these management innovators are overly attentive to key performance indicators at the expense of more practical matters. The (perhaps unintended) consequences of "managing by the numbers" include quality reduction (in the pursuit of "efficiency"), a stimulus to strategic behavior (whereby figures are recorded imaginatively to "meet the targets") and unimaginative decision-making (where risk is minimized and initiative discouraged). In effect measurement rewards those who do the least and count the most. So, while police management assumes that "you cannot manage what you cannot measure," police personnel work to the adage, "what gets measured counts." The successful production of measures may work without affecting the actually existing problems. Hence the implosion of SOCA because, in spite of the ability to produce management information, crime and insecurity remained and both the public and police insiders knew it.

The rhetoric of realism

The national intelligence model in the United Kingdom and, similarly, other models of the Intelligence Cycle elsewhere tend to founder and fail because of the ephemeral nature of the management information that animates them. The models persist because of the rhetoric of realism which the purveyors of the Intelligence Cycle routinely invoke.

In his book *Organized Crime and American Power* Michael Woodiwiss tells how the Washington-based Center for Strategic and International Studies sponsored a conference in 1994, the proceedings of which subsequently emerged as a book on global organized crime subtitled *The New Empire of Evil*.[31] The echo from the rhetoric of the Cold War was no accident. The conservative think tank's conference featured a number of barely recycled Cold Warriors, as well as the Director of the CIA, who affirmed that global mafias had replaced the Soviet Union as the leading national security threat to the USA. One of the participants was the journalist Claire Sterling (who in the Reagan era had advanced the thesis that international terrorism was all directed from Moscow). That same year, she published a book that purported to describe a new international *Pax Mafiosa*. Woodiwiss's point was that, globally, a new crescendo in the rhetoric surrounding the problem of organized crime had been reached.[32] Years later we can see that, despite the supposed realism, the analysis was rather wide of the mark.

Woodiwiss was one of a number of academic criminologists who noticed the long-term historical development of organized crime rhetoric which creates a sense of threat that is simultaneously ominous and ephemeral but nevertheless *realistic*.[33] Such analysis exposes the political or social construction of the "organized crime phenomenon" and its uses in the manufacture and support of perceived institutional vested interests, while also trying to maintain a balance because such critics do not suggest that the terminology is based on pure fiction. These points have, with due alteration of detail, also been made with regard to counter-terrorism discourse.[34] The point is that there is considerable harm associated with any number of forms of activity that might reasonably be said to constitute "organized crime," "terrorism" and "security threats" generally. So when this or that agency issues its annual Threat Assessment, the institutional facts it expresses are inevitably tinged with a halo of realism. Tales of the Russian

Mafia, Chinese Triads, Jamaican Yardies, Outlaw Motorcycle Gangs, criminal insurgents, narco-terrorists, fundamentalist terrorists and similar "suitable enemies"[35] propound stereotypes of the "criminal other." While appearing realistic, this type of imagery is nonetheless selective and steeped in politics, but this is only evident upon critical reflection, which is often difficult because of the urgency of the rhetoric.

The "threat" mantra has the seductive power to draw the press, win votes, acquire law enforcement resources, and gain public support for various legislative or enforcement crackdowns. The rhetoric disguises the diversity of activity the language of threat is stretched to cover and the things that are being left out. The hype, while tinged with realism, works to exclude consciousness of the institutional choices being made and it not-so-subtly underscores the plausibility of effectiveness claims. The rhetoric of realism lends urgency to its purveyors' message such that managerial efforts to quantify and measure "organized crime" and other "security threats" according to vague criteria of agency success can continue indefinitely, making ill-defined threats seem concrete and ill-conceived institutional responses seem rational.

The data delusion

In early 2012 the pages of *Wired* magazine revealed that contractors with top-secret clearances had nearly finished the construction of the Utah Data Center. This innocuously named erection was being built for the US National Security Agency (NSA) near a tiny town called Bluffdale, Utah. A project of immense secrecy, it was the final piece in a complex puzzle assembled over the decade since 9/11. Its purpose: to intercept and store vast swaths of data collected from foreign and domestic communications networks. An estimated five million square feet, the heavily fortified US$2 billion nerve center was complete with its own power plant for energy self-sufficiency. Flowing through its servers and routers and stored in near-bottomless databases would be a great mass of information including the complete contents of private emails, cell phone calls and Google searches, as well as all sorts of personal data trails – parking receipts, travel itineraries, bookstore purchases, library borrowings and other digital detritus. It was part of the realization of the "total information awareness program" created during the administration of George W. Bush – an effort that was killed by Congress in 2003 after it caused an outcry over its potential for invading Americans' privacy.[36]

The justification for this massive government intrusion into the private communications of the general populace, not only in the United States but around the world, is that we are now in the post-9/11 era.[37] The practices of policing and the security and intelligence services have become increasingly intertwined and counter-terrorism practice has had a tremendous knock-on effect within the policing sector.[38] The NSA is not the only intelligence-gathering organization to exhibit the massive expansionism associated with the data delusion; it is merely the most colossal. For example, in mid-2012 it emerged that the UK equivalent of the NSA, the Government Communications Headquarters (GCHQ), would again expand its infrastructure. Already GCHQ had moved to new quarters in 2003 – named "the Doughnut" because of its architectural shape – at a reputed cost of £330 million and in 2012 the cost of additional expansion of capacity was rumoured to be in excess of £2 billion.[39]

The lesson taken from the events of 9/11 concerned the evident inability of the policing intelligence and security communities to integrate information into a bigger picture, to "connect the dots." In institutions predicated on surveillance and data acquisition, any problem encountered can be answered only by calls for more surveillance and more data. It therefore follows that "a 'smart' government would integrate all sources of information to see the enemy as a whole."[40] This idea of "connecting the dots" has been taken to imply that there is a "plain as day" pattern; if only there was enough data to sift in order to be able to find it. The trouble is, 9/11 did not happen because there was a failure to gather enough data; it occurred because there was a failure to analyze and communicate on the basis of what was already known.[41] The pattern that became evident in retrospect, with the aid of 20/20 hindsight, would not have been clearer beforehand if there had been more data. If anything, it would have been more difficult to see. The belief that, in order to "connect the dots," we need more dots to connect is the data delusion.

A number of pathologies in intelligence systems are associated with this.[42] It is a symptom of "compulsive data demand," a reflex action in institutions whose *raison d'être* is collecting information. Problems induce demands for "more data" rather than "better data," or better *data analysis*. This leads to "intelligence overload" where the analytical strength of an organization is sapped by the demand to manage the weight of information coming in.[43] This exacerbates the problem of "noise": since "the probability that personnel working with 'raw' intelligence will come across a piece of 'high-quality' information is lower than the probability that they will receive something of relatively 'low quality'" the system can be overwhelmed.[44] "Noise" in an intelligence system makes it ever more difficult to "connect the dots."

These terms are not foreign to intelligence analysts. They are as common as the other well-known types of organizational pathology that plague their systems: "linkage blindness," "information silos," "intelligence hoarding" and others. None of these speak to a dearth of data. If anything they are a symptom of its superabundance. Why, then, when faced with evidence of system failure, does the Intelligence Cycle compulsively demand more data? The answer, in short, is the panoptic promise.

The panoptic promise

Michel Foucault's theoretical mediation on Jeremy Bentham's 'panoptic prison' rates as one of the most influential ideas in late-twentieth-century social theory. Bentham's "Panopticon" design for the prison (which was unrealized in its original form, but was nevertheless widely influential) postulated a system where a single guard could watch over many prisoners, while the guard remained unseen by the watched. For Foucault the panoptic gaze was the essential form of power-knowledge that distinguishes modern forms of discipline; it is the quintessence of social control. It is through panoptic surveillance, Foucault theorized, that modern society exercises its controlling systems. The panoptic promise pursues power on an increasingly individualized level, shown by the possibility of governmental institutions tracking individuals throughout their lives. Foucault posits a "carceral continuum" running through the social order – from the maximum security prison, through police, probation, social workers, teachers, right down to the everyday working and domestic lives of everyone. All are connected by the (witting or unwitting) supervision (i.e. surveillance and the application of norms of acceptable behavior) of some humans by others.

Foucault explained the promise of panoptic power thus:

> [T]he major effect of the Panopticon: to induce in the inmate a state of conscious and permanent visibility that assures the automatic functioning of power. So to arrange things that the surveillance is permanent in its effects, even if it is discontinuous in its action; that the perfection of power should tend to render its actual exercise unnecessary ... To achieve this, it is at once too much and too little that the prisoner should be constantly observed by an inspector: too little, for what matters is that he knows himself to be observed; too much, because he has no need in fact of being so. In view of this ... power should be visible and unverifiable ... The Panopticon is a machine for dissociating the see/being seen dyad ... one is totally seen, without ever seeing ... one sees everything without ever being seen.[45]

Thus, the previously discussed data delusion is masked and sustained by the promise of panoptic power. Panoptic power, where the few *surveille* the many, is precisely the mode of social control depicted in George Orwell's anti-utopia *1984*, curiously not mentioned in any of Foucault's writings.

The great advances in surveillance technology since Foucault's death in June 1984 have, arguably, both positive and negative implications[46] and, no doubt, participants in policing and security surveillance would emphasize the former over the latter. However, critics of the growth of "the surveillance state" in recent times have tended to focus attention onto the negative implications for privacy, civil liberty and the pursuit of (peaceful) democratic opposition promised by increased surveillance power.[47] Be that as it may, in considering the panoptic promise of power for social control and social ordering, what should also not escape mention is Foucault's insistence that every form of power-knowledge contains the seeds of its own resistance. So the dystopian promise of panoptic power – Big Brother-like total social control – is always already bound to fail on its own terms. Oppressive power breeds resistance. That is why, in addition to more or less overt forms of system surveillance pursued to inform the police Intelligence Cycle (which are motivated by the panoptic promise) there is an increasing dependence on covert forms of surveillance. Panoptic power needs back-up, and it gets it from the secret police.

Covert surveillance and anti-trust

The morass of ambiguity that surrounds undercover policing was opened up to scholarly scrutiny by the pioneering work of Gary T. Marx.[48] Broadly speaking, Marx suggests that, apart from what can be learned from electronic and other forms of direct surveillance, legal processes of search and seizure, post-hoc investigation and forensic examination, security operatives must inevitably engage in the practices of covert surveillance, lying and secrecy. He argues that covert policing is "double edged," by which is meant that it is both a danger to democracy and a necessary evil for maintaining it. However reluctantly, he concludes that there are conditions under which law enforcement officials practice deception for good reason, because, paradoxically, no virtue stands alone and every virtue is intertwined with its opposite. For Marx, it is unrealistic to prohibit law enforcement from ever taking actions that deceive (for example, while an investigation is ongoing); more than that: it would be socially harmful. Yet he remains aware that, in legitimating the use of deception in the name of better security, albeit in a circumscribed fashion, the risks are ever-present. He does not want Mephisto to sit at the head of the table, but grants him a seat above the salt. For him the problem is only a lack of adequate rules, accountability and oversight. That, however, is a stubborn problem because by definition covert practice, lying and deceit are "below the radar." When it comes to secret policing, lack of transparency is a given and therefore democratic accountability is problematic. As a result, in a putative democracy, its legitimacy is always questionable.

These general thoughts have considerable intellectual weight. However, when it comes to the functioning of the Intelligence Cycle there are additional considerations and the awareness of the moral ambiguity that Marx brings to the study of undercover policing needs to be brought to bear. In the world of intelligence-led policing there are different uses of the word "intelligence" that stem from different occupational practices. The term means different things to different kinds of intelligence practitioner and the subcultural expectations imbued in it can sometimes lead to working at cross-purposes. Police undercover detectives and personnel from the various secret intelligence services expect intelligence to be in the form of information acquired by covert means.[49] For them, secrecy is routine. Crime analysts working in support of the Intelligence Cycle as described in manuals for intelligence-led policing do not normally function with that expectation. For these professionals communicability and analysis are foremost.[50]

There is a conflict in the understanding of intelligence between those who construct it as an essentially covert and secret practice and those who construct it as an analytical task based on information sharing and communication. Hulnick also describes aspects of this subcultural conflict which he labels the "cops and spies dilemma."[51] In practice, the role expectations associated with covert practices tend to have more cachet within professional policing and security circles and so the Intelligence Cycle tends to become cloaked in an air of mystery, when not altogether shrouded in secrecy.[52] The strictures of secrecy required by covert practice trump the openness of intelligence sharing implied by the Intelligence Cycle model. More importantly, they make difficult (but perhaps not entirely impossible) the practices of transparency necessary for accountability and administrative oversight.

Police are symbolic of the social order, so deceptive policing has important implications for the institution or principle of trust. Trust, according to Francis Fukuyama, is very important for sociability.[53] High-trust societies are more successful, economically, politically and socially, and Fukuyama warned that the erosion of trust in western societies, particularly the United States, during recent decades may have undermined the basis for such success. When police institutions were established in Anglo-American societies at the beginning of the modern period there was a general distaste for the police spy, which was distrusted because of its association with undemocratic and oppressive political regimes.[54] Originally, the British Bobby and the American cop were "citizens in uniform," highly visible symbols of democratic social order embodying the spirit of an open society.[55] As night follows day, in the long process by which these symbolic guardians of social order – the police and other agents of "law enforcement" – became associated with the practices of systematic deception that are the basis of undercover policing, there were negative consequences for social trust more generally and thus for the legitimacy of police institutions.

The literature on the Intelligence Cycle and surveillance-led policing often ignores convert practice and certainly ignores the implications for trust that deceptive practice implies. It is necessary to recognize the fundamental concerns about trust and legitimacy that arise when things go wrong in intelligence-led policing due to secrecy and covert practices turned rotten. Consider the following:

- A number of UK undercover police officers tasked with maintaining undercover surveillance on groups of environmental activists are accused of sexual manipulation. It emerges that two of them fathered children with political campaigners they had been sent to spy on.[56]
- In a related case, allegations emerged that undercover police acted as *agents provocateurs*. In Parliament MPs demanded an investigation into suggestions that an undercover officer planted a firebomb in a department store in order to gain credibility with the people he was spying on.[57]
- FBI operatives are accused of operating a series of undercover stings that amount to "entrapment." It appears that undercover agents provided planning, means and encouragement to attack targets to persons who were only marginally disaffected and who would otherwise have remained so. Cases include "The Newburgh Four," "The Fort Dix Five" and "The Liberty City Seven." Muslim civil rights spokespersons speak of Muslim Americans being "hounded and threatened by the FBI."[58]
- In the case of "The Cleveland Five" the FBI faced allegations of entrapment of members of the so-called "Occupy Movement." Having furnished

bomb-making materials and facilitated illegal acts, it again seemed likely that covert agents were acting as *agents provocateurs*.[59]

• A botched sting operation by the US Bureau of Alcohol, Firearms and Tobacco (ATF) resulted in thousands of guns going missing in Mexico. In what turned into a scandal of state-sponsored gun-running, the ATF launched a "controlled delivery" operation aimed at tracing the criminal networks responsible for gun smuggling but lost the trail. The ATF did not inform partner agencies about the operation. Some of the guns were thought to have been implicated in an incident in which a US Border Patrol agent died, while others were implicated in multiple shooting incidents in Mexico that left many people dead.[60]

This is not a scientific sample of police covert operations and doubtless others could marshal many examples where covert policing produces laudable results. For instance, there is a case where an FBI/NYPD undercover operation exposed the actions of a group, including five serving NYPD officers and a number of other police officers, smuggling guns, cigarettes and stolen slot machines.[61] But mud sticks. Theories concerning the practice of intelligence-led policing remain incomplete when they fail to address the difficult ethical and social issues that covert intelligence operations entail. The general model of the Intelligence Cycle does not acknowledge the centrality of covert practice in contemporary intelligence-led policing and this is a major flaw.

The digital delusion, the panoptic promise and the deleterious effects of covert policing on social trust and the legitimacy of policing combine and contribute to a growing climate of fear. It might be thought that these obviously negative consequences would result in a roll-back of the cycle of intelligence-led policing. One of the primary reasons it has not is due to the persuasive power of the rhetoric of realism. Another has to do with the war fever that pervades policing and security practice.

War fever

In mid-2012 it emerged that for the previous decade training manuals circulating in US military, intelligence and law enforcement communities had taught that Islam was a "barbaric ideology" that "should not be tolerated."[62] While officials hurriedly moved to distance the Pentagon from revelations concerning courses that taught military officers to prepare for "total war" with Islam, it also became apparent from a six-month review launched by the FBI into their own agent training material that the problem was widespread. The FBI probe uncovered 876 Islamophobic statements used in 392 presentations, including a PowerPoint slide that said the bureau can sometimes bend or suspend the law in counter-terror investigations. The NYPD was also implicated in the scandal. American Muslim civil liberties groups were quick to point out that this Islamophobia in military, police and intelligence circles was actually detrimental to US national security interests because it contributed to the growing deficit of trust between the Muslim community and authorities.[63]

A key condition for the militarization of a conflict is the construction of us/
them identity categories and the identification and dehumanization of "the
enemy." It is useful to pay close attention to the psychological moves made in
the justification of war fever. Sociologists of the military have shown how beha-
vioral science has been used to desensitize and naturalize attitudes among
military personnel, heightening patriotic sensibilities and prejudice against a
target group on the basis of "othering."[64] This psychological move – the
dehumanization of the enemy – is considered essential for success on the battlefield, but research also suggests that this mindset is also fostered within broader
civilian populations because the inculcation of fear and insecurity in the individual psyches of civilians is instrumental in the incubation of war fever and so
sustains a posture of belligerence.[65]

According to Lucia Zedner, war language has come to define the security
scene.[66] War language provides a justification for the introduction of security
practices that would be indefensible during peacetime. The war fever that results
has helped to fuse together the practices of the security services, police institutions and military ones, and what is emerging is a transnational system of social
control.[67] The claim that the gravity of the threat is so grave that only an all-out
war will allow democratic societies to survive undermines the democratic conditions that (used to) define those societies. However, there is more to criticism
of war fever than this principled challenge. War fever, as the civil liberties
advocates rightly argue, actually serves to undermine the aim of the policing and
security services to prevent further conflict and this point is practically demonstrated by a rather opposite approach that seeks to lower the temperature – reassurance policing.[68] Practical police operations in the UK have already
demonstrated the utility of bridge-building approaches in reducing fundamentalist extremism, enhancing intelligence co-operation between police and communities and reassuring the public that conflict is not unmanageable. Community
based counter-terrorism projects that recognize that co-operation, not dehumanization, offers a better probability of preventing and deterring future forms of
such violence shows that putting human security thinking before national
security thinking is both practical and serviceable.

However, these lessons are not well known or well understood by the purveyors of intelligence-led policing models. That is because the language of war has
been percolating within the policing sector since it was introduced by the Nixon
administration in the late 1960s.[69] According to Jonathan Simon, this language
transformed American democracy and created a culture of fear. Instead of governing crime, state agencies are governing *through* crime.[70] War language in
crime fighting is now taken for granted and so too is the militarization of policing.[71] This language has been successfully exported to Europe and beyond.[72]
Exporting the harsh language of the war on crime has made the world-wide war
on terror possible.[73] With it has come the normalization of the exceptional.[74] By
normalization of the exceptional is understood a toleration for extraordinary
measures now routine in law enforcement in general and intelligence-led policing in particular. Such normalization also helps to elide the sorts of systemic

problem alluded to in the preceding sections, problems naturalized in the well-worn military acronym SNAFU.

There is no irony in the observation that war fever has undermined the conditions of democracy in the societies that harbor it. War fever creates confusion in the social body which helps sustain the conditions of failure described in this chapter. The cure for war fever is to confront the banal point so often made that "truth is the first casualty of war" and speak truth to power.

Conclusion

This chapter has been pursued on the basis that stinging critique is necessary before the policing sector can be moved beyond the Intelligence Cycle. Elsewhere I have argued that there is a need to re-orientate intelligence-led policing around the paradigm of human security.[75] The human security concept represents a qualitative change in thinking and it has been strongly endorsed as the basis of foreign and security policy.[76] It suggests that security should be oriented around processes of social inclusion that foster both freedom from fear and freedom from want. This chapter did not set out to formulate a new paradigm for intelligence-led policing, but clearly one is in order. The further elucidation of the principles of that new way of thinking for intelligence-led policing await future opportunities for discussion. Here I can do no more than summarize the main points of the critique of the currently existing police Intelligence Cycle.

This chapter has hinged on two meanings of the Intelligence Cycle. First, there has been the observation that the policing sector is in the grip of a form of managerialism that fosters more or less continuous organizational restructuring and rapid turnover of personnel. This cyclical phenomenon is not evenly spread across the policing sector, but it is generalized enough to matter. Coupled with this is the tendency within managerial *philosophy*, if one can use that term without being accused of being overly ironic, to favour what has been called variously "management by the numbers," "management by objectives" and "performance management." This aspect of the Intelligence Cycle was referred to here as management mythology. The central point of this criticism is that these aspects of existing intelligence-led policing practice tend to rob police organizations of their institutional memory. Arguably, if the institutional memory of the agencies that comprise the policing sector were not so flawed, then it would be possible to learn from mistakes. Instead, the managerial culture fostered within these agencies seems destined to repeat them.

The cycle of intelligence-led policing is wrong-headed in other respects. First and foremost is the "cart-before-the-horse" relationship between strategic intelligence analysis and policy-making. Rather than evidence-based strategic intelligence analysis informing policy, there is widespread recognition that analysis is expected to provide the justification for policy choices made in advance. Policy failure is further guaranteed by a number of other features of the cycle of intelligence-led policing. In this chapter, the data delusion – that what is needed is more data, not better data or better data analysis – was shown to be detrimental to "connecting the dots" in the strategic intelligence picture. That failure contributes to the inability of intelligence practitioners to challenge pre-existing policy with alternative suggestions; and some practitioners see this, but this recognition is difficult because of the rhetoric of realism infused into the language of threat assessment. The data delusion is further bolstered by the promise of panoptic power – that surveillance itself will be an effective form of social control minimizing harm and controlling risk. The effects of this are both unmeasurable and questionable. However, panoptic power creates insecurity due to a widespread cultural suspiciousness about the "power of Big Brother," and so covert policing practices are utilized as a sort of insurance policy. Still, covert policing is a tainted practice in societies that maintain an expectation of democratic norms and, despite often well-advertised examples of agency success in covert operations, the whiff of scandal is ever-present. This undermines the social trust which is a pre-condition for a well functioning social order, further de-legitimating the intelligence enterprise and, in turn, creating and sustaining the conditions for system failure. All of these problems seem to be sustained by the atmosphere of war fever which is a symptom of crisis and a contributor to it. The conclusion is that the result of the existing cycle of intelligence-led policing is an endless round of ineffectiveness masked as agency success.

What is required, ultimately, is a solidaristic and egalitarian motif in the practices of the security Intelligence Cycle.[77] In the long term, we shall find that human rights and security, along with democracy and social justice, are the best guard against the threats and insecurities of a rapidly changing world. Robust critique is only the first step along the road to this, hopefully better, model of policing with intelligence. Beyond critique, the field of Intelligence Studies will need to foster a new interdisciplinary body of knowledge that combines the views of civil liberties and human rights scholars and activists with those of security intelligence scholars and practitioners. There is a great deal of work to be done, but if the police Intelligence Cycle is to be moved beyond the current impasse, there is no avoiding it.

Notes

1 The author would like to acknowledge the support of the Oxford Centre of Criminology, which provided such a wonderful base of operations during the winter of 2012 when this chapter was written.
2 Home Office, *The National Crime Agency: A Plan for the Creation of a National Crime-Fighting Capability*, with an Introduction by Home Secretary Theresa May (London: Home Office, 2011).
3 Ibid., p. 5.
4 Ibid.
5 Ibid.
6 Ibid.
7 Ibid., p. 4.
8 Simon Jenkins, "A British FBI has got no chance against London's very own KGB," *The Guardian*, May 10, 2012.
9 Jean-Paul Brodeur, *The Policing Web* (Oxford: Oxford University Press, 2010).

10 James Sheptycki, "Police Ethnography in the House of Serious Organized Crime," in Alistair Henry and David J. Smith (eds.), *Transformations in Policing* (Aldershot: Ashgate, 2007), p. 51.

11 Martin Innes and James Sheptycki, "From Detection to Disruption: Intelligence and the Changing Logics of Police Crime Control in the United Kingdom," *International Criminal Justice Review*, Vol. 14, 2004, pp. 1–24; Peter Gill, Stephen Marrin and Mark Phythian (eds.), *Intelligence Theory: Key Questions and Debates* (London: Routledge, 2009); Jerry Ratcliffe, *Intelligence-Led Policing* (Cullompton: Willan, 2008); Jerry Ratcliffe (ed.), *Strategic Thinking in Criminal Intelligence* (2nd edn., Sydney: The Federation Press, 2009); Raymond A. Guidetti, "Policing the Homeland: Choosing the Intelligent Option" (unpublished MA Thesis, Monterey, CA: Naval Graduate School, 2006).

12 James Sheptycki, "Policing, Intelligence Theory and the New Human Security Paradigm: Some lessons from the field," in Gill, Marrin and Phythian (eds.), *Intelligence Theory*, pp. 166–87.

13 Arthur S. Hulnick, "What's Wrong with the Intelligence Cycle," *Intelligence and National Security*, Vol. 21 No. 6, 2006, pp. 959–79.

14 James Sheptycki, "Review of the Influence of Strategic Intelligence on Organized Crime Policy and Practice," London: Home Office Special Interest Paper No. 14, 2002.

15 HMIC, *National Criminal Intelligence Service, 1997 Inspection Report* (London: HMIC, 1997), p. 25.

16 Ibid., p. 22.

17 Ibid.

18 Ibid., p. 23.

19 Klaus von Lampe, "Making the Second Step Before the First: Assessing Organized Crime," *Crime, Law and Social Change* Vol. 42 Nos. 4–5, 2005, p. 236.

20 Petrus C. van Duyne and Maarten van Dijck, "Assessing Organised Crime: The Sad State of an Impossible Art," in Frank Bovenkerk and Michael Levi (eds.), *The Organized Crime Community: Essays in Honor of Alan A. Block* (New York: Springer, 2007), p. 102.

21 Petrus C. van Duyne, "Introduction: Counting clouds and measuring organised crime," in Almir Maljevic, Maarten van Dijck, Klaus von Lampe, James L. Newell and Petrus C. van Duyne, *The Organisation of Crime for Profit: Conduct, Law and Measurement* (Nijmegen: Wolf Legal Publishers, 2006), p. 5.

22 Malcolm Young, *An Inside Job: Policing and Police Culture in Britain* (Oxford: Oxford University Press, 1991).

23 Sheptycki, "Police Ethnography in the House of Serious Organized Crime."

24 Sean O'Neill, "Is Soca just too soft?" *The Times*, May 13, 2008.

25 Sean O'Neill, "Soca abandons hunt for crime lords," *The Times*, May 13, 2008.

26 Sandra Laville, "Gordon Brown steps in as Agency fails to tackle organised crime gangs," *The Guardian*, April, 27, 2009.

27 Laura Clout, "Soca is paralysed by bureaucracy," *Daily Telegraph*, January 24, 2007.

28 Simon Holdaway, "Modernity, Rationality and the Baguette: Co-operation and the management of policing in Europe," *European Journal on Criminal Policy and Research*, Vol. 1 No. 4, 1993, pp. 53–70.

29 Barry Loveday, "Policing Performance," *Criminal Justice Matters*, Vol. 40 No. 1, 2008, p. 24.

30 See, for example, A. J. P. Butler, *Police Management* (London: Gower, 1984).

31 Michael Woodiwiss, *Organized Crime and American Power* (Toronto: University of Toronto Press, 2001); Linnea P. Raine and Frank J. Cilluffo (eds.), *Global Organized Crime: The New Empire of Evil* (Washington, DC: Center for Strategic and International Studies, 1994).

32 See also Michael Woodiwiss and Dick Hobbs, "Organized Evil and the Atlantic Alliance: Moral panics and the rhetoric of organized crime policing in America and Britain," *British Journal of Criminology*, Vol. 49 No. 1, 2009, pp. 106–28.

33 Margaret Beare (ed.), *Critical Reflections on Transnational Organized Crime, Money Laundering and Corruption* (Toronto: Toronto University Press, 2003); William R. Geary, "The Legislative Recreation of 'RICO': Reinforcing the 'myth' of organized crime," *Crime, Law and Social Change*, Vol. 38 No. 4, 2002, pp. 311–56; James Sheptycki, "Global Law Enforcement as a Protection Racket: Some sceptical notes on transnational organised crime as an object of global governance," in Adam Edwards and Peter Gill (eds.), *Transnational Organised Crime: Perspectives on Global Security* (London: Routledge, 2003), pp. 42–59; James Sheptycki, 'Against Transnational Organized Crime' in Beare (ed.), *Critical Reflections on Transnational Organized Crime, Money Laundering and Corruption*, pp. 120–44; James Sheptycki, "The Governance of Organised Crime in Canada," *The Canadian Journal of Sociology* Vol. 28 No. 3, 2003, pp. 489–517; Petrus C. van Duyne, "The Phantom and Threat of Organized Crime," *Crime, Law and Social Change*, Vol. Vol. 24 No. 4, 1995–96, pp. 341–77.

34 David L. Altheide, *Terrorism and the Politics of Fear* (New York: AltaMira Press, 2006); Richard Jackson, *Writing the War on Terror; Language, Politics and Counter Terrorism* (Manchester: Manchester University Press, 2005); Alexander Spencer, *The Tabloid Terrorist; The Predicative Construction of New Terrorism in the Media* (London: Palgrave Macmillan, 2010).

35 Nils Christie, "Suitable Enemy," in Herman Bianchi and Rene von Swaaningen (eds.), *Abolitionism: Toward a Non-Repressive Approach to Crime* (Amsterdam: Free University Press, 1986), pp. 42–54.

36 James Bamford, "The NSA is building the country's biggest spy center (watch what you say)," *Wired*, March 12, 2012, pp. 78–85, 122–4.

37 Thomas Keen and Lee H. Hamilton, *The 9/11 Commission Report* (New York: W. W. Norton, 2004); Erin Kruger and Kevin D. Haggerty, "Intelligence Exchange in Policing and Security," *Policing and Society*, Vol. 16 No. 1, 2006, pp. 86–91.

38 See, for example, Peter Andreas and Richard Price, "From War-Fighting to Crime-Fighting; Transforming the American National Security State," *International Studies Review*, Vol. 3 No. 3, 2001, pp. 31–52; Antony Field, "Tracking Terrorist Networks: Problems of intelligence sharing within the UK intelligence community," *Review of International Studies (2009)*, Vol. 35 No. 4, 2009, pp. 997–1009.

39 Richard Norton-Taylor, "The Doughnut: The less secretive weapon in the fight against international terrorism," *The Guardian*, June 10, 2003; Christopher Booker, "Does the Government want to make GCHQ the 'Big Brother' for Europe?" *Daily Telegraph*, April 7, 2012.

40 Keen and Hamilton, *The 9/11 Commission Report*, p. 401.

41 Peter Gill, "Not Just Joining the Dots but Crossing the Borders and Bridging the Voids: Constructing Security Networks after 11 September 2001," *Policing and Society*, Vol. 16 No. 1, 2006, pp. 27–49.

42 James Sheptycki, "Organizational Pathologies in Police Intelligence Systems: Some contributions to the lexicon of intelligence-led policing," *The European Journal of Criminology*, Vol. 1 No. 3, 2004, pp. 307–32.

43 Ibid., p. 316.

44 Ibid., p. 315.

45 Michel Foucault, *Discipline and Punish: The Birth of the Prison* (New York: Vintage Books, 1995), pp. 195–6.

46 David Lyon, *The Electronic Eye: The Rise of Surveillance Society* (University of Minnesota Press, 1994); Jerome E. Dobson and Peter F. Fisher, "The Panopticon's Changing Geography," *Geographical Review* Vol. 97 No. 3, 2007, pp. 307–23.

47 Kevin D. Haggerty and Richard V. Ericson (eds.), *The New Politics of Surveillance and Visibility* (Toronto: University of Toronto Press, 2005).
48 Gary T. Marx, *Undercover: Police Surveillance in America* (Berkeley, CA: University of California Press, 1989); Cyrille Fijnaut and Gary T. Marx, *Undercover: Police Surveillance in Comparative Perspective* (The Hague: Kluwer, 1995).
49 Innes and Sheptycki, "From Detection to Disruption," pp. 6–7.
50 Nina Cope, "Intelligence Led Policing or Policing Led Intelligence? Integrating Volume Crime Analysis into Policing," *British Journal of Criminology*, Vol. 44 No. 2, 2004, pp. 188–203.
51 Hulnick, "What's Wrong with the Intelligence Cycle."
52 Sheptycki, "Review of the Influence of Strategic Intelligence on Organized Crime Policy and Practice"; Sheptycki, "Organizational Pathologies in Police Intelligence Systems."
53 Francis Fukuyama, *Trust: The Social Virtues and the Creation of Prosperity* (New York: The Free Press, 1996).
54 Mark Mazower (ed.), *The Policing of Politics in the Twentieth Century: Historical Perspectives* (New York: Berghahn Books, 1997).
55 Wilbur R. Miller, *Cops and Bobbies: Police Authority in New York and London, 1830–70*, (2nd edn., Columbus, OH: Ohio State University Press, 1999); Robert Reiner, *The Politics of the Police* (2nd edn., Oxford: Oxford University Press, 2000), pp. 56–7.
56 Rob Evans and Paul Lewis, "Undercover police had children with activists," *The Guardian*, January 20, 2012.
57 Rob Evans and Paul Lewis, "Call for police links to animal rights firebombing to be investigated," *The Guardian*, June 13, 2012.
58 Paul Harris, "Fake terror plots, paid informants; the tactics of FBI 'entrapment' questioned," *The Guardian*, November 16, 2011.
59 Arun Gupta, "Cleveland Occupy arrests are the latest in FBI's pattern of manipulation," *The Guardian*, May 12, 2012.
60 Rodrigo Camarena, "How the ATF's gun-running misfired for Calderón," *The Guardian*, March 18, 2011.
61 Karen McVeigh, "Eight New York police officers arrested in gun smuggling ring," *The Guardian*, October 11, 2011.
62 Ryan Devereaux, "Anti-Islam teachings 'widespread' in US law enforcement; activists point to past incidents in the FBI and NYPD after military course urged soldiers to prepare for 'total war' with Islam," *The Guardian*, May 11, 2012.
63 Ibid.
64 Ron Robin, *The Making of the Cold War Enemy: Culture and Politics in the Military-Intellectual Complex* (Princeton, NJ: Princeton University Press, 2001).
65 Jackie Orr, "The Militarization of Inner Space," *Critical Sociology* Vol. 30 No. 2, 2004, pp. 451–81.
66 Lucia Zedner, *Security* (London: Routledge, 2009), pp. 121–3.
67 Jean-Paul Brodeur, "High and Low Policing in Post-9/11 Times," *Policing: An International Journal of Policy and Practice*, Vol. 1, No. 1, 2007, pp. 25–37; Ben Bowling and James Sheptycki, *Global Policing* (London: Sage, 2012).
68 Martin Innes, "Policing Uncertainty: Countering Terror through Community Intelligence and Democratic Policing," *The ANNALS of the American Academy of Political and Social Science* Vol. 605 No. 1, 2006, pp. 222–41.
69 James Vorenberg, "The War on Crime: The First Five Years," *The Atlantic Monthly*, May 1972, pp. 63–9. Available at www.theatlantic.com/past/politics/crime/crimewar.htm, last accessed November 15, 2012.
70 Jonathan Simon, *Governing Through Crime: How the War on Crime Transformed American Democracy and Created a Culture of Fear* (New York: Oxford University Press, 2007).

71 Peter B. Kraska (ed.), *Militarizing the American Criminal Justice System: The Changing Roles of the Armed Forces and the Police* (Boston MA: Northeastern University Press, 2001).

72 Sophie Body-Gendrot, *The Social Control of Cities? A Comparative Perspective* (London: Palgrave Macmillan, 2008).

73 James Foreman Jr., "Exporting Harshness: How the war on crime helped make the war on terror possible," *New York University Review of Law and Social Change* Vol. 33, 2009, pp. 331–74.

74 Janne Flyghed, "Normalizing the Exceptional," *Policing and Society*, Vol. 13 No. 1, 2002, pp. 23–41.

75 James Sheptycki, "Policing, Intelligence Theory and the New Human Security Paradigm," in Gill, Marrin and Phythian (eds.), *Intelligence Theory*, pp. 166–87.

76 Mary Kaldor, Mary Martin and Sabine Selchow, "Human Security: A new strategic narrative for Europe," *International Affairs* Vol. 83 No. 2, 2007, pp. 273–88.

77 Cf. Ian Loader, "The Cultural Lives of Security and Human Rights," in Benjamin J. Goold and Liora Lazarus (eds.), *Security and Human Rights* (Portland, OR: Hart Publishing, 2007), pp. 27–43.

7 The Intelligence Cycle in the corporate world

Bespoke or off-the-shelf?

David Strachan-Morris

Introduction

This chapter examines the Intelligence Cycle in a commercial context, specifically in relation to political risk and security. Commercial organisations use intelligence in a very different way to governments or the military in that it informs their decisions on taking or avoiding risks. In this chapter I argue that, in fact, the Intelligence Cycle works fairly well in a commercial context because it directly supports business decisions, and the relationship between client and provider is much different to that in government or the military because the provider is as much an advisor as a simple source of intelligence. Rather than simply describe the workings of the Intelligence Cycle I will take as my starting point the criticisms that have been made of it by Arthur Hulnick and the work on the relationships between intelligence agencies and decision makers by Stephen Marrin.[1] This chapter will take the same basic approach as Hulnick throughout, by providing an individual perspective based upon personal experience, albeit in the corporate intelligence industry rather than in an intelligence agency. Although the issues have been discussed at length with colleagues throughout the industry, it is still one point of view, but hopefully one that will shed some light on a hitherto underexplored area of intelligence study – the corporate intelligence world.

In doing this I use the term 'corporate intelligence' to describe this activity rather than 'private sector intelligence' because the latter also encompasses outsourcing government intelligence work to private companies, whereas I am specifically focusing on the use of intelligence to support business activities. Similarly, I use 'corporate intelligence' rather than 'commercial intelligence' because 'commercial intelligence' is closer to competitor intelligence and is used to cover activities around market information and trying to find out what your competitors are up to, whereas this chapter is intended to examine the use of intelligence in support of business decisions relating to political and security risk management. The nature of corporate intelligence activity is very different to state or sub-state intelligence activity. Arguably, state intelligence agencies exist to enable states to collect and analyse information on other state and non-state actors in order to take some form of executive action – such as taking offensive action or committing resources to defence against a threat. Corporate intelligence activity exists mainly to provide information that will enable an organisation to take an opportunity or manage a risk. An example of this difference comes from Iraq: while the military needed intelligence to fight the war, civilian contractors only needed intelligence to be able to operate within the war. So, while the military would be interested in the membership and future intentions of an insurgent group that was emplacing improvised explosive devices (IED) along a particular stretch of road, it was enough for civilian security contractors to know that the stretch of road in question was prone to IED attack and, therefore, avoid travelling along it. Another example is the use of intelligence by pharmaceutical companies to monitor the threat posed by animal rights extremists: they collect information on the future intentions of these groups and trends within animal rights in order to plan their security response but they are not seeking to make arrests or take executive action against the groups (although they do co-operate with the police and do take legal action against the groups concerned – mainly in the form of injunctions to restrict the level of protest at their premises).[2]

William Shakespeare's *The Merchant of Venice* provides a useful illustration of the role of intelligence in the business world, albeit a fictional one. The main male characters, Antonio (the eponymous merchant), Bassanio (a rich playboy) and Shylock (a money lender) all use intelligence, in one form or another, in support of their risky ventures. For a start, they all get 'current intelligence' in the form of open source information to keep up-to-date with the latest business news; the question 'What news upon the Rialto?' is asked a number of times by various characters as they attempt to get the latest gossip from the business community.[3] This is how Shylock hears that one of Antonio's ships has been wrecked at a key point in the play.[4] When Bassanio asks Shylock for a loan, with Antonio standing as the guarantor, it is clear that Shylock has carried out a due diligence credit check on Antonio; he knows that Antonio has four ships at sea, with all the perils associated with that, and that he may default on the loan if his ships fail to return with their goods because all of his money is tied up in the venture. Shylock is also well aware of how Antonio feels about him and his people, so he is willing to take the risk of Antonio defaulting on the loan so he can 'feed fat the ancient grudge' he bears towards Antonio.[5] Also, he thinks he can afford the loss. Thus, Shylock believes he can win either way, but in fact he overreaches himself and ends up losing everything because he fails to understand how far the others will go to ruin him. The reason for the loan is so that Bassanio can continue his pursuit of the wealthy heiress, Portia. He has already spent a considerable sum of money and now needs more. This is a considerable risk as failure means he loses everything and will be considerably indebted to Antonio. In order to win Portia's hand he must choose the right box from three put in front of him, one of which bears the inscription 'Who chooseth me must give and hazard all he hath'.[6] This plain lead box is, of course, the correct one and the other two more decorative boxes are there to entrap those who consider looks more important than content. When he comes to make his 'hazard' he picks up on the vital clues, or 'warning intelligence', given to him by Portia in their bantering exchange and by her household in the song they sing as he ponders his choice.[7]

In current risk management methodology the four ways to 'treat' risk are to avoid, reduce, share or accept.[8] The characters in *The Merchant of Venice* engage in three of these, supported by the information they can collect. Bassanio *shares* his financial risk with Antonio. Antonio and Shylock both *accept* the full risk of the loan and its potentially harmful terms. Finally, Bassanio's risk is considerably *reduced* compared with Portia's other suitors as it appears that he is aware of the fact that he is being given clues, when in the banter with Portia before he makes his choice he says 'O happy torment, when my torturer doth teach me answers for my deliverance.'[9] None of the main characters actually appears to *avoid* a risk when one is presented, maybe because they feel they have sufficient information to proceed.

But the corporate world has moved on from the relatively simple business dealings of Shakespeare's time, when merchants knew each other personally and could gather all the information they thought they needed 'upon the Rialto' or in the coffee houses of London. We now live in an age in which vast multinational oil companies, banks, airlines – even Walt Disney and Wal-Mart – have their own intelligence function. Servicing their intelligence needs, and those of companies with no internal intelligence department of their own, is a plethora of commercial organisations that can provide a full range of products, from strategic-level political analysis to tactical threat assessments. This range of activity has increased dramatically in the last few years, mainly as the result of the increased threat from terrorism directed against western interests since 9/11. A series of attacks against hotels around the world in the first decade of the twenty-first Century, in Amman (2005), Islamabad (2008), Mumbai (2008) and Jakarta (2003 and again in 2009), caused businesses to consider the risks in what were previously 'safe' parts of the world and fuelled an increased need for intelligence in the corporate world. To give some idea of the scale of the corporate intelligence industry, the Aprodex website, a directory of security providers, lists 213 companies that claim to provide some form of intelligence gathering and analysis.[10] Even this list is not comprehensive, as there are several companies I am aware of that do not appear there. The vast majority of this corporate intelligence activity takes place openly and relies on open-source information. As Dominick Donald points out, most of it is very innocuous and consists of analysts sitting in offices looking at open sources.[11] It is to avoid the connotation of secrecy, or even underhandedness, that some intelligence providers use hybrid terms such as 'Research and Intelligence', 'Analysis and Assessments' or 'Global Strategic Analysis' when listing their services.[12] Many analysts working in the corporate intelligence fields do not have 'traditional' intelligence backgrounds at all. To pick examples from three corporate intelligence providers, Oxford Analytica, Aegis and Diligence LLC all advertise on their websites that their analysts have backgrounds in academia, journalism, law and finance in addition to those who have served with the intelligence services.[13] The implication of this, of course, is that a great number of the people who work in corporate intelligence services have not been trained, or indoctrinated, in the use of the Intelligence Cycle; it has grown organically as the best model for servicing the needs of their clients.

The title of this chapter alludes to the two types of service provided by the corporate intelligence market. There is 'bespoke' reporting, which is commissioned specifically for a client in response to a particular requirement, and there is 'off-the-shelf' reporting, often consisting of subscriptions to reports that are written generically to satisfy more general requirements. Clients will sign up for daily, weekly or monthly intelligence reports that are of a very generic nature in order to get an overview of the situation in a particular part of the world or to get an understanding of the current standing of a particular issue. These reports may or may not completely satisfy their need for information. Most of the time they do but often they do not. Many off-the-shelf daily, weekly or monthly corporate intelligence reports are little more than an aggregation of the media reporting with not much in the way of comment. At the other end of the scale, companies such as Stratfor or Control Risks Group offer subscriptions to some very sophisticated analyses on complex issues that can often be used with little or no extra 'bespoke' analysis to support it.

In his classic article, 'What's wrong with the intelligence cycle', Hulnick identifies four different types of intelligence product: warning intelligence; current intelligence; in-depth studies; and the estimate.[14] The analysis that follows will be concerned mainly with bespoke reporting, which consists of products that generally match the four categories given by Hulnick.

The direction phase: the relationship between policy maker and intelligence provider

Hulnick starts his critique of the Intelligence Cycle by describing the relationship between policy makers and intelligence managers in the direction phase of the Intelligence Cycle. He says that policy makers do not often, in fact, give guidance to intelligence managers. While some may give guidance on areas of concerns or indicate the direction they want to take in their policy, intelligence managers often have to take the initiative and make their own decisions when it comes to directing the intelligence effort. While this is sometimes not too difficult, often the main driver is 'filling in the gaps' in existing intelligence rather than reacting to the specific direction of policy makers.[15] Marrin takes these criticisms of this stage in the process a step further, arguing that rather than policy makers 'pulling' information from intelligence agencies, the agencies often 'push' information that they think policy makers should know.[16]

In the corporate intelligence world, direction is often much more clear from the start. When a business is looking to take an opportunity, such as investing in a new venture or starting a new project, it will want a clear understanding of the threats and risks. Where direction is unclear or ambiguous, in my experience, intelligence managers have considerable scope to work with the policy maker to understand how exactly they intend to use the information to inform their decision. As with political policy makers, the decision may already have been made by the time any direction is given to the intelligence manager and the direction is given in order to decide how to proceed with the new venture or project. In the security field, for example, it is likely that the business wants to get an idea of how much to budget for security and therefore needs to understand what the risks are and how to mitigate them. With an internal intelligence department in an oil company or bank, for example, the intelligence manager will (or should) have a good feel for the type of detail required when given direction to provide reports in support of a business decision. When the business goes to an external provider of intelligence they will often seek one with existing expertise in their industry and select a provider through a process of requesting proposals, seeking bids and negotiating the final contract. Throughout this time, the requirements are made clear to the prospective provider. There is, of course, a certain 'push' element to the corporate intelligence world as intelligence providers try to get new business, but this still differs from the government model. An intelligence provider will approach a prospective client and make the case that the client needs their services, either replacing their current provider or supplementing the services of their current provider. But it is still the client ultimately who decides the size, scope, scale and content of the reports that are subsequently provided. Of course, this is not to say that all users of corporate intelligence give good direction. Those that do tend to be the more business-oriented organisations, such as banks, oil companies and pharmaceutical companies. The difference between businesses and governments in giving directions can arise because businesses only ask for intelligence when they feel they need it and when they are prepared to pay for it and, having decided they want to pay for it, they know what it is they want for their money. They also have more focus than a government, in terms of the range of issues they face and the number of countries they face them in. They are only interested in what affects them and their business and do not have to try to cope with the vast range of issues that a government does.

In the direction phase, then, the decision maker has a clearer idea of what they want from an intelligence provider, and the relationship is such that the provider can seek greater guidance where there is ambiguity. The fact that direction is more focused is a product of the fact that intelligence is often specific to the needs of a particular industry and the intelligence provider is not required to cover the wide range of issues that a government intelligence agency is expected to cover. Even when clients from a different industry purchase intelligence services, the actual range of issues tends not to differ that much in relation to political risk or security intelligence. This relative 'leanness' in terms of requirements greatly assists the collection and analysis phase, and is discussed next.

The collection and analysis phase: the Intelligence Cycle as a tandem

Hulnick also finds fault with the next two stages, collection and analysis. Rather than occurring as two separate stages, in which all the information is gathered and then it is processed, he points out that these often happen at the same time.

The two processes take place in parallel, independently of each other, often with no communication or co-ordination between the respective groups carrying out each stage of the process. Aside from this, raw information is often passed directly to the policy makers, despite the fact that in can be contradictory or wrong, and the policy makers often take this raw information to be evaluated intelligence.[17]

To take Hulnick's first point and apply it to the corporate intelligence world, the collection and analysis phases very often do take place in tandem rather than in parallel. This is because in almost all cases the collector and the analyst are in the same team and very often are the same person. The analyst tasked with writing the report in a corporate intelligence environment will be expected to use their own expertise, research skills and network of contacts to acquire the information they need to write their report. In many cases, they will have been hired because of their existing expertise in a region or issue. Language skills are at a premium in corporate intelligence providers so their analysts can exploit local sources, including the news media. While this removes many of the problems associated with independent collection and analysis processes, such as raw intelligence going straight to the policy maker, it does introduce a new problem. The collection effort is almost entirely dependent upon the ability of the analyst to collect information. If they have poor research skills, lack personal contacts, or their organisation won't pay for collection resources (subscriptions to information sources, travel to the region, attendance at conferences, etc.), then the collection effort will be very limited and the analysis will be lower in quality. If 'raw' or 'unevaluated' information is passed to the client then this says more about the quality of the intelligence provider than it does about the Intelligence Cycle itself – there are organisations that do little more than aggregate news reports on a daily or weekly basis and pass these on as intelligence products. This is more common in 'generic' reporting, however, than in the bespoke intelligence report market.

An issue that falls between the direction and analysis/collection stages is that of 'time lag' caused, according to Hulnick, by the need to ensure that the right sources are available when direction is given to report on a particular topic. He gives the example of HUMINT, in which it can take years to develop the right source, or IMINT, in which the policy maker may have to wait for the imagery platforms to be re-calibrated to cover the required area. He uses this issue to support his argument that it is intelligence managers who are driving collection, in order to cover this time lag and any other information gaps that exist.[18] At this point I would take a step back from the Intelligence Cycle and argue that intelligence work and the Intelligence Cycle need to be separated out. Intelligence work encompasses all the processes that ensure that as much as possible of the right information is available at the right time. To this end, intelligence managers do need to be driving their own internal processes and need to anticipate the needs of their clients, whether government, military or corporate. This is, after all, why they are called intelligence managers. I don't believe it was ever the intention of those who first devised the Intelligence Cycle, or those who continue to be guided by it, that intelligence agencies should sit and do nothing until specifically asked a question. They should always be pursuing current and likely future government policy to ensure they are ready to respond. They should be 'horizon scanning' and watching indicators for threats. The Intelligence Cycle does not dictate intelligence work – it is a tool to enable policy makers to make the best use of intelligence. The old saying that it is a poor workman who blames his tools is true to a certain extent in this case. Policy makers do not make best use of this tool and intelligence managers, in many cases, do not teach policy makers well how to use it. In their chapter in this volume Peter Gill and Mark Phythian propose a model of intelligence that is more of a web than a linear process.[19] Their model of a complex series of interactions that comprise intelligence work as a whole seems to be an accurate one. I would argue that if any elements of the Intelligence Cycle may need changing, they are the collection and analysis (or processing) stages. These are perhaps more accurately depicted as a 'black box' step that encompasses Gill and Phythian's web.

The issue of raw, unevaluated intelligence going straight to policy makers has no real counterpart in the corporate intelligence world. There is no classified, single-source HUMINT or SIGINT to be treasured as a sign of a policy maker's 'intelligence virility' or the superiority of one agency over another. Perhaps the closest equivalent is when a corporate decision maker reads or hears a news story about an event that may have an impact upon their business. Even that may have some analysis attached, albeit usually fairly shallow, but it is usually followed by a fairly rapid request for analysis – thereby starting the Intelligence Cycle. Corporate intelligence providers often compete to be the first to provide comment on a major event, either in 'quick look reports' which provide immediate analysis, or in less formal ways such as an email, phone call, blog post or media item. Also, where a corporate intelligence provider does not have the expertise or resources to conduct its own collection, this is often sub-contracted to another specialist corporate provider. Even in major corporations that have their own internal intelligence departments, this kind of work is often contracted out. The internal or external intelligence provider, therefore, acts as a cut-out between the collector and the decision maker, who is often unaware that this has been sub-contracted out. A prime example of this is the pharmaceutical industry, which often requires surveillance or inside knowledge of the activities of single-issue extremist groups. Most corporate intelligence providers lack their own capability to provide this level of service and the work is contracted out by the pharmaceutical company's own security department or their external security or intelligence provider.[20]

The collection and analysis phases in corporate intelligence do not operate in separate stages. They do, however, operate in tandem rather than as entirely separate parallel stages, as Hulnick argues they do in government intelligence. Again, this is partly due to the much smaller size of corporate intelligence organisations, in which much of the work is done by a relatively small team, or even by one person. There is no separate organisation for collection and another for analysis, thus there is no competition between the two to be 'first with the story' to the policy maker. This results in a more unified product, so the policy maker is often presented with one assessment of the issue and not multiple, sometimes contradictory, versions of the 'truth'.

The dissemination phase: where analysis meets decision making

It is probably at the dissemination stage that the greatest difference appears between government intelligence and corporate intelligence. According to the Intelligence Cycle, the finished intelligence product is disseminated to policy makers, who make a decision or generate further requirements.[21] But, as Hulnick says, this 'is a distortion of what really happens'.[22] The reaction of policy makers often depends on the type of product. Warning intelligence very rarely gives sufficient advance notice, making it more of an alert than a warning, but 'rarely misses the start of a crisis'. However, it does not then give advice to policy makers on how to proceed.[23] Current intelligence, such as daily reports, mainly exists to provide background on events or an overview of issues that may be outside an official's normal area of expertise. According to Hulnick this is often the most useful intelligence product, but it rarely informs policy.[24] The next set of products are in-depth studies, which, as the name suggests, provide a higher-level analysis of a particular issue, normally used by mid-level or operational-level policy officials, although Hulnick points out that many are only read internally by agency staff, if they are read at all.[25] Finally there is the estimate, which is supposed to be 'a forecast of the future' used by senior government decision makers to decide policy.[26] Very often, however, these decision makers have already made up their minds and will only accept those estimates that support their decisions. Hulnick says:

> Although one would think that policy makers would want to know when they were heading in the wrong direction, this is not usually the case. Policy makers do not welcome intelligence that is non-conforming, perhaps because the large egos that brought them into positions of power do not permit admissions of ignorance.[27]

This somewhat gloomy view of the final stage of the cycle has some parallels in the corporate intelligence world, but there are also some key differences.

The closest parallel to warning intelligence or an estimate in the corporate world is probably the risk assessment and risk register. Technically speaking, a risk assessment is not only an intelligence document. In standard Enterprise Risk Management, the whole business unit, at whatever level, is involved in the risk assessment process. According to *A Structured Approach to Enterprise Risk Management (ERM) and the Requirements of ISO 3100*:

> An enterprise-wide approach to risk management enables an organisation to consider the potential impact of all types of risks on all processes, activities,

stakeholders, products and services. Implementing a comprehensive approach will result in an organisation benefiting from what is often referred to as the 'upside of risk'.[28]

But in reality, political and security risk assessments are normally carried out in their entirety by the security intelligence provider (or internal department) and the political risk intelligence provider (which may be the same as the security intelligence provider). These products act as a kind of warning intelligence in that they provide assessments of the risks to a project before it begins and during its lifetime. These reports include an assessment of the likelihood of a particular risk occurring and the impact it will have upon the project or the business as a whole.[29] Another product that fulfils the purpose of warning intelligence or an estimate is the indicators and warnings chart, sometimes referred to as a 'boiling frog chart'. These charts contain a list of indicators, either political or security-related, and ratings on each one. These ratings show the current security and political situation. For a stable country with no internal strife and a low crime rate all of the indicators may be shown as 'Normal'. For an unstable country with a civil war and high crime, the indicators will be set to reflect the situation. The point is that if one of these indicators changes – i.e. the situation improves or gets worse in the country of interest – then the business is informed of the change and this may trigger a decision-making process: either to remain and possibly increase investment or, in extreme cases, evacuate the country.[30] Of course, these products can only cover part of the equation, Donald Rumsfeld's famous 'known knowns' and 'known unknowns', but they cannot predict 'unknown unknowns'.[31] The extent to which intelligence can ever do that is, however, the subject of a much wider debate.

The key difference between these products and their government intelligence counterparts is that they come with policy advice. This can be in the form of mitigation measures in the case of the risk assessment and risk register or, in the case of the indicators and warnings chart, a link to a decision that needs to be made. By this I mean that when the indicators reach a certain level then management is informed that they need to decide on a course of action, either to evacuate or increase security provision, for example. This advice does not tell management what course of action should be taken. For example, during the flu epidemic in 2009 major oil companies in the UK did not initiate their pandemic protocols despite the World Health Organization officially declaring the outbreak to be a pandemic. Clearly this was identified in their risk management procedures but it is likely they carried out independent assessments of the situation and decided that there was no need to implement their procedures.[32] There have also been occasions when businesses have behaved in the same manner as the policy makers described by Hulnick. I was once fired as the political risk consultant to one major corporation that thought my assessments of a certain region of a war-torn country were too pessimistic, and rather than taking my advice and engaging a security firm they informed me that all they needed to succeed there was 'hard work and the right attitude'.[33]

In the corporate world, the parallel with current intelligence is to be found in subscriptions to periodic reports, usually daily, weekly or monthly. For the most part these are available as generic products, which are dealt with later, but many organisations require specifically tailored reports that cover a specific part of a country or a specific issue. Unlike the government intelligence world, these are used to inform policy, but usually at a relatively low level. For example, one client wanted monthly reports on a country but only needed a general overview and then detail on two specific locations where they had employees working on a project. The reports were used to determine whether any changes were needed to existing security procedures. Another client used monthly reports on the levels of terrorist incidents in a capital city, and when incidents fell below a certain level for several months in a row they intended to authorise the establishment of a permanent office there. A pharmaceutical company with a global presence only wanted reports on the activity of animal rights groups in certain cities, all gained from open sources. This would be used to provide warnings to employees of forthcoming animal rights protests or new protest techniques, as individuals would often be targeted during campaigns against the pharmaceutical industry.

The intelligence products with the most direct input into policy in the corporate world are arguably the bespoke reports, the equivalent of the in-depth studies. These are specially commissioned reports that directly support a decision or, more usually, support decision implementation. As with government, overarching business policy is often set regardless of the intelligence. For example, an international oil company may take the strategic decision to go into Iraq and then work out how to realise that decision. In this case, intelligence would be used to determine how best to seize the opportunity while keeping the risks within acceptable margins. An example of this kind of report is one I prepared for a major construction company before they began building an oil refinery in the Far East. The company wanted a report that detailed the political risks involved in doing business in the country, as they had never operated there before, but they also needed travel advice for their employees going from the capital city to the project site, which was a few hundred kilometres away from a main airport, and it needed to cover the local situation there as well. There had been some protests at the site by local people who had been displaced and felt they had not been adequately compensated for their land. These protests had resulted in at least one death and as a result local ill-feeling toward the project had increased considerably. Rather than such reports being simply read internally or written for the sake of it, corporations pay a great deal of money for in-depth studies of this kind and they expect a return. They expect to be able to base their business decisions upon the analysis contained within the report and they expect to see recommendations – as far as they are concerned these reports are written by subject-matter experts. The report in this example informed strategic-level decisions, helped the company's travel department and allowed the security department to plan and budget appropriately.

One area that does lend itself to the same kind of drive to 'find the right answer' or get intelligence to fit the policy is security intelligence. When the intelligence provider and the physical security provider are one and the same there is the danger that pressure could be exerted upon the intelligence team to provide an answer or amend their assessment in a way that allows the business to sell its physical security services. This is not the same as the intelligence team and the physical security team sitting down together and looking at the risks to come up with a workable solution to mitigate them and allow the client to perform their business. The latter is a legitimate part of the provision of expertise and, in most cases, is exactly what the client has asked them to do. What I mean here relates to those very rare occasions when an assessment could lead to a client not going ahead with a particular project or cancelling a current project and, therefore, not needing the physical security service. Equally, an assessment may indicate that the threat is much less than it was previously and, therefore, the client may feel they can scale down their physical security. On those occasions, management may put pressure on the intelligence team to moderate their assessment to prevent this from happening. I must point out, however, that these occasions are incredibly rare and it has only happened to me once in my career. In organisations where this occurs, anecdotal evidence from conversations with colleagues shows that it is normally because they are trying to scale the physical security to match the threat and not the risk. What I mean by this is that the intelligence team may, for example, have produced a threat assessment that shows high levels of terrorist activity in a particular country, but not in the area where the client intends to operate and not directed against foreigners. The subsequent risk assessment may then place the risk well within the risk tolerance of the client but still show the need for physical security measures to mitigate the risk. Equally, the threat assessment may have shown that there is only a fairly low threat of some kind of attack, but that these attacks are almost exclusively directed against foreign businesses, thereby driving the risk up, requiring extra mitigation measures. My point is that this is far more likely where the external security and intelligence provider has no real understanding of the difference between threat and risk although, of course, there are still cases where the external provider is just interested in selling its physical security measures regardless of the threat or risk.

There have been cases in my experience where the language used in an assessment can have an inadvertent effect on a client, and corporate intelligence providers often have to carefully match their language to the client's risk appetite. On one occasion I recall providing an assessment in which I said the threat was low in a particular city because there were only between three and five terrorist attacks per day. My assessment was based upon previous levels of activity that had been as high as 30 attacks per day only two years before. The client, with an extremely low appetite for risk, was on the verge of dismissing my assessment until I managed to explain the background and context. On the opposite end of the scale, there have been clients (usually news media organisations but also on one occasion an energy company) who have dismissed assessments as being too doom-laden and have insisted that a project continue regardless – to its credit, the security company I worked for at the time refused to take contracts where this happened.

It is at the dissemination phase that analysis meets decision making. Marrin begins by looking at the 'standard model' of intelligence that exists within the scholarship, in which objectivity and the separation of intelligence and decision making are the key features. In this model, decision makers ask for intelligence, get a product and then make a decision.[34] He takes a deeper look into the literature and finds, however, that most of the evidence shows that intelligence very rarely changes minds, or is ignored if it doesn't fit with the policy maker's decision.[35] This certainly fits with Hulnick's experiences in the CIA. Marrin offers up a number of explanations for this. First, he points out that, according to the literature, there are serious consequences to changing policy mid-stream – politicians do not want to be accused of 'flip-flopping' or be found to have made a mistake.[36] He also finds an argument that policy makers feel they have sufficient expertise and general knowledge of their own upon which to base a decision, only requiring intelligence to update their facts but not to give an opinion.[37] So Marrin asks what politicians do base their decisions on, if it is not intelligence. His answer is that decision makers are not data driven, but base their decisions on 'concepts, theories or mind-sets that affect their interpretation and use of raw data as well as analysis'.[38] Political policy making is values driven, based as much on political philosophy as it is upon hard facts and figures. Thus it can be argued that intelligence based upon more scientific methodology is not speaking the same 'language' as political policy makers.[39] Policy makers are also aware that intelligence analysis is not an exact science but contains uncertainty and ambiguity.[40] This gives politicians a 'get-out clause' – it is easier for them to ignore intelligence that doesn't fit the policy because it does not give them the certainty they require, while at the same time allowing them to use intelligence that does seem to forecast some measure of success. Marrin does offer some glimmer of hope, though, suggesting that intelligence can have an indirect impact upon policy through 'the decision-maker's creation of policy alternatives and adjustments'.[41] In conclusion, Marrin argues that the current model of intelligence scholarship that concentrates upon the accuracy of the intelligence product should be replaced by one that concentrates upon its usefulness.[42] This is effectively how corporate intelligence works, but this is a product of the differences between the political and business worlds.

Business decisions are very different from political decisions. They are not based upon political philosophy or values; they are based upon seizing opportunities or taking risks in order to maximise profits. In 1947 Herbert Simon argued that business executives make decisions with 'bounded rationality', meaning they make decisions that they believe are 'good enough' based on the information available.[43] Business decisions, in the era of Enterprise Risk Management, are based on assessments of financial, reputational and security risks. Not every decision involves a high degree of risk – in fact businesses often spread their risk, mixing in high-risk decisions with many low-risk ones so that losses are minimised. Businesses can also insure against risk with companies such as Zurich, which claims it can 'help you manage exposures such as expropriation, political violence, currency inconvertibility and non payment with our global footprint and experience as you conduct business in markets across the world'.[44] The point is that businesses are constantly operating in an atmosphere of risk, and the consequences of taking a risk or changing a decision if it becomes too risky are very different from those in the political world. Intelligence in the corporate world, with its assessments couched in 'words of estimative probability', to use Sherman Kent's phrase, is speaking a language that business can understand. Its products, as described here, are intended to highlight potential risks and give mitigating advice. Corporate intelligence products say, in essence, 'if you are going to do this, these are the potential risks and this is what you can do to mitigate them'.

Conclusion

This chapter has shown that the corporate intelligence world operates very differently to the government intelligence world and the Intelligence Cycle is used in a different way. The direction phase is heavily dependent upon the relationship between the decision maker and the intelligence provider. In the corporate world, the intelligence provider has a much clearer understanding of the decision and how the intelligence product needs to support the process underpinning that decision. As in the political world, the decision has often been taken at a strategic level, but intelligence has the job of facilitating that decision. The direction can then be much more clearly focused upon specific issues. I have shown that the collection and analysis phases are conducted in tandem, and here there are similarities with the more orthodox critiques of the Intelligence Cycle that argue that the two phases never really occur in sequence. Here I would agree with the body of intelligence scholars who argue that the phases should be combined. Gill and Phythian's 'web' model of intelligence is a much closer approximation of how intelligence work is actually done. Of course collection and analysis in the commercial world are far less complex than in the government world. They are carried out by much smaller organisations with far fewer issues to cover; this is largely a product of the much more focused direction that prevails in the corporate world. In the dissemination phase, analysis meets decision making. In the government world this creates tensions but in the corporate world decision makers expect to get solutions presented alongside problems; and that the intelligence products they get, either in the political risk or security realm, come with mitigating suggestions or security solutions.

Like Arthur Hulnick's article, this analysis is a largely personal perspective based upon observation of the Intelligence Cycle in practice. I may have been lucky and seen it work, while others may have different experiences. My aim here has been to apply the critiques of government intelligence and see how they stand up in the commercial world. Although this by no means covers every eventuality, I have found that the Intelligence Cycle works fairly well in the corporate world but there is one key difference between the Intelligence Cycle and the way intelligence work is done. The Intelligence Cycle does not dictate intelligence work; it only provides guidance on how to get benefit from intelligence.

Finally, I have highlighted the major difference between the role of intelligence in the corporate world and the role of intelligence in the government world; it's all about uncertainty in seizing opportunities and mitigating risks.

Notes

1 Arthur S. Hulnick, 'What's wrong with the Intelligence Cycle', *Intelligence and National Security*, Vol. 21 No. 6, 2006, pp. 959–79; Stephen Marrin, 'Intelligence Analysis and Decision-Making: Methodological Challenges', in Peter Gill, Stephen Marrin and Mark Phythian (eds), *Intelligence Theory: Key Questions and Debates* (London: Routledge, 2009), pp. 131–50.
2 Both examples are from the author's personal experience in Iraq (2004–2008) and in the United Kingdom (2008–2010).
3 William Shakespeare, *The Merchant of Venice*, Act One, Scene III and Act Three, Scene I.
4 Ibid., Act Three, Scene I.
5 Ibid., Act One, Scene III.
6 Ibid., Act Two, Scene VII.
7 Ibid., Act Three, Scene II.
8 International Standards Organisation, *Draft International Standard ISO/DIS 31000:2009, Risk Management – Principles and Guidelines on Implementation* (Geneva: International Standards Organisation, 2008), p. 12.
9 Shakespeare, *The Merchant of Venice*, Act Three, Scene II.
10 Aprodex website, www.aprodex.com/intelligence-gathering-and-analysis-281-sc. aspx, last accessed 20 October 2012.
11 Dominick Donald, 'Private Security and Intelligence', in Andrew Alexandra, Deane-Peter Baker and Marina Caparini (eds), *Private Military and Security Companies: Ethics, Policies and Civil–Military Relations* (London: Routledge, 2008), pp. 135–8.
12 Ibid. One global head of intelligence for a multinational organisation has suggested to the author that the term 'research and analysis' should be used for all corporate intelligence activity for this very reason.
13 See www.aegisworld.com/index.php/aria/who-we-are, http://www.oxan.com/Analysis/Team/Default.aspx?about=true/ and www.diligence.com/our-team.html. All last accessed 15 October 2012.
14 Hulnick, 'What's wrong with the Intelligence Cycle', p. 964.
15 Ibid., pp. 959–60.
16 Marrin, 'Intelligence Analysis and Decision-Making', p. 131.
17 Hulnick, 'What's wrong with the Intelligence Cycle', p. 961.
18 Ibid., pp. 960–1.
19 Peter Gill and Mark Phythian, Chapter 2 in this volume.
20 This can have its own problems, though, in terms of ethics and legality. The 2010 Mark Kennedy case called into question the activities of specialist companies in the single-issue extremism field. Rob Evans, Amelia Hill, Paul Lewis and Patrick Kingsley, 'Mark Kennedy: Secret Policeman's Sideline as Corporate Spy', *The Guardian*, 13 January 2011; Neil Tweedie, 'Eco Infiltrator Mark Kennedy: The Great Betrayal', *Daily Telegraph*, 15 January 2011.
21 Hulnick, 'What's wrong with the Intelligence Cycle', p. 964.
22 Ibid.
23 Ibid., p. 965.
24 Ibid.
25 Ibid., p. 966.
26 Ibid.
27 Ibid.

28 Institute of Risk Management, *A Structured Approach to Enterprise Risk Management (ERM) and the Requirements of ISO 3100* (London: AIRMIC, Alarm, IRM, 2010), p. 2.
29 For a more detailed analysis of how risk assessments are carried out and used by organisations see David Strachan-Morris, 'Threat and Risk: What's the Difference and Why Does it Matter?', *Intelligence and National Security*, Vol. 27 No. 2, 2012, pp. 172–86.
30 For a publicly available example of this kind of political risk product see Control Risks Group, *Risk Map. 2012* (London: Control Risks Group, 2012), www.control-risks.com/OurThinking/CRsDocumentDownload/RiskMap_2012_report.pdf,   last accessed 15 October 2012.
31 Donald Rumsfeld, Press Briefing, US Department of Defense, 12 February 2002.
32 Author's recollection from a meeting with a senior security manager from an energy company in late 2009.
33 Email to the author. For the record, the security situation in that area is now far worse than even I predicted due to the outbreak of civil war in a neighbouring country.
34 Marrin, 'Intelligence Analysis and Decision-Making', p. 135.
35 Ibid., p. 136.
36 Ibid., p. 137.
37 Ibid., p. 138.
38 Ibid., p. 140.
39 Ibid., p. 142.
40 Ibid., p. 143.
41 Ibid., p. 146.
42 Ibid., pp. 147–8.
43 Herbert Simon, *Administrative Behavior: a Study of Decision-Making Processes in Administrative Organizations* (New York: Simon and Schuster, 1997). This is, of course, a vastly simplified version of Simon's conclusions.
44 Zurich website, www.zurichna.com/zna/creditandpoliticalrisk/creditandpoliticalrisk.htm, last accessed 15 October 2012.

8   Is it time to move beyond the Intelligence Cycle?

A UK practitioner perspective

David Omand

The conventional diagram of the Intelligence Cycle embodies three different ideas, each one of which has been subject to challenge by the authors contributing to this volume. For the practitioner, accepting the continued use of the cycle itself in intelligence teaching and studies is of lesser importance than establishing the validity and relevance of the arguments over these three basic ideas themselves, and their implications for the work of intelligence communities in the twenty-first century.

The first concept is that of an intelligence narrative: sequencing functional activities to create a narrative that links the steps said to be involved in producing intelligence, starting with collection of raw material from agents, signals interception, imaging satellites and so on, and leading after processing (validation, collation, analysis and assessment) to some form of intelligence reporting to an end user, be they policy maker, military commander or law enforcement officer. For the modern practitioner, the nature of the intelligence narrative and its public acceptability has become a pressing concern in an age of domestic counter-terrorism, internet surveillance and drone strikes. Likewise, the effectiveness of independent oversight of the inherently secret activity of intelligence agencies becomes an issue for the democracies.

The second concept is that of professional intelligence identity: the separation of the identity of the intelligence professionals from that of their various user communities, especially the policy makers. The cycle shows intelligence being disseminated by producers to the consumers of intelligence (be they end users or analysts in other parts of one's own or liaison intelligence communities) who then provide feedback on the value of the product in order to refine collection strategies. It is this idea of intelligence having an added value in public policy terms expressed in user response that curls the linear intelligence narrative back on itself in a feedback loop or cycle. For the practitioner, estimating where the greatest added value of future intelligence activity is likely to lie is of the essence in organizing the analytic effort, in direction of priorities, in resource allocation, and in planning and justifying future investment.

The third (meta-) concept is that of the model of intelligence: that it is indeed possible sensibly to model intelligence activity, specifically by capturing in a cyclical model the specific functional activities that reveal the essence of what intelligence activity is all about. The reach of the model is governed by the choice of which activities to include in the cycle. That choice is, of course, as contributors to this volume have pointed out, equally a choice to exclude others and to define 'intelligence' accordingly, a point of some importance for the practitioner in terms of the boundaries, organization and development of the intelligence community of the future.

Each of these fundamental ideas is examined in more detail in the sections that follow, concluded by an examination of the implications for the future practice of intelligence.

The intelligence narrative

The idea of identifiable steps leading to the production of intelligence goes back to the military lessons of the American Civil War, the Franco-Prussian War and, for the British, the Boer War – in which Lord Wolseley's *Pocket-Book for Field Service* in 1886 provided detailed instructions for the field commander and his staff on how to choose an intelligence officer and how to set up a field intelligence organization. Three phases of intelligence work were covered: collection, analysis and reporting.[1] These steps became the basis of the modern military intelligence doctrine with its sequence of direction, collection, processing and dissemination (DCPD).[2]

From the experience of these nineteenth-century campaigns the roles of the general staff branches developed, and with that the idea that it is not enough for the commander to observe the lie of the land and listen to the reports from his scouts. Specialized activities are needed to provide reliable topographical information on the terrain ahead such as the navigability of rivers, condition of fording places, bridges and roads, and later the state of the railways as well as intelligence on the movements of enemy formations themselves.

Systematic description of what is involved in the production and use of intelligence was thus developed by the pioneers of military intelligence before the First World War, distinguishing between what is involved at the acquisition stage from that of the tasks of classifying and disseminating the product to field units.[3] British Admiralty intelligence in Room 40 during the First World War introduced analysis as a separate function from collection and processing (presaging the later initiative of Sherman Kent in the newly formed CIA to split the 'processing' function identified in the military version of the cycle into further separate steps in order to highlight the importance of intelligence analysis as a professional function in its own right, a practice followed to this day by the US Agencies). Wilhelm Agrell has drawn my attention to German experience as described in Max Ronge's *Kriegs und Industriespionage*, printed in Vienna in 1930. Ronge was a former intelligence officer and the last director of the intelligence department of the Austrian–Hungarian general staff in the First World War and he provides an early example of a visual illustration of an intelligence system, with all-source analysis at the centre (called *Feind-Evidenz*).

By the end of the Second World War, as Michael Warner explains in Chapter 1 of this volume, the sequence of intelligence functions was well established in military circles. For example, the 1940 US Army Air Corps Manual FM 1-40 describes the functions of an intelligence officer on the staff of an air commander as following a routine sequence that when viewed as a whole illustrates a coordinated and continuing process involving a 'sequence or cycle of intelligence procedure for any specific tactical mission'. The War Office in London published in 1944 updated versions of its field manuals on military intelligence, of which No. 1 similarly covers the principles of acquisition, collation, communication and liaison.[4] The visual representation of the cycle itself came into use in the United States to illustrate this in intelligence teaching in the late 1940s. Although in the UK intelligence community the cycle metaphor does not seem to have caught the imagination in quite the same way, the logical relationship between the intelligence functions was well understood. The first official Cabinet Office booklet describing British intelligence was titled *Central Intelligence Machinery* and did not use the cycle.[5]

The classic US Intelligence Cycle provided a readily comprehensible Cold War intelligence narrative. Its intuitive public appeal is well demonstrated in the film *Thirteen Days*[6] when at the heart of the Cuban missile crisis photo-recce sorties are ordered over the island (no doubt leaving cinema audiences on the edge of their seats over the danger to the pilots), the resulting raw imagery is processed (with audience tension building over the wait) and interpreted by expert analysts (with the will-they, won't-they-spot-the-Soviet-missiles moment), and the resulting intelligence assessment of the state of preparedness of the Soviet missile deployments is delivered by the Director of Central Intelligence in person to a tense National Security Council to help the President decide how much time he has to avert war before the missiles become operational (satisfyingly demonstrating the power of intelligence to shape events).

Recent technical developments, especially in support of military counter-insurgency and counter-terrorist operations, have, however, also reduced the need for steps in the cycle to be followed strictly sequentially. Modern communications allow fast interaction: targets geo-located by SIGINT or other intelligence and identified as hostile by intelligence analysts can have their coordinates uploaded onto precision guided missiles already airborne carried by drones or combat aircraft in orbit. Valuable intelligence can now come from accessing and mining digital data in government and commercial databases with examples ranging from immigration records to mobile telephone records and airline bookings as well as many other examples from open sources. Such data can be exploited to reveal clues to the identities, location, movements, finance and associations of suspects. Such intelligence exploitation of protected personal data, for which I have coined the term PROTINT,[7] makes the intelligence officer more akin to a detective on a fast-moving case than the classic intelligence analyst analysing the characteristics of the strategic weapons systems of potential adversaries. Most recently, the explosive growth in social media use on the internet has begun to provide another source of intelligence, for which the term SOCMINT seems appropriate[8] and which can, for example, provide near-real-time insight into the sentiment of demonstrators against a regime.

The steps in the Intelligence Cycle have never mapped neatly onto the responsibilities of individual agencies. The exact form of the cycle if shown in detail would look different, for example, in imagery, signals intelligence and human intelligence. The now extensive links with overseas liaison services, as well as differing national organizational structures, also mean that the standard cycle is unlikely to capture precisely any given nation's intelligence production processes. It may well be that the standard cycle reflects the Anglo-Saxon cultural prejudices of its originators and that in China or India, for example, their different philosophical traditions would lead them to a different model. It may nevertheless help newcomers to intelligence work, for example in the burgeoning commercial intelligence sector, to have in their minds all the steps and different skills that have to be brought to bear in a systematic way to produce traditional intelligence analytic products.

Given modern developments, it is harder than in the past to construct a comparably simple narrative for modern intelligence work. Of course, conventional inter-State intelligence can be assumed to continue, but after 9/11 the emphasis has been on intelligence for immediate action, whether to protect deployed military forces or identify and locate terrorists, as well as other current priorities to interdict embargo breaking or proliferation activities, interrupt narcotics supply or to trigger other forms of operational military, police or border security activity. The key relationships over the last decade have been as much those between analysts and military commanders as policy makers, and increasingly and notably with law enforcement officers.

Intelligence is, however, not evidence, and given the inherent need for maintaining secrecy over sources and methods there will always be limitations on – and controversy over – how far intelligence can be converted into admissible evidence in a proper court of law. The intelligence narrative has therefore in the public mind become clouded by questions over the methods used to obtain intelligence by our own and liaison services, both from the point of view of allegations of violations of individual rights through coercive interrogation and ill-treatment of suspects and by violation of privacy rights through potentially invasive methods of surveillance and investigation. Strains are evident regarding the rules of evidence and judicial procedure to allow secret material to be admitted securely if cases are to proceed to court. Concerns arise too over the limits of direct action taken on the basis of intelligence, such as drone strikes. The public is clearly prepared to place a high value on its own security, but as yet lacks a consensus on what should be the limits on intelligence work to deliver it, an issue with which parliamentary and other independent oversight bodies of intelligence communities will have to wrestle in the years to come.

The interaction with the user and professional intelligence identity

By comparison with the early recognition of the sequence of steps in military intelligence production the adoption of a cyclic model to describe the whole process is relatively recent. As Michael Warner has suggested in Chapter 1 of this volume, the cyclic representation probably arose in intelligence teaching from the influx of large numbers of wartime recruits from academia. It thus dates from the era of the newly discovered popularity of the notion of cybernetic systems and optimization theories. In passing we can note that in the field of economics it was the same era that gave rise to neo-classical welfare theory with its conclusion that the net result of the personal optimization decisions of individuals pursuing their own self-interest will lead inexorably to a social optimum.[9]

The optimizing mechanism in the classic Intelligence Cycle is the feedback loop at the end by which comments from customers inform and regulate the next round of the collection cycle. Such feedback will certainly still be sought by intelligence agencies, for example seeking a scoring of individual reports as 'major contribution to policy', 'of value in policy making', 'of background value', or even 'of little or no value'. But modern digital communications also enable intelligence products to be available on demand, changing the relationship between the intelligence analyst and the military staff or policy customer. Databases of intelligence product (written reports, indexes, watch lists, multispectral images, annotated digitized mapping, equipment schematics and the like) can be searched securely online and then downloaded as required by the user. This 'pull' complements the traditional Intelligence Cycle's direction of 'push' of product and is a major conceptual development beyond the classic cycle in understanding how modern intelligence works.[10]

Most versions of the cycle therefore add numerous short-circuits and feedback loops,[11] emphasizing that intelligence flows are not linear and that there are direct interactions between the policy makers and the tasking process over specific requirements such as an approaching ministerial visit or an international negotiation. There are also many operational connections to refine search parameters or provide names of individuals of intelligence interest for border security and law enforcement. Practitioners also know that policy makers are often too busy – and often not sufficiently expert – to spell out their 'needs' in advance and that it is mostly up to the collecting agencies to be sufficiently in contact with the world of the policy maker to know what will make a difference to the quality and timeliness of their decisions and judgements.[12] In a comparable way, in 'target-centric' versions of the Intelligence Cycle[13] the components of the cycle can be connected together in a network, with the participants collaborating to produce a shared picture of the target.

What no simple version of the cycle can render visually is the cumulative value of assessed intelligence. The assembled whole can reveal far more than the reading of individual intelligence reports that are by their nature usually fragmentary and incomplete. This drawback is at least partially overcome (although at the price of added complexity and thus providing a less comprehensible intelligence narrative) by the stocks and flows approach of systems analysis,[14] highlighting the importance to the analyst of having a base of useable intelligence.

Most nations have developed processes to capture the requirements and priorities of customers as well as feedback on reporting, such as the US National Intelligence Topics and the UK annual Joint Intelligence Committee (JIC) Intelligence Requirements, based on a prioritization exercise in which departmental customers are forced to rank their ambitions for intelligence reporting. Such customer-driven priorities ought always to include authorization to the intelligence community to invest on its own initiative in intelligence to forewarn government of unexpected, and usually unwelcome, surprises even where these arise from countries or circumstances that were not high (or even were missed) on a prioritized current requirements list.

On the one hand, therefore, as already noted the end user may not appreciate what intelligence might, if commissioned, be able to deliver. On the other hand, a customer's top priority may not be achievable if there is a high degree of security around the target, and given the inevitably constrained means available to devote to any one target. In practice a balance is needed between having high probability of good coverage of second order targets and lower probability of success with high-priority but hard targets.

The practitioner must also be aware of the long-run extra costs, which are likely to be very substantial, to open up a new overseas station (plus the time taken to build agent networks) or to make the necessary investment in satellite observation platforms or interception and processing capability for new modes of communication. By contrast, the short-run marginal costs of switching priorities can be low if the necessary capability is already in being, allowing agents in place to be re-tasked with new questions or allowing different targets to be intercepted successfully. The planning and directing component of the cycle has therefore to operate both at a strategic level, to give direction for future investment in assets, and at a tactical level, to try to meet operational requirements as a situation develops or circumstances change. The British intelligence requirements system has also always recognized that there are requirements on which intelligence is to be actively sought and resources expended and there are those on which intelligence should be reported on an opportunity basis.[15] The balancing of these considerations can only be done within the intelligence community itself at the level of the specialist agency, where the necessary detailed knowledge and experience lies.

The 2002/03 Iraq experience re-ignited old debates within intelligence communities about the importance of intelligence assessments (such as those from the JIC) being regarded as professional advice on a par with professional military or medical advice. Governments need not act on such advice, but have to accept it for what it is and not cherry pick from it to fit policy. The danger of politicization of intelligence reporting if analysts and their customers get too comfortable in their relationship has been a concern since the days of Sherman Kent in the CIA, but the practitioner knows that real life requires a balanced relationship.

The nuanced British attitude to the Kent school of thought was well summed up in advice from Cabinet Secretary Burke Trend to Prime Minister Harold Wilson at the time of re-organization in the 1960s:

[T]hey [the United States] take the attitude that the job of an intelligence machine is to produce the best 'technical' evaluation it can; to deposit this on the policy-maker's desk; and then to wash its hands of what happens. Intelligence is a matter for purists, whose objectivity should not be contaminated by unduly close contact with political considerations; and the producers of intelligence should therefore work at relative arm's length from the makers of policy ... We have always believed that the intelligence machine must be geared actively and positively into the policy-making machine, that both machines must be given the fullest opportunity to react on each other, and that the responsibility for the recommendation which is ultimately submitted to Ministers in any particular case is something which both machines in some sense share. The JIC itself is the formal expression of this view.[16]

This is the case because the JIC has both intelligence professionals and senior Whitehall policy makers as full members and all members share responsibility for the final assessment.

The reach of the model of intelligence

A relatively narrow definition of the purpose of intelligence is to help improve the quality and timeliness of decision taking by reducing ignorance; secret intelligence can be said to achieve that purpose in respect of information that others wish to remain hidden – and usually that you do not want them to know that you know.[17] The use of secret intelligence is of great antiquity, but organizing intelligence activity as a specialist domain separate from those who have the responsibility for taking action on it is in historical terms a relatively new concept. For Walsingham in the sixteenth century, for example, protecting Queen Elizabeth I from the intrigues of the Catholic monarchies in Europe, as for the later British colonial leaders, the collection and assessment of secret intelligence was simply part of the task of taking action to preserve state security. The wartime British Chiefs of Staff did not hesitate to ask the JIC to rewrite intelligence assessments submitted to them whose conclusions they disagreed with. The popularization of the Intelligence Cycle is a product of the Cold War, no doubt owing much to the perceived need in the United States to build up the respectability of the new central intelligence machine and to emphasize the distinctions between the new professional breed of civilian and military intelligence analyst and their policy customers and the evident need to maintain the independence of the former from the policy outlook of the latter.

What the classic Intelligence Cycle, based on a narrow definition of intelligence activity, leaves out is a significant part of the activity of intelligence communities including counter-intelligence and security intelligence.[18] British intelligence effort over several centuries supported the civil power in maintaining security in British colonies and dependencies.[19] Colonial intelligence was at the heart of anticipating, and then policing, unrest, and the same could be said for the intelligence support in the British counter-terrorist campaigns in Northern

Ireland or the French in Algeria. The fundamental role of MI5 in the UK and its dependent territories is to be a security service, rather than an intelligence service in the sense implied by the Intelligence Cycle. So MI5 from the outset has been the principal consumer of its own intelligence product for the purposes of disrupting and neutralizing threats to the security of the UK and its dependencies, and only relatively recently with the growth of international terrorism has it been a full intelligence-generating participant in the JIC.

Examples of leveraging secret intelligence to disrupt hostile activities include the use of deception and sting operations, by intercepting illegal arms shipments and by arresting those involved in terrorist, proliferation or criminal networks. External intelligence services can therefore double as external action services, increasingly with support from Special Forces units within defence. As Hulnick has pointed out, policy makers want not just more information bearing on their decisions, they want to know what can be done to achieve their goals by utilizing the more intimate knowledge Western intelligence officers may have of the personalities and politics of the leadership of a country of interest, or of opposition groups, than may be possible through conventional diplomatic channels, and what opportunities there may be for using agents of influence.[20]

The classic Intelligence Cycle does not encompass such work, nor does it illustrate the inherent conflict between gathering intelligence (which requires acting as unobtrusively as possible) and direct action (which can result in very visible results, as in the French sinking of the Greenpeace ship, *Rainbow Warrior*, or the US mission to capture or kill Bin Laden). A nod in that direction is given in my own updating of the Intelligence Cycle[21] by the inclusion in the cycle of the function of 'action-on', as the siginters term the process of gaining authority to take action on intelligence reporting, as well as placing the user of intelligence at the centre of the cycle, interacting with every stage of the intelligence process.

The new cyber domain also provides a new (or, more accurately, greatly enhanced) operational opportunity for the intelligence community. Iain Lobban, the Director of the UK's SIGINT agency, GCHQ, in his first public speech[22] suggested that good cyber security can solve 80 per cent of vulnerabilities through keeping software patches up to date, educating staff on good practice in information assurance, good personnel security to counter the 'insider' threat and so on. But tackling the remaining 20 per cent of the severe persistent threat is going to involve active detection using intelligence capabilities to illuminate the capabilities and intentions of the attacker, for example discriminating between attacks for criminal gain, for intelligence gathering and industrial espionage, or as a means of planting Trojan attacks on critical systems to be activated at time of need. Such intelligence can trigger international law enforcement investigation and in future may also provide active means for disrupting the attacker and even of striking back. To do this requires the leverage provided from the intelligence and law enforcement space, and that involves highly classified and sometimes commercially very sensitive information and a near-real-time response. There will be equities to be balanced between the interests of intelligence gathering, of law enforcement and of the protection of national infrastructure. Operating at cyber speed will be of the essence in using such intelligence, for which the classic Intelligence Cycle is an inadequate model.

Conclusions for the practitioner

The advent of the UK National Security Strategy (NSS)[23] shows that the British security establishment has recognized the importance of the intelligence function to future national policy in ways that include but go beyond the classic Intelligence Cycle. Thus the first task identified in the NSS is the identification and monitoring of national security risks and opportunities, specifically to produce:

- strategic intelligence on potential threats and opportunities for the UK to act;
- coordinated analysis and assessment of the highest priorities;
- investment in technologies to support the gathering of communications data for national security and law enforcement;
- intelligence assets to support the core requirements and economic prosperity;
- secure borders and counter-terrorism capability.

From having been in earlier centuries the covert exercise of the sovereign's prerogative powers in defence of the realm, intelligence in the UK National Security Strategy has now become an avowed, statutory component of modern government, in domestic as well as in foreign affairs, in law enforcement as much as in statecraft or military operations. With a historical perspective, we can see an underlying three-fold logic to this fundamental shift, even if at the time those involved may well have felt themselves simply responding to the pressure of events, not least from media revelations and human rights pressures.

The starting point was an increasing awareness, as the Cold War came to an end, of a variety of threats to human security, displacing the earlier dominating preoccupation with the security of the state from Soviet aggression and subversion of democratic institutions. National security now begins to be seen as a state of confidence that the response to the major risks facing the citizen – both malign threats such as terrorism and natural hazards such as pandemics – is being managed to allow normal life to continue, with markets stable and investment being encouraged. This benign state contrasts with the conditions of insecurity, on the other hand, that are readily identifiable in those countries where economic and social developments are held back through armed conflict, civil strife and religious war, insurrection and terrorism.

Accepting that the goal of national security, as seen from the point of view of the citizen, is thus about protection from all major risks (both threats and hazards) a second step in constructing modern national security policy is to apply the tools of risk management. Thus the use of risk registers and risk matrices and applying risk analysis to rank threats, acknowledging that the response has to be framed in terms of risk management not risk elimination. Here the magnitude of the risk to be managed can be assessed as the product of several factors that are capable of being influenced by government: the likelihood of the disruptive risk arising; the degree of vulnerability of the nation and its inhabitants to the danger; and the initial impact and duration of danger and disruption should the risk crystallize.

An example of such risk management in practice is given by the longstanding British '4P' counter-terrorism strategy, CONTEST,[24] designed to reduce the likelihood of attempted attacks (by strategic campaigns to improve the ability to PURSUE terrorists and PREVENT violent radicalization), to reduce vulnerability (by a strategic campaign, PROTECT, to identify and correct weaknesses in protective security of the critical national infrastructure including aviation security), and to reduce the impact and duration of disruption (by investment to PREPARE blue-light services, community resilience and exercise crisis management). The overall aim is to reduce the threat so that normal life can continue, freely and with confidence. The dissolving of the previous hard boundary between the overseas and domestic domains when it comes to intelligence and security reinforces the need for risk-management thinking as events abroad impact on domestic communities and vice versa. Looking for ways to work upstream of problems to pre-empt, or at least minimize, risks of instability and conflict that could affect national interests is well embedded in UK national security thinking.

Taking a human view of overall national security thus leads naturally to an increased demand for intelligence to support risk analysis. If, for example, strategies such as CONTEST are to be pursued successfully then intelligence must be brought to bear on each of the factors in the risk equation. This has happened in the post-9/11 expansion of intelligence and law enforcement capabilities to detect terrorist networks and frustrate impending plots. But intelligence is also needed to help understand the ideology of the terrorists and explain their motivations and thus help focus work to prevent radicalization and enhance community cohesion. Different types of intelligence must in addition be brought to bear to support investment in protective security, based on deep technical analysis of terrorist capabilities and future intentions. Different again is the type of horizon scanning and strategic notice needed to support contingency planning and prepare the emergency services, looking not just at prediction of the probable forms of future disruption but at the spread of risk of unlikely but high-impact events.

Here we see a broader 'intelligence' function not captured in the classic Intelligence Cycle: to provide government with strategic notice of possible emerging risks (and opportunities). The intelligence analysts have an important contribution to make to generating strategic notice of possible future threats, and thus avoiding strategic surprise, but so do the scientists and technologists with their horizon scanning, the geologists looking at oil and mineral resources, the climatologists modelling future climate change and water stress, the astronomers looking for coronal mass ejections and stray asteroids, and the social scientists and anthropologists studying the growth of hostile ideologies and the problems of rapidly increasing global urbanization. Where in government does a National Security Council look for consolidated assessment of short- and long-term risks, covering both threats and hazards and using open-source and traditional secret sources? To be useful clearly such work has to be fundamentally inter-disciplinary, and to break out of the stockade of secrecy around most Intelligence Cycle activity.

The intelligence community has, for example, to be prepared to assess the worst, or near-worst cases of possible terrorist attack as well as report on the most likely form they will take. The former takes us into the territory of low-probability, high-impact scenarios with non-Gaussian fat-tailed distributions (of a type government has not traditionally been good at recognizing); the latter takes us into central 'most probable' outcomes that are the staple of JIC and NIE intelligence assessments. To counter the former, policy makers may construct a Minimax strategy of minimizing the maximum level of damage the adversary can cause, for example by investing in protective security at nuclear sites and water treatment plants and in laboratories handling toxins. To counter the latter, the authorities may invest in Maximin strategies to maximize the minimum general level of security offered to the public, for example in crowded public places such as railway stations and sports stadiums, through such measures as CCTV coverage and armed policing. Different forms of intelligence work have therefore to be brought to bear on each of these factors, with the common thread that the interaction between all-source intelligence analysts and policy makers will need to be continuous and close, and certainly not following a stereotyped Intelligence Cycle.

The UK National Security Strategy used such risk analysis to identify four types of 'top tier' risk to UK interests: the validity of the method can be judged by the fact that examples of all four have arisen since the strategy was published in October 2010: international terrorism (such as the failed printer cartridge bombs plot emanating from Al-Qaeda in the Arabian Peninsula (AQAP) in Yemen); cyber attack (a worsening persistent threat driven by espionage and criminal gain); international military crises (as in Libya during 2011); and major accidents or natural hazards (the Fukushima reactor failure in Japan in March 2011, with its knock-on effects on global industry through just-in-time logistics chains and international market confidence).

There are of course limits to the reliance that can be placed on risk identification. There will always be surprises: the most significant example over the last few years of failure of strategic notice and consequent risk blindness has been the global financial crisis, a threat that did not figure on the risk registers of the UK or other nations. Nevertheless, modern national security policy provides a strong rationale for greater investment in national intelligence capability. There is perhaps a further reason, evident to the policy makers, even if given less stress in public. Over the next decade financial austerity resulting from the need to overcome successive global economic and financial crises will mean reduced levels of expenditure on both hard and soft power capabilities and reductions in the numbers available for domestic law enforcement. Thinking smarter will have to be given priority.

One result of the need to do more with less is the harnessing of technical developments in managing and moving data efficiently within intelligence agencies. Now the search is for ways better to integrate and fuse all elements of the process.[25] Intelligence agencies are now knowledge management industries coming to terms with the cultural and structural transformations of the postmodern world.[26]

With such thinking in mind we can derive from a modern practitioner perspective a more detailed model of future intelligence analysis (using intelligence in its broadest sense) to support national security decision making. The model is best thought of as consisting of four levels of reasoning.[27]

The first level is that of situational awareness. The primary use of intelligence, and by far the greatest in terms of volume of effort involved, will continue to be what I term *building situational awareness*, to answer questions of 'what, where, who?' Intelligence reporting is always fragmentary, incomplete and must be assumed even after validations sometimes turn out to be just plain wrong. But used systematically over a period, government and its various organs will be in a position to take better decisions than by simply relying on chance or political whim.

A second essential dimension in using intelligence in supporting decision making is, however, in building an *explanatory* theory of past and present behaviour, answering the questions 'why and what for?' Such explanatory theories are important in understanding and, more importantly, not misunderstanding the behaviour of foreign states; for example, whether military deployments should be taken as indicators of defensive or offensive intent of nations, and of the motives of non-state groups such as insurgents or terrorists.

Good intelligence assessment thus has explanatory value in helping deepen real understanding of how a situation has arisen, the dynamics between the parties and what the motivations of the actors involved are – *as they, not we, see them* – and thus how they might be perceiving our side's moves. Providing such satisfactory explanation requires a detailed knowledge of the country concerned, the languages, personalities, local cultures, history, commerce and topography. Developing expert analysts capable of such deep understanding represents a major challenge for all intelligence communities. What is required at this level of thinking about security is deep understanding of the phenomena in question, and their roots and causes and possible future development, expressed in ways that will help the military or policy staffs develop options for decision makers.

Having a satisfactory explanation of events is a necessary precondition to producing well-founded predictive assessments since the third dimension of intelligence judgement is *prediction*, answering the questions 'what next?' or 'where next?' Prediction is the desired end product of much intelligence activity. It could be fundamental to grand strategy, such as estimates of the likelihood of conflict over oil exploration in the South Atlantic or South China Sea, or of tactical significance, such as identification of the intended target of a terrorist attack. Prediction need not be a 'point estimate' but could also be the forecasting of a limited range of outcomes that would still usefully focus down the options for the policy maker. It could be a predictive assessment based not on specific intelligence reporting but on judgements made about a developing situation that extends the explanatory into the predictive. In the case of failure to predict revolutionary change (such as in Iran in 1979 and in Berlin in 1989) what is likely to matter is the 'feel' that the analyst has for the interactive dynamics of the developing situation rather than any specific secret intelligence.

Intelligence prediction beyond a short time ahead is next to impossible. A fourth, separate, category is needed in this model of modern intelligence to support national security planning, and that is '*strategic notice*' of possible future risk-related developments (hazards as well as threats, and threats that might develop from hazards), especially where these might invalidate the explanations and predictions being made by the analysts in their risk matrices. These are possible futures worthy of attention, but not predictions that they will necessarily come about. One of the most important benefits of good strategic notice is in enhancing the ability of government to commission full intelligence assessments or longer-term scientific and other research to illuminate the phenomena, which should be done systematically as a cross-government exercise. Open sources come into their own here.

Strategic notice will be needed, for example, of potential relevant developments in the fields of technology (such as the further development of bio- and nano-technologies or of quantum computing), in diplomacy (such as the development of potential new alliances or groupings of nations), in nature (such as the effects of global warming on scarce resources), or in other aspects of security (such as the possible development of new violent ideologies) or prospective shifts in public and international attitudes to security. To achieve this, intelligence organizations will have to become more strategic, engaging more with outside experts, and developing a more rigorous intelligence community training programme.[28]

Such a four-level model complements the traditional military intelligence distinction between capabilities and intentions, as well as the elaboration by Professor R. V. Jones of the distinction between secrets and mysteries. There is a further subtlety here. We do not just have secrets to uncover and mysteries to divine but also a third category: *complexities* to unravel, the wicked problems when the prediction of what is going to happen depends not just on the capabilities and intentions of the adversary but on how our own policies and those of our allies impact on the perceptions and actions of the adversary. Thus, for example, the assessment of whether Iran will assemble a nuclear weapon in the next five years is not a pure 'intelligence' judgement – much depends on our honest assessment of how effective will be our own counter-proliferation policies, what the Iranian leadership on the day is likely to think of potential international reaction, and the interaction between the respective strategic narratives that Iran and the Western nations tell each other.

There is at the heart of intelligence work a simple truth. The most basic purpose of intelligence today remains the same as it was centuries ago, to help improve the quality of decision making by reducing ignorance. The nature of those decisions has changed over time, and today is governed by the demands of national security strategy to manage a wide range of major risks. The speed of technological change challenges our ability to adapt, with the pervasiveness of the technology reaching into every aspect of our lives – and thus providing new opportunities for intelligence gathering. And that increase in potential supply is coinciding with an increase in demand for real-time intelligence on so-called non-state actors, terrorists and the like. It is a matter for debate whether these urgent demands drew forth the means of supply or it was the potential to supply that enabled and encouraged the demand. What is clear is that we have seen an increasing impact over the last ten years on our intelligence communities from the potential of cyber.

As already noted, the purpose of the *secret* component of intelligence is simply to improve decision taking with information that other people do not want you to have, from which flow all of the characteristic moral hazards associated with the world of intelligence so beloved of fiction. Secret intelligence cannot be obtained without using techniques that overcome the will of the person with the secrets who is determined to keep them secret. That inconvenient fact could be ignored by most governments running intelligence operations during the twentieth century; intelligence in the twenty-first century is, however, no longer an ethics-free zone and the democratic acceptability of its methods may well end up shaping much of the future development of the intelligence community.

We can expect further changing patterns of demands for intelligence to support future national security; the impact of rapid developments in technologies relevant to intelligence access and analysis; and the influence on the acceptability of intelligence of changing social attitudes to privacy and human rights over what methods should be judged acceptable in the production of intelligence by ourselves and by our partners. The future development of intelligence communities is thus likely to be governed by the net effect of these pressures external to the classic Intelligence Cycle.

Notes

1 David Omand, 'The Intelligence Cycle', in Robert Dover, Michael S. Goodman and Claudia Hillebrand (eds), *Routledge Companion to Intelligence Studies* (London: Routledge, 2013).
2 See Philip H. J. Davies, Kristian Gustafson and Ian Rigden, Chapter 4 in this volume.
3 David Henderson, *Field Intelligence: Its Principles and Practice* (London: HMG Government Printer, 1904).
4 I am grateful to Lt Col. Trygve Smidt, Norwegian Army, for these references.
5 Cabinet Office, *Central Intelligence Machinery* (London: HMSO, 1993).
6 Dir. Roger Donaldson, 2000.
7 See David Omand, *Securing the State* (London: Hurst and Co. 2010).

8 David Omand, Jamie Bartlett and Carl Miller, *#Intelligence* (London: DEMOS, 2012). Available at www.demos.co.uk/files/_Intelligence_-_web.pdf?1335197327, last accessed 15 November 2012.

9 Kenneth J. Arrow and Gerard Debreu, 'Existence of an Equilibrium for a Competitive Economy', *Econometrica* Vol. 22 No. 3, 1954, pp. 265–90.

10 Peter Scharfman, 'Intelligence Analysis in the Age of Electronic Dissemination', *Intelligence and National Security* Vol. 10 No. 4, 1995, pp. 201–11.

11 Rob Johnston, *Analytic Culture in the US Intelligence Community: An Ethnographic Study* (Washington, DC: Center for the Study of Intelligence, 2005). Available at www.fas.org/irp/cia/product/analytic.pdf, last accessed 15 November 2012.

12 Gregory F. Treverton, *Reshaping National Intelligence in an Age of Information* (RAND Studies in Intelligence, Cambridge: Cambridge University Press, 2001).

13 Robert M. Clark, *Intelligence Analysis: A Target-Centric Approach* (Washington, DC: CQ Press, 2003).

14 Johnston, *Analytic Culture in the US Intelligence Community*.

15 Cabinet Office, *Central Intelligence Machinery*.

16 Minute from Burke Trend to Harold Wilson, 13 March 1967, cited in John W. Young, 'The Wilson Government's Reform of Intelligence Co-ordination,1967–68', *Intelligence and National Security*, Vol.16 No.2, 2001, pp.133–51.

17 See the discussion in Omand, *Securing the State*.

18 Arthur S. Hulnick, 'What's Wrong with the Intelligence Cycle', *Intelligence and National Security*, Vol. 21 No. 6, 2006, pp. 959–79; and Hulnick, Chapter 9 in this volume.

19 Rory Cormac, 'Organizing Intelligence: An Introduction to the 1955 Report on Colonial Security', *Intelligence and National Security* Vol. 25 No. 6, 2010, pp. 800–22.

20 Hulnick, 'What's Wrong with the Intelligence Cycle'.

21 Omand, *Securing the State*, Ch. 5.

22 Iain Lobban, *GCHQ's Perspective on Cyber Security*, 12 October 2011. Available at www.gchq.gov.uk/Press/Pages/IISS-CyberSpeech.aspx, last accessed 15 November 2012.

23 Cabinet Office, *National Security Strategy: A Strong Britain in an Age of Uncertainty* (London: HMSO, 2010).

24 The latest version is: Home Office, *Counter-Terrorism Strategy (CONTEST)* (London: Home Office, 2012). Available at www.homeoffice.gov.uk/counter-terrorism/uk-counter-terrorism-strat/, last accessed 15 November 2012.

25 Alan Dupont, 'Intelligence for the Twenty-First Century', *Intelligence and National Security*, Vol. 18 No. 4, 2003, p. 34.

26 Andrew Rathmell, 'Towards Postmodern Intelligence', *Intelligence and National Security*, Vol. 17 No. 3, 2002, p. 99.

27 Omand, *Securing the State*.

28 Roger Z. George, 'Reflections on CIA Analysis: Is it Finished?' *Intelligence and National Security*, Vol. 26 No. 1, 2011, pp. 72–81.

9 Intelligence theory

Seeking better models

Arthur S. Hulnick

In the fall of 1957, as a newly minted Air Force officer, I arrived at the Air Force Intelligence School in Wichita Falls, Texas, full of enthusiasm and excitement. I was to spend four months there, before reporting to my first duty station in Korea. All of the students were either fledgling officers like myself, or were moving into intelligence from other career fields. Most of us already had our assignments, while others were waiting to see what fate awaited when the school ended in December. None of us knew much about intelligence, so we were eager to learn what this business was about.

Of course, our instruction began with the study of the Intelligence Cycle, already long accepted as the best theoretical model of the intelligence process, and enshrined in the literature we were given to study. We dutifully wrote it down, studied it, then quickly moved on to the more practical business of learning how to become intelligence officers. The rest of the four months passed quickly as we practiced various intelligence techniques, the intricacies of intelligence reporting, and the more puzzling aspects of intelligence analysis. The Intelligence Cycle was quickly forgotten, and in the subsequent seven years of my Air Force career, I don't remember it ever being raised or recalled.

Joining the Agency

In 1965, after leaving the Air Force, I joined the Central Intelligence Agency and was told that I would spend most of the next year in training. I was assured that I should forget everything that I had learned about intelligence in the Air Force – the CIA would teach me all that I needed to know. This was, of course, nonsense, but I went along, knowing that my previous experience would probably pay off down the road. In the first few months, our training would take place in classrooms near CIA Headquarters, before moving to more serious work at 'The Farm', the CIA training facility. One of our first lectures, after studying how to get rid of classified trash, was about the Intelligence Cycle. Nothing had changed.

Again, I dutifully wrote down the basics, but spent most of my training involved in learning how the CIA did things. Of course, my Air Force experience served me well, although I did have to learn some new terms for doing the same work. When I emerged from training and went on to my first assignment as an analyst, the Intelligence Cycle was again quickly forgotten, and did not appear again until much later in my career.

In one of my last assignments in the CIA, I became head of a unit in Public Affairs that dealt with the outside world, including the public at large and the academic community. As the Agency's Briefing Officer, I often met with senior officials to explain what I could about the Agency's work. In my package of briefing materials I found once again a pictorial about the Intelligence Cycle. We included it in a fancy brochure about the Agency, and various other materials for public consumption. By now, after 25 years in CIA, and 32 years altogether as an intelligence officer, I realized that the Intelligence Cycle was a fairly poor and simplistic explanation of how the intelligence system really worked. But, it was the accepted gospel, and I was expected to brief it to my audiences as written.

Academic outreach

One of my tasks was to visit colleges and universities as part of my academic outreach function. In a visit to the University of Georgia in Athens, Georgia, I spent time with Professor Loch Johnson, one of the first academics to teach a course on the intelligence process. Prof. Johnson had served on the staff of the Church Committee, the investigation of U.S. intelligence led by Senator Frank Church of Idaho in the 1970s. Church thought the intelligence system, especially the CIA, was a 'rogue elephant' running amok. His investigation, of course, proved otherwise. Prof. Johnson often was critical of the CIA in his written works, but was quite friendly and open to me. He invited me to speak to his classes, which I was happy to do, thinking that I could correct some of the mistaken ideas some of Prof. Johnson's students had picked up about the CIA.

To my surprise, Prof. Johnson invited me to write an academic paper for the American Political Science Association annual convention, and my colleagues at the CIA thought this was another good opportunity to tell the Agency's story without giving away any secrets. I spent some time thinking about what I could tell a group of academics, some of whom were clearly hostile to the Agency, which would fit within the framework of the convention. I discussed this as well with some of my co-workers who had doctorates in Political Science, and were more in tune with this sort of exercise. In the end, I decided to write an alternative theoretical model of intelligence that would at the same time explain what was wrong with the Intelligence Cycle. My superiors at the CIA did not mind this heresy, as long as I did not divulge secret information.

Officer-in-residence

The paper was not only a great success, but I was invited to publish it in a new journal, *Intelligence and National Security*.[1] Again, the CIA's Publications Review Board had no trouble with this effort, since it contained no classified information and was not critical of the Agency, the U.S. Government, or anything other than its condemnation of the Intelligence Cycle as bad theory. In fact, the publication enhanced my credentials with the academics I visited, and invitations to speak on campus increased. The article, along with some other materials I had published, made it easier to garner an invitation to become a CIA Officer-in-Residence at Boston University, whose then President John Silber welcomed me to the newly established International Relations faculty headed by the late Ambassador Hermann Eilts.

In 1992, my time as an Officer-in Residence was complete and I faced the unpleasant prospect of returning to Washington to try to find a new assignment in CIA Headquarters. This would have meant giving up my teaching and writing on intelligence issues, and leaving Boston, a city we had come to love. Fortunately, Ambassador Eilts stepped in once again to offer me the opportunity to remain on the faculty as a Lecturer, and continue my teaching career. The Agency's retirement counselors helped me move from the Agency to my new position at Boston University and so I became, for the first time in my professional life, a real civilian.

Intelligence Studies

As a member of the faculty, I could seek more opportunities to write and present academic papers, especially to support the establishment and growth of the Intelligence Studies Section (ISS) of the International Studies Association (ISA). The ISS was in its infancy, and some more established members of ISA actually objected to its inclusion in the ISA conventions. Nonetheless, the early leaders of the ISA, including Professor Roy Godson of Georgetown University, persevered in setting up panels at the conventions, and I was happy to be able to support this effort. This gave me the opportunity to refine and revise my original paper on intelligence theory, while writing about other issues related to intelligence. Finally, I decided to incorporate my revised theory into my first book, *Fixing the Spy Machine*, which appeared in 2000.[2] This led to my appointment as Associate Professor, and my deepening involvement in Boston University.

Over the years since then, I have had the opportunity, along with several colleagues, many of whose work appears in this volume, to refine my ideas about intelligence theory. As readers can see from the previous chapters, and from other literature, there are three main schools of thought about theoretical models of intelligence and all have relevance. The traditional Intelligence Cycle model, the one espoused by Loch Johnson and taught to this day in government training courses, may not be a good fit for the general run of intelligence systems, but it is a fairly accurate model for tactical intelligence in field operations, and for the private sector in business intelligence. I am troubled by the fact that neither Johnson nor those who teach intelligence in government have recognized that alternative views about the Cycle even exist.

Alternative views

The modified cycle model described in previous chapters does make an effort to deal with the shortfalls in the traditional model, but is still off the mark in my view. As more and more modifications are made to the traditional model, the diagrams become almost incomprehensible, and perhaps misleading. While we cannot dispense completely with the Intelligence Cycle model in its various forms because it does have certain utility in limited cases, there ought to be a better way to develop a general theory. I am especially concerned that in all their various forms, the Intelligence Cycle models leave out two key functions in intelligence, those of Counter Intelligence and Covert Action.

The matrix model

I propose that we try to meld the traditional models with what I have come to call the 'matrix model' of intelligence, a theory that I first wrote about in my early work and have come to modify since. This theory posits that there are four main functions in intelligence. These are Collection, Analysis, Counter Intelligence, and Covert Action. Each function operates somewhat differently from the other three. This leads to the notion that there are actually two main variables in intelligence. The first is that of Process, which covers the main elements of each of the functions. The second variable is Sequence, and deals with the ways in which the functions interact with each other.

We can begin by looking at the Process variable, and its four main components. All intelligence services and units must have at least of two of these functions, and many state services have all four.

The Intelligence Cycle suggests that policy officials drive the intelligence process by involving intelligence managers in planning and direction of the intelligence processes. In reality this rarely happens. Instead, policy officials rely on intelligence managers to figure out what ought to be done, and who should do it. Efforts to seek requirements from policymakers have often proven to be fruitless. Policy officials want intelligence to tell them what they should be worried about. The result is that intelligence managers direct the various functions based on a variety of requirements, some inferred from policy officials, but most derived internally within the intelligence system. The requirements usually vary according to the function. We can begin there.

The collection function

The first function is that of Collection. All intelligence systems must have this function to be effective. The Collection function has some familiar elements, although they may not always work in the same way. The basic goal of intelligence collection is to fill gaps in existing knowledge, and unearth new information. All intelligence services, small and large, state-run or private, will pursue open sources – OSINT in U.S. terminology – as the least expensive and easiest method of filling the gaps. Open sources are, of course, subject to false information, disinformation, and propaganda, but discerning collectors usually learn which sources to trust. The explosion of information on the internet has complicated OSINT because there is more information out there than can easily be absorbed. Thus, intelligence collectors have to develop screening algorithms to sort out what might be valuable.[3]

Intelligence services increasingly rely these days on technical sensors to obtain information. These range from satellite images freely available on the internet to intercepts of communication, the latter made easier by the expanding use of cell phone technology. More sophisticated services may even be able to use drone imagery, or other high-tech devices.

Finally, many services are able to take advantage of espionage networks, if they have the personnel to handle the work. The techniques of this arcane business are well known, but establishing a human resource network is expensive, the training is complicated, and because espionage is usually illegal there is a certain level of danger in employing it. This is especially true in the private sector. While state-run intelligence services can provide some measure of protection to their officers by giving them diplomatic status, private intelligence services may find themselves either enmeshed in expensive law suits, or subject to criminal proceedings if they are caught 'with their hands in the cookie jar'.

Collation

An important step in the Collection function, not well recognized in the literature, is that of Collation. This is the process of turning the raw bits and pieces derived from the various collection systems into usable intelligence. For example, it has been widely reported that Chinese intelligence units gather up small bits of information to bring back to their headquarters where a 'mosaic' is created to reveal significant intelligence. In the U.S. system, collection management officers – they used to be called reports officers – turn raw intelligence into usable intelligence.[4] All of this effort leads to intelligence reporting, usually in a standardized format, keyed to the requirements laid out by intelligence managers.

In theory, especially in the Intelligence Cycle, the collection reports pass to analysts who evaluate the reports before creating intelligence products such as daily briefs, in-depth studies, or estimates of the future. In reality, especially in the U.S. governmental system, the collection reports often go to policy offices as well as to analysts. This creates a problem because policy officials who see these collection reports do not always realize that they have not been evaluated, may be fragmentary, or may be incorrect.

In tactical military intelligence, the collection data may be evaluated in the field and go directly to military commanders – no additional analysis may take place. In the private sector, the intelligence professionals who collect the data may be the same ones who analyze them and create the product contracted by the people who hire them. These latter two categories fit the Intelligence Cycle exactly, the main reason why Cycle Theory cannot be discarded entirely.

Research and analysis

While the Collection function does not vary much from what I have described, the Research and Analysis function is quite a bit more variable. The requirements for analysis may indeed be driven, at least in part, by policy officials as well as by intelligence managers. While the U.S. intelligence system often draws a clear line between collectors and analysts, and both functions are somewhat detached from policy officials, in many national intelligence systems the relationship between policymakers and analysts is closer. This happens because the analytic component of intelligence is located within the policy system, and not in intelligence. For example, in Great Britain, analysts are located in the Foreign and Commonwealth Office, and a similar arrangement exists in Canada.

In the private sector, because intelligence is contracted to produce certain results, the relationship between the CEO who hires a professional intelligence organization, usually on a consultant basis, and the analysts who do the work is often quite close. The same might be true for military commanders in the field. It would be better for intelligence analysts if they all could have close relationship with their policy consumers, but there are significant obstacles to making this work.[5]

There is an ongoing debate these days about how intelligence analysts should evaluate the reports they receive from the collection systems. In the United States there is growing pressure to use more rigorous methodologies in intelligence analysis, fostered by a growing body of literature on the subject.[6] In other countries, analysis may still be done the conventional way, using history, trend lines, and expert advice. Some intelligence systems only use analysts to evaluate collection reports and do not actually produce independent evaluations, but it appears that this is changing, as more and more intelligence services try to copy the U.S. or British models.

The final products of the Research and Analysis function include warning intelligence, daily reports, in-depth studies, and estimates of the future. According to the Intelligence Cycle, these products are distributed – 'disseminated' in U.S. jargon – to policy officials, and in that case, the Cycle is quite correct. In the United States, because of the large number of intelligence agencies, similar products may be sent to the policy community and duplicate each other. There are some products, however, such as National Intelligence Estimates (NIEs), that are coordinated among the agencies to deal with differing or dissenting views. Most national services, because they are so much smaller and may have only one intelligence agency, should not have the problem of duplication or coordination.

The last phase

The last phase of the Intelligence Cycle is where the greatest problem lies. The Cycle suggests that the delivery of intelligence triggers policy decision making. Nothing could be further from reality. We have no accurate measurement of how much influence intelligence products have on policy, but anecdotal evidence and some studies indicate that most policy decisions are made without a great deal of intelligence input. Decision makers are influenced by a great many things, including their own political agenda, pressure from special interest groups, and their existing knowledge of world affairs. Policy officials may react to warning intelligence, if it gets to them early enough to help them deal with a crisis, and daily reports may keep them up to date on world events, but longer studies and estimates of the future seem to matter little in policymaking.

Clearly, there are some benefits to a good intelligence system. It educates staffs and policy officials at the working level, and the intelligence may indeed filter up to the top level through staff action. It provides an independent and expert center of knowledge, immune from political pressure or public opinion. It would be useful to have more accurate measurement of the impact of intelligence on policy, a target for future intelligence research.

Parallel functions

While the Intelligence Cycle claims that the Collection and Analysis functions operate in sequence, in the main, they are actually parallel functions, operating somewhat independently of each other, at least in intelligence systems that have co-equal but separate Collection and Analysis units. This should not be surprising. Collection systems have a great many more targets, or gaps in the data bases, than they can fill, so collection managers are constantly trying to recruit new sources, or target technical systems. They do not need to wait for new targeting.

Analytic units already have huge data bases, either accumulated over many years, or, if they are newer systems, taken from the internet or partner intelligence services. These units do not have to wait for new inputs to make judgments about world events. Thus, new inputs from the Collection system are added to the data base, and rarely create entirely new subjects for analysis. Therefore, I argue that the Collection and Analysis functions are parallel functions, and not sequential. Only in tactical military intelligence and in the private sector are the functions sequential, mostly because the officers who do the collection are likely then to analyze what they have collected, and deliver the product.

The downside of this parallel functioning is that it tends to create 'stovepipes' that isolate collectors from analysts. This has been a serious problem in the U.S., especially in the larger agencies, where cultural differences as well as security concerns exacerbate the situation. This may also occur in intelligence services where the Collection function is in the intelligence service, but the Analytic function lies elsewhere. In smaller services, and in military intelligence, this problem is less likely. In both the latter cases, intelligence personnel may well perform all the various functions of intelligence during a career, instead of being isolated into only one function.

Counter intelligence

Now we come to one of the great conundrums of the Intelligence Cycle, the functions that the Cycle fails to recognize. The first of these is Counter Intelligence. Most of the literature on this subject focuses on threats to intelligence, and precious little tries to develop a theoretical model.[7] I believe this approach is too narrow, and that the Counter Intelligence function should really encompass defense against all the major threats to national security, including espionage, terrorism, global organized crime, subversion, and narcotics flows. In my view, the Counter Intelligence function attacks each of these threats in similar ways, and it is possible to develop a model that explains this function.[8]

The first part of the Counter Intelligence function involves recognizing specific threats and identifying the people or groups involved. More general threats to national security would have already been highlighted by the Intelligence Collection and Analysis Functions. The intelligence inputs in Counter Intelligence may come from sources developed by specialized counter intelligence collectors, from law enforcement, or even from the public. In many countries, a separate counter intelligence agency, or internal security service, carries out this specialized activity. Of all the major industrialized countries, only the U.S. does not have such a service, relying instead on law enforcement agencies to provide the identification inputs.

The second part of the Counter Intelligence function is both offensive and defensive in nature. On offense, counter intelligence specialists attempt to stop the workings of foreign espionage, terrorism, and the other threats by either penetrating their operations – recruiting assets on the inside of these groups – or through surveillance of the adversary operatives. This surveillance may be physical in nature, or carried out through the use of technical sensors, mostly electronic. The goal is to identify the specific individuals or groups, so that action can be taken against them.

On defense, security methods of various kinds are employed to protect the targets of the enemy operations. This may include physical security, such as restricted entry to government facilities, armed guards, security sensors, or enhanced barrier devices. Personnel security seeks to prevent penetration by enemy operatives, by careful hiring and vetting practices, and restrictions on the behavior of government employees. Classification of data, restricted handling of sensitive materials, and monitoring of personnel may also be used. Defensive measures may even include restrictions on the public, such as the effort to prevent terrorists from flying on commercial aircraft by treating almost everyone as a potential terrorist.

Cops and spies

The third part of the Counter Intelligence function is also bifurcated, and perhaps the most controversial. After counter intelligence officers have identified, located, and gathered intelligence about adversary spies, terrorists, or others suspected of threatening national security, these people must be stopped. This means intelligence must turn to law enforcement to carry out the next step. Intelligence professionals are sometimes reluctant to do this, because bringing in the 'cops' usually brings an end to any possible intelligence gathering. Intelligence officers would prefer to exploit their sources, including the 'bad guys' themselves, because once law enforcement enters the picture the targets would certainly stop providing intelligence to protect their legal rights.

This conundrum of intelligence versus law enforcement has become known in the literature as the 'cops and spies' dilemma. In most countries, the domestic security or intelligence service does not have police power, and must turn its cases over to law enforcement to stop the adversary operations. This gives intelligence some control over the decision to end collection operations, and to turn to the police. The United States does not have a domestic intelligence service, however, and so faces a somewhat different situation. Because the Federal Bureau of Investigation combines both law enforcement and intelligence, the decision about when to move against the targets is an internal one. Since the FBI's intelligence arm is relatively weak, and its intelligence personnel lack the power and prestige of the Special Agents who run the FBI, the decision is almost always biased toward law enforcement.

The final step

Once the targets have been arrested, the final step in the Counter Intelligence function is usually to make public the success of the system against its targets. While the traditional Collection and Analysis functions try not to make their successes public in hopes of repeating them, declaring victory in counter intelligence has both a certain tradition and a logic. It sends a clear message to other potential evil-doers that the system is working against them, and, as one former FBI Agent said, it adds to the prestige and aura of the Bureau, or their counterparts elsewhere.

The Counter Intelligence function, like the Collection and Analysis functions, operates in parallel with the others. Of course there are some connections between the functions, although in most services, counter intelligence is largely independent. The Counter Intelligence function has traditionally operated independently in the military. In the United States, each of the military services has long had a counter intelligence corps of some kind. In the private sector, counter intelligence lies in the hands of whatever security systems firms employ to protect themselves. Private firms must also turn to law enforcement when the need arises, since private security firms have only limited jurisdiction in preventing threats.

Covert action

The final function, and perhaps the least well understood, is that of Covert Action. Strictly speaking, covert action is not intelligence. It is the use of intelligence resources to carry out the foreign or security policy of the nation in such a way that the hand of the nation is not readily visible. It has deep roots in history. Sun Tzu, the famous Chinese military philosopher, wrote about the use of secret agents to confuse or deceive an enemy, and there are many examples of such activity all over the world. Why are intelligence services tasked with covert action? The answer is simple. Intelligence services have the special resources, from secret agents to safe houses, from clandestine communications to unmanned aerial vehicles, to carry out covert action. Although such activity could also be managed by specialized military units, there are advantages to using civilian agencies for the task in certain cases.[9]

Whether covert action is a military operation or run by a civilian intelligence service, the theoretical model looks very much the same. It looks a bit different from the other functions because covert action is really a sub-set of policy formulation and implementation. We know from long experience as well as from historic examples that covert action will only work if it is part of some larger scheme of policy. By itself, it cannot carry the day. We also know that short term objectives using covert action may lead to long-term unintended consequences. Despite its shortcomings, for those countries with the capability to carry out the Covert Action function, policy officials may be tempted to seek its use.

The function begins when policy officials turn to either their intelligence service or their specialized military units to incorporate a covert action in policy implementation. This should generate a dialogue about whether or not the action is workable, appropriate, and what the long-term consequences might be. In reality, intelligence or military managers often salute smartly and run off to try to carry out the wishes of the policy officials without raising the issues I've suggested. This almost always creates problems.

There are many ways to carry out covert action, from the use of so-called 'agents of influence' to drone strikes. Covert action can range from deception or disinformation operations to support for paramilitary units. All of the covert action operations are supposed to mask the hand of the operators, but this is very difficult to do. In the United States, there was a time when covert action was set up to give the President so-called 'deniability'; that is, a way to plead ignorance about covert action, but the U.S. Congress put a stop to that by demanding that the President report to the Intelligence Oversight Committees when he wanted such an operation. In other countries, deniability may still work.

Covert action and the public

Inevitably, many covert actions become public, especially if they go wrong, but even if they work successfully. In theory, the policy officials who ordered the covert action should take responsibility when it becomes public, but the reality is somewhat different. It is much easier to let the intelligence service or military unit take the heat, in hopes that they will remain silent. This does not always work, and then intelligence managers or military commanders may be forced to justify the actions thrust on them by policymakers.

The result of all of this is that covert action becomes the part of intelligence that the public tends to remember rather than the other functions. Covert action becomes the stuff of movie thrillers or spy novels, and may well distort the entire process. Intelligence services or specialized military units are thought to be independent operators, rather than units doing the bidding of policy officials. It was just such thinking that caused Senator Church to lead his investigation into covert action in the 1970s in the United States. He thought the CIA was a 'rogue elephant' but his investigation proved that the CIA was only carrying out the wishes of the White House, blessed in part by members of Congress.

Conclusion

The foregoing is what I have been calling the Matrix Model of the Intelligence Process, consisting of four distinct but related functions. It contrasts with the traditional Intelligence Cycle, either in its original or its modified form. I have welcomed the opportunity to include it in this volume, because all of the chapters in this book should lead to a continuing dialogue about intelligence theory. Clearly, more work needs to be done in regard to what I have described as the key variables, Process and Sequence. In addition, we need more theoretical work on the inter-operability of the Functions. The relationship between Intelligence and Policy is a fertile field for more research.

I am also hopeful that those who teach about intelligence, whether in official training programs or in the academic world, will move beyond the early formulations about the Intelligence Cycle, and at least discuss the modified models as well as the new ones in this volume. At least we can say that, since the field of Intelligence Studies has grown into a legitimate academic discipline, the development of a theoretical base for such studies should be welcomed by serious scholars in the field.

Notes

1 Arthur S. Hulnick, 'The Intelligence Producer-Policy Consumer Linkage: A Theoretical Approach', *Intelligence and National Security* Vol. 1 No. 2, 1986, pp. 212–33.
2 Arthur S. Hulnick, *Fixing the Spy Machine: Preparing American Intelligence for the Twenty-First Century* (Westport, CT: Praeger, 2000).
3 For a more detailed view, see Arthur S. Hulnick, 'The Dilemma of Open Source Intelligence: Is OSINT Really Intelligence?' in Loch K. Johnson (ed.), *The Oxford Handbook of National Security Intelligence* (Oxford: Oxford University Press, 2009), pp. 229–41.
4 See Joseph Wippl with Donna D'Andrea, 'The CMO in the CIA's National Clandestine Service', *International Journal of Intelligence and CounterIntelligence*, Vol. 23 No. 3, 2010, pp. 521–33.
5 Arthur S. Hulnick, 'Intelligence Producer-Consumer Relations in the Electronic Era', *International Journal of Intelligence and CounterInitelligence*, Vol. 24 No. 4, Winter 2011–12, pp. 747–56.
6 See, for example, Richards J. Heuer and Randolph H. Pherson, *Structured Analytic Techniques for Intelligence Analysis* (Washington, DC: Congressional Quarterly Press, 2010).

7 For one effort to develop a theoretical model of counter intelligence, see John Ehrman, 'Toward a Theory of CI: What Are We Talking About When We Talk About Counter-intelligence?' *Studies in Intelligence* Vol. 53 No. 2, 2009, pp. 5–20.

8 Arthur S. Hulnick, 'Home Time: A New Paradigm for Domestic Intelligence', *International Journal of Intelligence and CounterIntelligence* Vol. 22 No. 4, Winter 2009, pp. 569–85.

9 A useful discussion of Covert Action is contained in Loch K. Johnson (ed.), *Strategic Intelligence Vol. 3 – Covert Action: Beyond the Veils of Secret Foreign Policy* (Westport, CT: Praeger Security International, 2007).

Select bibliography

Andreas, Peter and Richard Price, 'From War-Fighting to Crime-Fighting: Transforming the American National Security State', *International Studies Review*, Vol. 3 No. 3, 2001, pp. 31–52.

Betts, Richard K. 'Analysis, War and Decision: Why Intelligence Failures Are Inevitable', *World Politics*, Vol. 31 No. 1, 1978, pp. 61–89.

Bowling, Ben and James Sheptycki, *Global Policing* (London: Sage, 2012).

Brenner, Joel, *America the Vulnerable: Inside the New Threat Matrix of Digital Espionage, Crime, and Warfare* (New York: Penguin Press, 2011).

Brenner, Susan W. '"At Light Speed": Attribution and Response to Cybercrime/Terrorism/Warfare', *The Journal of Criminal Law and Criminology*, Vol. 97 No. 2, 2007, pp. 379–475.

Brodeur, Jean-Paul 'High and Low Policing in Post-9/11 Times', *Policing: An International Journal of Policy and Practice*, Vol. 1, No. 1, 2007, pp. 25–37.

Brodeur, Jean-Paul, *The Policing Web* (Oxford: Oxford University Press, 2010).

Lord Butler, *Review of Intelligence of Weapons of Mass Destruction* (London: TSO, 2004).

Central Intelligence Agency, *A Consumer's Guide to Intelligence* (Washington, DC: National Technical Information Service, 1993).

Clark, Robert M. *Intelligence Analysis: A Target-Centric Approach* (Washington, DC: CQ Press, 2003).

Clarke, Richard A. and Robert K. Knake, *Cyber War: The Next Threat to National Security and What to do About It* (1st edn, New York: Ecco, 2010).

Clausewitz, Carl von, *On War*, translated by Michael Howard and Peter Paret (Princeton, NJ: Princeton University Press, 1989).

Cope, Nina, 'Intelligence Led Policing or Policing Led Intelligence? Integrating Volume Crime Analysis into Policing', *British Journal of Criminology*, Vol. 44 No. 2, 2004, pp. 188–203.

Cullather, Nick, 'Bombing at the Speed of Thought: Intelligence in the Coming Age of Cyberwar,' *Intelligence and National Security*, Vol. 18 No. 4, 2006, pp. 141–54.

Davies, Philip H. J. 'Intelligence and the Machinery of Government: Conceptualizing the Intelligence Community, *Public Policy and Administration*, Vol. 25 No. 1, 2010, pp. 29–46.

Davies, Philip H. J. *Intelligence and Government in Britain and the United States: A Comparative Approach* (Santa Barbara, CA: Praeger Security International 2012).

Donald, Dominick, 'Private Security and Intelligence', in Andrew Alexandra, Deane-Peter Baker and Marina Caparini (eds), *Private Military and Security Companies: Ethics, Policies and Civil-Military Relations* (London: Routledge, 2008), pp. 131–42.

Dupont, Alan, 'Intelligence for the Twenty-First Century', *Intelligence and National Security*, Vol. 18 No. 4, 2003, pp. 15–39.

Ehrman, John, 'Toward a Theory of CI: What Are We Talking About When We Talk About Counterintelligence?' *Studies in Intelligence*, Vol. 53 No. 2, 2009, pp. 5–20.

Evans, Geraint, 'Rethinking Military Intelligence Failure – Putting the Wheels Back on the Intelligence Cycle', *Defence Studies*, Vol. 9 No. 1, 2009, pp. 22–46.

Farson, Stuart, 'Security Intelligence Versus Criminal Intelligence: Lines of demarcation, areas of obfuscation, and the need to re-evaluate organizational roles in responding to terrorism', *Policing and Society*, Vol. 2 No. 2, 1991, pp. 65–87.

Farson, Stuart, Peter Gill, Mark Phythian and Shlomo Shpiro (eds), *PSI Handbook of Global Security and Intelligence: National Approaches: Volume 1 – The Americas and Asia/Volume 2 – Europe and the Middle East* (Westport, CT: Praeger Security International, 2008).

George, Roger Z. 'Reflections on CIA Analysis: Is it Finished?' *Intelligence and National Security*, Vol. 26 No. 1, 2011, pp. 72–81.

Graaf, Beatrice de, 'How the MfS' Worldview Affected the Intelligence Cycle: A study based on operations against the Netherlands', in Thomas Wegener Friis, Kristie Macrakis and Helmut Müller-Enbergs (eds), *East German Foreign Intelligence: Myth, Reality and Controversy* (London: Routledge, 2010), pp. 162–81.

Gill, Peter, *Rounding Up the Usual Suspects? Developments in Contemporary Law Enforcement Intelligence* (Aldershot: Ashgate, 2000).

Gill, Peter, 'Not Just Joining the Dots but Crossing the Borders and Bridging the Voids: Constructing Security Networks after 11 September 2001', *Policing and Society*, Vol. 16 No. 1, 2006, pp. 27–49.

Gill, Peter, 'Intelligence, Threat, Risk and the Challenge of Oversight', *Intelligence and National Security*, Vol. 27 No. 2, 2012, pp. 206–22.

Gill, Peter, Stephen Marrin and Mark Phythian (eds), *Intelligence Theory: Key Questions and Debates* (London: Routledge, 2009).

Gill, Peter and Mark Phythian, *Intelligence in an Insecure World* (2nd edn, Cambridge: Polity, 2012).

Glass, Robert R. and Philip B. Davidson, *Intelligence is for Commanders* (Harrisburg, PA: Military Service Publishing, 1948).

Healey, Jason, 'Claiming the Lost Cyber Heritage', *Strategic Studies Quarterly*, Vol. 6 No. 3, Fall 2012, pp. 11–19.

Herman, Michael, *Intelligence Power in Peace and War* (Cambridge: Cambridge University Press, 1996).

Herman, Michael, 'Counter-Terrorism, Information Technology and Intelligence Change', *Intelligence and National Security* Vol. 18 No. 4, 2003, pp. 40–58.

Heuer, Richards J. and Randolph H. Pherson, *Structured Analytic Techniques for Intelligence Analysis* (Washington, DC: Congressional Quarterly Press, 2010).

Hulnick, Arthur S. 'The Intelligence Producer-Policy Consumer Linkage: A Theoretical Approach', *Intelligence and National Security*, Vol. 1 No. 2, 1986, pp. 212–33.

Hulnick, Arthur S. *Fixing the Spy Machine: Preparing American Intelligence for the Twenty-First Century* (Westport, CT: Praeger, 2000).

Hulnick, Arthur S. 'What's Wrong with the Intelligence Cycle', *Intelligence and National Security*, Vol. 21 No. 6, 2006, pp. 959–79.

Hulnick, Arthur S. 'Intelligence Producer-Consumer Relations in the Electronic Era', *International Journal of Intelligence and CounterInitelligence*, Vol. 24 No. 4, Winter 2011–12, pp. 747–56.

Johnson, Loch K. 'A Framework for Strengthening US Intelligence', *Yale Journal of International Affairs*, Vol. 1 No. 2, 2006, pp. 116–31.

Johnson, Loch K. *National Security Intelligence* (Cambridge: Polity, 2012).

Johnson, Loch K. (ed.), *Strategic Intelligence Vol. 2 – The Intelligence Cycle: The Flow of Secret Information from Overseas to the Highest Councils of Government* (Westport, CT: Praeger Security International, 2007).

Johnson, Loch K. (ed.), *Strategic Intelligence Vol. 3 – Covert Action: Beyond the Veils of Secret Foreign Policy* (Westport, CT: Praeger Security International, 2007).

Johnston, Rob, *Analytic Culture in the US Intelligence Community: An Ethnographic Study* (Washington, DC: Center for the Study of Intelligence, 2005).

Keen, Thomas and Lee H. Hamilton, *The 9/11 Commission Report* (New York: W. W. Norton, 2004).

Kent, Sherman, *Strategic Intelligence for American World Policy* (Princeton, NJ: Princeton University Press, 1966).

Klimburg, Alexander, 'Mobilising Cyber Power,' *Survival*, Vol. 53 No. 1, 2011, pp. 41–60.

Laqueur, Walter, *A World of Secrets: The Uses and Limits of Intelligence* (New York: Basic Books, 1985).

Lowenthal, Mark M. *Intelligence: From Secrets to Policy* (3rd edn, Washington, DC: CQ Press, 2006).

Lowenthal, Mark M. 'Towards a Reasonable Standard for Analysis: How Right, How Often on Which Issues?' *Intelligence and National Security*, Vol. 23 No. 3, 2008, pp. 303–15.

Marrin, Stephen, 'Intelligence Analysis and Decision-Making: Methodological challenges', in Peter Gill, Stephen Marrin and Mark Phythian (eds), *Intelligence Theory: Key Questions and Debates* (London: Routledge, 2009), pp. 131–50.

Ministry of Defence Development, Concepts and Doctrine Centre, *JDP 2-00: Understanding and Intelligence Support to Joint Operations* (3rd edn, Shrivenham, UK: DCDC, 2011).

Omand, David, *Securing the State* (London: Hurst & Co., 2010).

Omand, David, 'The Intelligence Cycle', in Robert Dover, Michael S. Goodman and Claudia Hillebrand (eds), *Routledge Companion to Intelligence Studies* (London: Routledge, 2013).

Omand, David, Jamie Bartlett and Carl Miller, *#Intelligence* (London: DEMOS, 2012).

Phythian, Mark, 'Policing Uncertainty: Intelligence, Security and Risk', *Intelligence and National Security*, Vol. 27 No. 2, 2012, pp. 187–205.

Pillar, Paul R. *Intelligence and U.S. Foreign Policy: Iraq, 9/11, and Misguided Reform* (New York: Columbia University Press, 2011).

Ratcliffe, Jerry, *Intelligence-Led Policing* (Cullompton: Willan, 2008).

Ratcliffe, Jerry (ed.), *Strategic Thinking in Criminal Intelligence* (2nd edn, Sydney: The Federation Press, 2009).

Rathmell, Andrew, 'Towards Postmodern Intelligence', *Intelligence and National Security*, Vol. 17 No. 3, 2002, pp. 87–104.

Richards, Julian, *The Art and Science of Intelligence Analysis* (Oxford: Oxford University Press, 2010).

Richards, Julian, *A Guide to National Security: Threats, Responses and Strategies* (Oxford: Oxford University Press, 2012).

Scharfman, Peter, 'Intelligence Analysis in the Age of Electronic Dissemination', *Intelligence and National Security*, Vol. 10 No. 4, 1995, pp. 201–11.

Sheptycki, James, 'Organizational Pathologies in Police Intelligence Systems: Some contributions to the lexicon of intelligence-led policing', *The European Journal of Criminology*, Vol. 1 No. 3, 2004, pp. 307–32.

Sheptycki, James, 'Policing, Intelligence Theory and the New Human Security Paradigm: Some lessons from the field', in Gill, Marrin and Phythian (eds), *Intelligence Theory*, pp. 166–87.

Sims, Jennifer, 'Defending Adaptive Realism: Intelligence theory comes of age', in Gill, Marrin and Phythian (eds) *Intelligence Theory*, pp. 151–65.

Steele, Robert David, 'Open Source Intelligence', in Loch K. Johnson (ed.), *Handbook of Intelligence Studies*, (London: Routledge, 2009), pp. 129–47.

Strachan-Morris, David, 'Threat and Risk: What's the Difference and Why Does It Matter?', *Intelligence and National Security*, Vol. 27 No. 2, 2012, pp. 172–86.

Treverton, Gregory F. *Reshaping National Intelligence in an Age of Information* (RAND Studies in Intelligence, Cambridge: Cambridge University Press, 2001).

Treverton Gregory F. and Wilhelm Agrell (eds), *National Intelligence Systems: Current Research and Future Prospects* (Cambridge: Cambridge University Press, 2009).

Treverton, Gregory F., Seth G. Jones, Steven Boraz and Philip Lipscy, *Toward a Theory of Intelligence: RAND Workshop Report* (Santa Monica, CA: RAND, 2006).

US Government, *International Strategy for Cyberspace: Prosperity, Security, and Openness in a Networked World* (Washington, DC: White House, 2011).

US Joint Chiefs of Staff, *Joint Publication 2-01: Joint and Military Intelligence Support to Military Operations* (Washington, DC: Joint Chiefs of Staff, January 2012), www.dtic.mil/doctrine/new_pubs/jp2_01.pdf, last accessed 14 February 2013.

Vitt, Elizabeth, Michael Luckevich and Stacia Misner, *Business Intelligence: Making Better Decisions Faster* (Washington, DC: Microsoft Press, 2002).

Lampe, Klaus von, 'Making the Second Step Before the First: Assessing Organized Crime', *Crime, Law and Social Change*, Vol. 42 Nos.4–5, 2005, pp. 227–59.

Wark, Wesley K. 'Introduction: Learning to Live with Intelligence', *Intelligence and National Security*, Vol. 18 No. 4, 2003, pp. 1–14.

Warner, Michael, 'Wanted: A Definition of "Intelligence"', *Studies in Intelligence*, Vol. 46, No. 3 (2002), https://www.cia.gov/library/center-for-the-study-of-intelligence/csi-publications/csi-studies/studies/vol46no3/article02.html, last accessed 14 February 2013.

Warner, Michael, 'Reflections on Technology and Intelligence Systems', *Intelligence and National Security*, Vol. 27 No. 1, 2012, pp. 133–53.

Williams, Phil, Timothy Shimeal and Casey Dunlevy, 'Intelligence Analysis for Internet Security', *Contemporary Security Policy*, Vol. 23 No. 2, 2010, pp. 1–38.

Zhang, Weiwu, Thomas J. Johnson, Trent Seltzer and Shannon L. Bichard, 'The Revolution will be Networked: The Influence of Social Networking Sites on Political Attitudes and Behavior', *Social Science Computer Review*, Vol. 28 No. 1, 2010, pp. 75–92.

Index